# Measuring, Understanding and Improving Wellbeing Among Older People

Sefa Awaworyi Churchill · Lisa Farrell ·
Samuelson Appau
Editors

# Measuring, Understanding and Improving Wellbeing Among Older People

palgrave
macmillan

*Editors*
Sefa Awaworyi Churchill
School of Economics, Finance and Marketing
RMIT University
Melbourne, VIC, Australia

Lisa Farrell
School of Economics, Finance and Marketing
RMIT University
Melbourne, VIC, Australia

Samuelson Appau
School of Economics, Finance and Marketing
RMIT University
Melbourne, VIC, Australia

ISBN 978-981-15-2352-6 ISBN 978-981-15-2353-3 (eBook)
https://doi.org/10.1007/978-981-15-2353-3



This Palgrave Macmillan imprint is published by the registered company Springer Nature Singapore Pte Ltd.
The registered company address is: 152 Beach Road, #21-01/04 Gateway East, Singapore 189721, Singapore

*To all those who value longevity*

# Contents

# Notes on Contributors

**Esenam Agyekumhene** is a Commonwealth Scholar and holds an M.Sc. in Environment and Development from the London School of Economics, UK. She has experience in communications having worked as a strategic communications officer for 5 years. She is currently a management consultant for two non-profit organisations focusing on women's development and health. Her research interests include development communications, wellbeing and gender.

**Dillys Amega** is a Doctor of Optometry currently practising in Ghana for the past five years. She has a keen interest in understanding issues that influence the wellbeing of vulnerable groups, and takes a practical approach to dealing with such issues. Her practice provides free community eye care services to people in rural communities as well as to thousands of school children annually. Her research interests focus on understanding retinal diseases process and the wellbeing of vulnerable groups.

**Samuelson Appau** is a Lecturer in Marketing at RMIT University. He holds a Ph.D. from the University of Melbourne. His research focuses on the impact of marketing, religion, culture and poverty on individual and group wellbeing and marketplace engagement. Samuelson's research sits at the intersection of transformative consumer research, development economics and consumer culture theory. His scholarly research has appeared in reputable scholarly outlets, such as the *Journal of Public Policy & Marketing, Journal of Business Research, Applied Economics* and *Empirical Economics.*

**Sefa Awaworyi Churchill** is a Senior Research Fellow in the School of Economics, Finance and Marketing at RMIT University, Australia. He holds a Ph.D. in Economics from Monash University. His interdisciplinary research focuses on development economics, addictive behaviour, ethnic diversity, wellbeing and other issues related to sociology, health and economics. He has experiences working on consultancy projects for various policy agencies and international development organisations.

**Sook Ning Chua** is a Lecturer at the National Institute of Education, Nanyang Technological University, Singapore. She completed her Ph.D. in Clinical Psychology at McGill University. Sook Ning's recent research focuses on how to promote positive personal and systemic changes. She is also actively involved in developing an effective mental healthcare system in Malaysia.

**Ashton de Silva** is an applied economist/econometrician in the School of Economics, Finance and Marketing, RMIT University Australia. He is an associate professor specialising in the analysis of the housing sector, household credit & financial markets, regional (including cultural) economies as well as government policy. He has published papers in leading international and domestic academic journals. Ashton has a strong record of engagement which includes conducting research in partnership with industry as well as being commissioned by private and public sector entities to lead specialised investigations. His current projects include the interaction between wellbeing and economics across various cohorts.

**Meg Elkins** is a Senior Lecturer in Economics at RMIT University. She holds a Ph.D. in Economics from La Trobe University. She is an applied economist with a focus on wellbeing and cultural economics. Meg's research methods include microeconomic analysis to evaluate programs and policies in the areas of international development, social protection, homelessness, youth curiosity and arts programs. Meg has published in high quality research journals in the area of development and communications. She has received research grants to conduct research for the City of Melbourne and Higher Education Research and Development Society of Australia (HERDSA).

**Lisa Farrell** is Professor and Deputy Head Research and Innovation in the School of Economics, Finance and Marketing at RMIT University. Her research field is in the area of applied microeconomics, with a particular focus on important contemporary social issues such as subjective wellbeing, decision-making under uncertainty and lifestyle choice behaviours. Her work has spanned both the theoretical and microeconometric aspects of risk and wellbeing, and the academic impact of this work is clear from the important contributions she has made leading to publications in high quality international economic journals.

**Paolo Franco** is a Ph.D. candidate in the Department of Management and Marketing at the University of Melbourne, Australia. His research investigates the intersections between families and the technologies that become part of their everyday lives. Through drawing upon relational approaches to study consumption in assemblage and Actor-Network Theory, his work aims to uncover what this intersection can tell us about new product adoption, family relationships and the impacts of non-human elements in consumption.

**Jane Fry** is a researcher with over 25 years of experience in the private sector, public sector and academia. She has conducted applied research in various areas of economics, econometrics and marketing, writing reports and publishing in several high-ranking academic journals. Her research interests lie broadly in econometrics and data analysis. Jane has a Masters of Economics degree from Monash University and is currently undertaking her Ph.D. at the Centre for Health Economics at Monash University.

**Asadul Islam** is currently Professor in the Department of Economics at Monash University in Australia. His research interests are primarily in the areas of development economics and demography. His recent research focuses on education, health, social networks, microfinance and long-term effects of shocks. His research works span in a number of countries including Bangladesh, India, Pakistan, China, Cambodia, Uganda and Tanzania. He has published widely in leading journals including *Economic Journal*, *European Economic review*, *Journal of Development Economics*, *Journal of Environmental Economics and Management*, *Journal of Banking and Finance*, *Journal of Economic Behavior and Organization*, and *Demography*.

**Richard Koestner** is Professor of Psychology at McGill University where he has conducted research on personality and human motivation for over 30 years. Richard Koestner did his Ph.D. research at the University of Rochester with Edward Deci and Richard Ryan and subsequently completed a post-doctoral fellowship at Harvard University with David McClelland. Richard's recent work focuses on using self-determination theory to understand how individuals can effectively select and pursue personal goals.

**Foula Kopanidis** is an Associate Professor in the School of Economics Finance and Marketing at RMIT University. Her research is anchored across the three disciplines of marketing, education and psychology and her methodology is primarily quantitative. Foula's research interests relate to consumption, choice behaviour and social marketing including ageing, middle-aged health, wellbeing and quality of life. Foula has been involved in a number of projects in the wellbeing field and has published in *Higher Education, Research and Development*, *Higher Education Policy and Management* and *Women & Aging* and has co-authored textbooks in Consumer Behaviour and Marketing.

**Matthew Gmalifo Mabefam** is currently a tutor and Ph.D. candidate in the School of Social and Political Sciences at the University of Melbourne. Matthew has experiences with local and international NGOs in Ghana and Australia. In the past decade, he has engaged in mobilising and advocating for and with local communities, and groups in negotiating spaces for their wellbeing. His research focuses on the impact of the relationship between development actors—both state and non-state actors and the wellbeing of people in Africa. His work lies at the intersection of wellbeing of vulnerable groups, especially women who have been displaced from their communities as a result of violent ethnic, chieftaincy and cultural conflicts.

**Anne-Laure Mention** is the Director of the Global Business Innovation Enabling Capability Platform at RMIT, Melbourne, Australia, and Professor in the College of Business. She is also a Visiting Professor at University of Tampere, Finland, and a FinTech Research Fellow at Singapore University of Social Sciences. Her research focuses on open and collaborative innovation, innovation in business to business services, with a particular focus on financial industry and fintech, technology management and business venturing. She is the co-founding editor of the open access multidisciplinary *Journal of Innovation Management*. She has been awarded twice the prestigious IBM Faculty Award for her research on innovation.

**Janet Ocloo** holds a master's degree in public health promotion from Leeds Beckett University. She has over 15 years of experience working in the health sector in Ghana. She currently works with the Korle-Bu Teaching Hospital, Accra. Her research focuses on issues of public health. Much of her current research focuses on determinants of subjective wellbeing and health in general.

**Paul Raschky** is Associate Professor of Economics in the Department of Economics at Monash University, Australia. His research interests are in the fields of political economy, environmental economics, insurance economics and development economics. His research has been published, among others, in the *Quarterly Journal of Economics*, *Journal of Development Economics*, *Journal of the Association of Environmental and Resource Economists*, *Journal of Environmental Economics and Management*, and *Journal of Public Economics*. He is the founding director of datainspace, co-founder of the IP Observatory and SoDa Labs, and co-founder and one of the directors of KASPR Datahaus PTY LTD.

**Sarah Sinclair** is an Applied Economist in the School of Economics Finance and Marketing at RMIT University. She has a strong research interest in the residential housing sector, in particular the effect of policy on household behaviour and housing outcomes. Her current research relates to the consumption choice over the life cycle, given certain social situations, interfamily interactions and public policy frameworks. Decision and situations studied include family formation and size, divorce and the role of child support in the housing consumption choices of lone parents, retirement planning and facilitating ageing in place.

**Russell Smyth** is Professor of Economics and Deputy Dean (Academic Resourcing) in the Monash Business School, Monash University, Australia. He has honours degrees in Economics and Law from Monash University and a Ph.D. in Economics from the University of London. His research interests include energy economics, empirical legal studies and subjective wellbeing. Much of his work has a geographic focus on China. He has published widely on these topics in a variety of outlets.

**Stuart Thomas** is an Associate Professor in the School of Economics, Finance and Marketing at RMIT. Prior to his academic career, he worked in business advice and consulting for a "Big 5" accounting and business advisory firm and before that in the IT industry. He has a diverse portfolio of research interests including student performance, innovation economics and industrial dynamics in the finance sector and in the sports industry, and more recently in private retirement funding through alternatives to superannuation.

# List of Figures

# List of Tables

## Chapter 6



## Chapter 7



## Chapter 8



## Chapter 11

## Chapter 12

# 1

# Wellbeing Among Older People: An Introduction

Samuelson Appau, Sefa Awaworyi Churchill and Lisa Farrell

## 1 Introduction and Overview

The concept of wellbeing is an important theme in international academic research and in public policy agenda. Increasing governmental interests in measuring Subjective Wellbeing (SWB) (see, e.g., Hicks, Tinkler, & Allin, 2013; Stiglitz, Sen, & Fitoussi, 2010) and extensive interdisciplinary work on the subject over the last few decades attest to the importance of wellbeing (Blanchflower & Oswald, 2011; Linton, Dieppe, & Medina-Lara, 2016). The importance of wellbeing and its

S. Appau · S. Awaworyi Churchill (✉) · L. Farrell
School of Economics, Finance and Marketing, RMIT University, Melbourne, VIC, Australia
e-mail: sefa.awaworyichurchill@rmit.edu.au

S. Appau
e-mail: samuelson.appau@rmit.edu.au

L. Farrell
e-mail: lisa.farrell@rmit.edu.au


S. Awaworyi Churchill et al. (eds.), *Measuring, Understanding and Improving Wellbeing Among Older People*,
https://doi.org/10.1007/978-981-15-2353-3_1

implications for various outcomes have been discussed in the fields of sociology, economics and psychology, among others. Studies across these fields also examine various determinants of wellbeing (see, e.g., Awaworyi Churchill & Mishra, 2017; Cummins, 2000; Diener & Chan, 2011; Diener & Oishi, 2000; Diener, Oishi, & Lucas, 2003; Diener, Sandvik, Seidlitz, & Diener, 1993; Frankel & Hewitt, 1994; Fredrickson, 2002; Hudson, 2006; Okun, Stock, Haring, & Witter, 1984; Winkelmann, 2009; Zhang & Zhang, 2015). These studies have examined, among others, factors such as income (Headey, Muffels, & Wooden, 2008; Headey & Wooden, 2004), social capital (Hooghe & Vanhoutte, 2011), mode of travel and transport poverty (Awaworyi Churchill & Smyth, 2019; Bergstad et al., 2011), consumption (Hudders & Pandelaere, 2012; Wang, Cheng, & Smyth, 2019), life events (Luhmann, Hofmann, Eid, & Lucas, 2012) and various socioeconomic factors (Haring-Hidore, Stock, Okun, & Witter, 1985; Van der Meer, 2014; Witter, Stock, Okun, & Haring, 1985), as determinants of SWB. Dolan, Peasgood, and White (2008) provide a useful review on the factors associated with wellbeing.

Sitting alongside the broader literature on the determinants of wellbeing are studies that focus on elderly people. Particularly, the theme of "ageing well" in the gerontology and geriatrics literature (see, e.g., Aberdeen & Bye, 2013; Bowling, 2005; Cosco, Matthew Prina, Perales, Stephan, & Brayne, 2014) has increased interest in understanding the wellbeing of older people (Davey, 2007; Lau & Morse, 2008; Smith, Sim, Scharf, & Phillipson, 2004). The World Health Organization's (WHO) declaration of "ageing well" as a global health priority coupled with the rapid increase in the relative number of older people worldwide lends support to the importance of understanding the determinants of cognitive function and wellbeing of older people.

With this book, we seek to build on the existing literature and expand our knowledge of wellbeing among the elderly. As many countries are faced with the challenges of an ageing population, further insights into what influences the wellbeing of the elderly are required to ensure appropriate policies are formulated for healthy ageing. Recent development in the field of wellbeing research as demonstrated in Bache and Scott (2018) places politics centre stage and provides fresh insights that aid our understanding of the significance of wellbeing. Specifically, Bache and Scott (2018) provide a unique collection of chapters that examine the politics of wellbeing and emphasize the state of research on wellbeing in public policy. However, none of the chapters provide insights into the wellbeing of older persons.

The purpose of this book then is to present a series of authoritative case studies that demonstrate how scientific research can discover important insights into the wellbeing of older persons, and so contribute to policies that can expand their capabilities for wellbeing. The case studies have been chosen to include examples from developed and developing countries, and they involve a variety of interdisciplinary research methods. Taken together, the chapters in this book demonstrate the rich opportunities for further research and policy development in this field. Findings from this book are also timely for policymakers across developed and emerging countries interested in promoting the wellbeing of the elderly.

## 2 The Concept of Wellbeing

The extant literature is yet to reach a consensus on what constitutes a general definition of wellbeing, although within the policy literature, indicators of wellbeing are often divided into subjective measures and objective measures. Regarding subjective measures, one strand of the literature has defined wellbeing as a person's evaluation of their life with respect to emotion and cognition. This dimension of wellbeing reflects one's feelings and overall judgement about how satisfying life is. It represents the evaluative, reflective and cognitive aspect of wellbeing (Awaworyi Churchill & Mishra, 2017; Diener, 1984, 1994; Pinquart & Sörensen, 2000). Wellbeing, along these lines, also referred to as SWB (Diener, 1984), is argued to encompass a complex subjective state and has thus been measured using constructs such as self-reported life satisfaction, happiness and self-esteem, among others. The simplest measures of wellbeing in this tradition consist of single-item happiness and life satisfaction questions, which are often included in large-scale surveys. For instance, the question, "All things considered, how satisfied are you with your life as a whole" or its variants are routinely used as measures of wellbeing. Similar questions are used to capture feelings of happiness and depression, among others. Multi-item or composite versions of these measures have also been used in the literature. These include similarly worded questions that attempt to capture various dimensions of one's feelings and life (Diener, Emmons, Larsen, & Griffin, 1985; Lucas, 2018; Lyubomirsky & Lepper, 1999). Objective measures have included constructs such as income, employment and health, among others.

The definition of wellbeing has also been driven by different perspectives of national and international policy drivers. For instance, from the perspective of international organizations such as the WHO, mental health is a component of wellbeing. In addition to the emotional dimension, wellbeing is said to also encompass how people feel physically, and thus, measures of physical health have also been used in the literature to measure wellbeing (Lindert, Bain, Kubzansky, & Stein, 2015). Others have considered wellbeing more broadly to refer to economic progress (Fleurbaey, 2009) while some studies suggest that expressions such as smiling (Harker & Keltner, 2001) are good indicators of wellbeing.

Studies in this book have examined wellbeing across various dimensions including general health, mental health, life satisfaction, happiness and other related composite measures. More precisely, the collection of studies in this book mostly focuses on SWB measures.

## 3 Summary of Chapters in the Book

The studies collected in this book are truly interdisciplinary and focus on quantitative and qualitative methods. The chapters also focus on a broad scope with coverage on wellbeing of the elderly in developed and developing countries as well as international perspectives using cross-country data. Four chapters focus on developed countries, three chapters on developing countries and another three presenting international perspectives.

Paolo Franco examines how older people experience independence as influenced by their adoption and consumption of everyday technologies such as smartphones, tablets and computers. His ethnographic study focuses on residents of a retirement village in Melbourne, Australia, and finds that technologies can impact on the independence of older people. Franco also finds that older people face various challenges in seeking and receiving tech-help from others which can enable their uses of everyday technologies. The findings from Franco's study suggest the need for policies that aim at empowering older people through influencing their adoption and consumption of everyday technologies.

Housing insecurity and homelessness have recently been the focus of international research. Meg Elkins, Lisa Farrell and Jane Fry use the Journeys Home data set, which is a unique longitudinal data set specifically designed to examine issues relating to homelessness or instability in housing/accommodation in Australia. They use information on accommodation type, start date and duration of accommodation spells, to construct a sequence spanning 2.5 years for individuals aged 40 years and over. They examine the sequences for patterns in the type, order, timing and duration of spells in various types of accommodation, and investigate the relationship between housing insecurity and wellbeing for older individuals. Elkins, Farrell and Fry present results that shed light on longer-term housing experiences and their correlation with individual wellbeing. They present policy discussions that are relevant for countries that are dealing with issues on homelessness and ageing populations.

The importance of social support for older people cannot be overstated. Samuelson Appau and Sefa Awaworyi Churchill use the Household, Income and Labour Dynamics in Australia (HILDA) survey data to examine the association between social support and wellbeing. They argue that social support can be very useful; however, not all social ties are helpful or desirable. They adopt quantitative methods to analyse 16 waves of longitudinal data focused on Australians above 55 years. Their findings support the importance of social support for the SWB of older people. Their findings also imply that the Australian government should focus on ways to improve both the quantity and quality of social support that older people have over time.

Sefa Awaworyi Churchill and Lisa Farrell also use data from the HILDA survey to examine the association between gambling and the wellbeing of older people. A growing number of studies examine gambling behaviour as a determinant of SWB. Awaworyi Churchill and Farrell, however, make a distinct contribution by focusing on Australia, which makes for an interesting case study because of its per capita gambling expenditure, known to be the highest in the world. To motivate their study, and show why gambling is an important factor to consider in understanding the wellbeing of older people, they show that compared to the Australian adult population regular gambling participants are substantially over-represented among people over the age of 50. They adopt multiple measures of gambling behaviour including the Problem Gambling Severity Index (PGSI), gambling risk spectrums based on PGSI scores, gambling expenditures and the number of gambling activities older people engage in. They find evidence of negative effects of gambling on different indicators of wellbeing including life satisfaction, the Mental Health Inventory (MHI-5) scale and the Kessler Psychological Distress Scale (K10). Although their chapter focuses on correlations rather than causality, they discuss significant policy implications worth considering in enhancing the wellbeing of the elderly in countries with high gambling rates.

Certain jobs can become so integral to employees' lives and identities that their sense of wellbeing becomes attached to their employment. What happens when these employees retire? To answer this question, Samuelson Appau, Sefa Awaworyi Churchill and Lisa Farrell use seven waves of the English Longitudinal Survey of Ageing (ELSA) to examine the impact of labour market attachments on SWB and quality of life (QoL), during employment and retirement. They find that permanent employees (as opposed to temporary employees) and self-employed (as opposed to paid employees) report higher levels of SWB and QoL throughout their working lives. However, in retirement, withdrawal from the labour market represents a loss of this identity, and thus, permanent employees and self-employed people tend to experience a significant drop in SWB and QoL during retirement.

We have three studies that focus on developing countries. Asadul Islam, Paul Raschky and Russell Smyth examine the wellbeing of elderly people from the health dimension using the China Health and Retirement Longitudinal Survey (CHARLS). Their study contributes to the literature that has considered height as a marker of health with significant implications for various outcomes later in life (Case, Paxson, & Islam, 2009; Gao & Smyth, 2010; Schultz, 2002). They find that taller people have less difficulty engaging in Activities of Daily Living (ADL) in old age, and thus enjoy better health in China. Their study presents significant policy implications for several reasons. First, they focus on China, an important developing country. It is estimated that over a third of the world's population aged 60 or above are expected to live in China or India by 2050. Second, the effects of an ageing population are likely to be more severe in developing countries given that they usually have limited resources compared to high-income countries. Lastly, the study of the relationship between height and health is more relevant for developing countries given that they are more likely to experience much harsher effects of undesirable early childhood experiences.

Ethnic diversity and discrimination are important social factors that influence SWB. Esenam Agyekumhene, Dillys Amega, Samuelson Appau, Sefa Awaworyi Churchill and Janet Ocloo examine the interplay between ethnic diversity, discrimination and SWB among older Chinese using data from the World Values Survey (WVS). They find a negative effect of ethnic diversity on wellbeing. Additionally, using a wide range of measures that capture various dimensions of discriminatory attitudes, the study reports on a negative effect of prejudice on wellbeing. The authors show that the negative effect of ethnic diversity on wellbeing could be as a result of ethnic diversity's negative influence on social capital, which is known in the literature to be a major determinant of wellbeing.

Mathew Gmalifo Mabefam and Samuelson Appau analyse qualitative data to examine the relationship between culture and the wellbeing of elderly persons in Ghana. Their ethnographic study examines witchcraft and people's perception of witchcraft and accused witches as unique cultural issues in Northern Ghana. They find that wellbeing is negatively impacted for the elderly when they are accused of witchcraft and violently banished from their communities to live in *witch camps*, which are secluded camps that are meant to serve three basic purposes: (1) verification of people accused of witchcraft to confirm their innocence or guilt, (2) cleansing of the powers of confirmed witches and, (3) providing residence for confirmed and cleansed witches. Their study touches on the importance of policy to focus on addressing cultural practices that legitimize the ill-treatment of elderly people.

Sarah Sinclair, Ashton de Silva, Foula Kopanidis and Stuart Thomas provide a useful review of the literature to motivate their argument that good housing characterized by good location and design is important for ageing well. They argue that in the context of ageing populations, housing that supports social and physical care needs is increasingly becoming important, yet long-term strategies to support the development of housing which are appropriate to these needs are not well developed.

Very few studies have examined the determinants of SWB in a cross-country setting. Two chapters included in the book add unique perspectives to the literature on cross-country determinants of SWB. Sook Ning Chua, Sefa Awaworyi Churchill and Richard Koestner examine the effects of personal and country-level freedom in the wellbeing of older people across 93 countries. It has been long recognized that a sense of personal control is essential to health and wellbeing in the aged, especially as experiences related to control are likely to increase during old age (Baltes, Wahl, & Schmid-Furstoss, 1990; Smith et al., 2000). However, no study has examined the individual and interactive effects of individual freedom and national freedom on wellbeing among the elderly. Chua, Awaworyi Churchill and Koestner bring together data from three sources, namely the WVS, the World Bank's World Development Indicators (WDI) database and the Freedom House database to examine how the interaction between individual and country-level freedom impacts on the wellbeing of the elderly. They focus on subjective happiness and life satisfaction as measures of wellbeing. Their findings suggest that people with low personal control have greater life satisfaction when living in countries with limited political and civic liberties, compared to living in free countries. Their study highlights the importance of ensuring the political and civil liberties of nations.

Sefa Awaworyi Churchill and Anne-Laure Mention present the second cross-country study in the book. They examine the relationship between country-level innovation and SWB. They focus on 58 countries using individual-level data from the WVS and country-level innovation measures including the Global Innovation Index (GII) and patents. Their findings show that country-level innovation tends to enhance the wellbeing of the elderly. Their cross-country study builds on the previous literature that has investigated the innovation–wellbeing relationship in a single country setting (see, e.g., Dolan and Metcalfe [2012] and their survey of the British population).

In a concluding chapter, Appau and Awaworyi Churchill reflect on the chapters of the book and provide critical discussions on how policy aimed at improving the wellbeing of older people can be more effective. The authors examine the role of discourses of ageism in scientific and popular discourse and how these discourses can negatively influence and affect even well-intended policies and interventions. They further advocate for policies and interventions aimed at improving the wellbeing of older people to adopt an intersectionality lens to better capture disadvantages older people may have due to various vulnerable social identities.

## 4 Conclusion

The gradual eradication of mass poverty, development of technology and better health systems have ensured that life expectancy is at an unprecedented high globally. This has resulted in record ageing populations, with the number of people aged 60 years and above having tripled in the last half-century alone. Overall, the chapters in this book provide an expansive and insightful collection of knowledge on measuring and understanding the wellbeing of this ageing population. All the authors have also thoughtfully reflected on their findings to offer useful and practical directions to policy makers and practitioners to improve the wellbeing of older persons across developing and developed contexts. It is our hope that this book and the chapters within will add to and encourage more scholarly interest in understanding and improving the wellbeing of ageing people everywhere in the world.

## References


Aberdeen, L., & Bye, L.-A. (2013). Challenges for Australian sociology: Critical ageing research–ageing well? *Journal of Sociology, 49*(1), 3–21.

Awaworyi Churchill, S., & Mishra, V. (2017). Trust, Social Networks and Subjective Wellbeing in China. *Social Indicators Research, 132*(1), 313–339. https://doi.org/10.1007/s11205-015-1220-2.

Awaworyi Churchill, S., & Smyth, R. (2019). Transport poverty and subjective wellbeing. *Transportation Research Part a: Policy and Practice, 124,* 40–54. https://doi.org/10.1016/j.tra.2019.03.004.

Bache, I., & Scott, K. (Eds.). (2018). *The politics of wellbeing: Theory, policy and practice.* London: Palgrave Macmillan.

Baltes, M. M., Wahl, H.-W., & Schmid-Furstoss, U. (1990). The daily life of elderly germans: Activity patterns, personal control, and functional health. *Journal of Gerontology, 45*(4), P173–P179. https://doi.org/10.1093/geronj/45.4.P173.

Bergstad, C. J., Gamble, A., Gärling, T., Hagman, O., Polk, M., Ettema, D., et al. (2011). Subjective well-being related to satisfaction with daily travel. *Transportation, 38*(1), 1–15.

Blanchflower, D. G., & Oswald, A. J. (2011). International happiness: A new view on the measure of performance. *Academy of Management Perspectives, 25*(1), 6–22.

Bowling, A. (2005). *Ageing well: Quality of life in old age.* Berkshire, UK: Open University Press.

Case, A., Paxson, C., & Islam, M. (2009). Making sense of the labor market height premium: Evidence from the British Household Panel Survey. *Economics Letters, 102*(3), 174–176.

Cosco, T. D., Matthew Prina, A., Perales, J., Stephan, B., & Brayne, C. (2014). Whose "successful ageing"?: Lay-and researcher-driven conceptualisations of ageing well. *The European Journal of Psychiatry, 28*(2), 124–130.

Cummins, R. A. (2000). Personal income and Subjective Well-Being: A review. *Journal of Happiness Studies, 1*(2), 133–158.

Davey, J. A. (2007). Older people and transport: Coping without a car. *Ageing & Society, 27*(1), 49–65.

Diener, E. (1984). Subjective Well-Being. *Psychological Bulletin, 95*(3), 542–575. https://doi.org/10.1037/0033-2909.95.3.542.

Diener, E. (1994). Assessing subjective well-being: Progress and opportunities. *Social Indicators Research, 31*(2), 103–157.

Diener, E., & Chan, M. Y. (2011). Happy people live longer: Subjective well-being contributes to health and longevity. *Applied Psychology: Health and Well-Being, 3*(1), 1–43.

Diener, E., Emmons, R. A., Larsen, R. J., & Griffin, S. (1985). The satisfaction with life scale. *Journal of Personality Assessment, 49*(1), 71–75. https://doi.org/10.1207/s15327752jpa4901_13.

Diener, E., & Oishi, S. (2000). Money and happiness: Income and Subjective Well-Being across nations. In E. D. E. M. Suh (Ed.), *Culture and Subjective Well-Being* (pp. 185–218). Cambridge, MA: The MIT Press.

Diener, E., Oishi, S., & Lucas, R. E. (2003). Personality, culture, and subjective well-being: Emotional and cognitive evaluations of life. *Annual Review of Psychology, 54*(1), 403–425.

Diener, E., Sandvik, E., Seidlitz, L., & Diener, M. (1993). The relationship between income and Subjective Well-Being: Relative or absolute? *Social Indicators Research, 28*(3), 195–223.

Dolan, P., & Metcalfe, R. (2012). The relationship between innovation and Subjective Wellbeing. *Research Policy, 41*(8), 1489–1498.

Dolan, P., Peasgood, T., & White, M. (2008). Do we really know what makes us happy? A review of the economic literature on the factors associated with Subjective Well-Being. *Journal of Economic Psychology, 29*(1), 94–122. https://doi.org/10.1016/j.joep.2007.09.001.

Fleurbaey, M. (2009). Beyond GDP: The quest for a measure of social welfare. *Journal of Economic Literature, 47*(4), 1029–1075.

Frankel, B. G., & Hewitt, W. (1994). Religion and well-being among Canadian university students: The role of faith groups on campus. *Journal for the Scientific Study of Religion, 33*(1), 62–73.

Fredrickson, B. L. (2002). How does religion benefit health and well-being? Are positive emotions active ingredients? *Psychological Inquiry, 13*(3), 209–213.

Gao, W., & Smyth, R. (2010). Health human capital, height and wages in China. *The Journal of Development Studies, 46*(3), 466–484.

Haring-Hidore, M., Stock, W. A., Okun, M. A., & Witter, R. A. (1985). Marital status and Subjective Well-Being: A research synthesis. *Journal of Marriage and the Family, 47*(4), 947–953.

Harker, L., & Keltner, D. (2001). Expressions of positive emotion in women's college yearbook pictures and their relationship to personality and life outcomes across adulthood. *Journal of Personality and Social Psychology, 80*(1), 112.

Headey, B., Muffels, R., & Wooden, M. (2008). Money does not buy happiness: Or does it? A reassessment based on the combined effects of wealth, income and consumption. *Social Indicators Research, 87*(1), 65–82.
Headey, B., & Wooden, M. (2004). The effects of wealth and income on Subjective Well-Being and ill-being. *Economic Record, 80,* S24–S33.
Hicks, S., Tinkler, L., & Allin, P. (2013). Measuring Subjective Well-Being and its potential role in policy: Perspectives from the UK office for national statistics. *Social Indicators Research, 114*(1), 73–86.
Hooghe, M., & Vanhoutte, B. (2011). Subjective well-being and social capital in Belgian communities. The impact of community characteristics on subjective Well-Being indicators in Belgium. *Social Indicators Research, 100*(1), 17–36.
Hudders, L., & Pandelaere, M. (2012). The silver lining of materialism: The impact of luxury consumption on Subjective Well-Being. *Journal of Happiness Studies, 13*(3), 411–437.
Hudson, J. (2006). Institutional trust and Subjective Well-Being across the EU. *Kyklos, 59*(1), 43–62.
Lau, R., & Morse, C. A. (2008). Health and wellbeing of older people in Anglo-Australian and Italian-Australian communities: A rural–urban comparison. *Australian Journal of Rural Health, 16*(1), 5–11.
Lindert, J., Bain, P. A., Kubzansky, L. D., & Stein, C. (2015). Well-being measurement and the WHO health policy Health 2010: Systematic review of measurement scales. *European Journal of Public Health, 25*(4), 731–740. https://doi.org/10.1093/eurpub/cku193.
Linton, M.-J., Dieppe, P., & Medina-Lara, A. (2016). Review of 99 self-report measures for assessing well-being in adults: Exploring dimensions of well-being and developments over time. *British Medical Journal Open, 6*(7), e010641.
Lucas, R. (2018). Reevaluating the strengths and weaknesses of self-report measures of subjective well-being. In E. Diener, S. Oishi, & L. Tay (Eds.), *Handbook of Well-being.* DEF Publishers: Salt Lake City, UT.
Luhmann, M., Hofmann, W., Eid, M., & Lucas, R. E. (2012). Subjective Well-Being and adaptation to life events: a meta-analysis. *Journal of Personality and Social Psychology, 102*(3), 592.
Lyubomirsky, S., & Lepper, H. S. (1999). A measure of subjective happiness: Preliminary reliability and construct validation. *Social Indicators Research, 46*(2), 137–155. https://doi.org/10.1023/a:1006824100041.
Okun, M. A., Stock, W. A., Haring, M. J., & Witter, R. A. (1984). Health and Subjective Well-Being: A meta-analysis. *The International Journal of Aging*

*and Human Development, 19*(2), 111–132. https://doi.org/10.2190/qgjn-0n81-5957-haqd.
Pinquart, M., & Sörensen, S. (2000). Influences of socioeconomic status, social network, and competence on Subjective Well-Being in later life: A meta-analysis. *Psychology and Aging, 15*(2), 187–224. https://doi.org/10.1037/0882-7974.15.2.187.
Schultz, T. P. (2002). Wage gains associated with height as a form of health human capital. *American Economic Review, 92*(2), 349–353.
Smith, G. C., Kohn, S. J., Savage-Stevens, S. E., Finch, J. J., Ingate, R., & Lim, Y.-O. (2000). The effects of interpersonal and personal agency on perceived control and psychological well-being in adulthood. *The Gerontologist, 40*(4), 458–468. https://doi.org/10.1093/geront/40.4.458.
Smith, A. E., Sim, J., Scharf, T., & Phillipson, C. (2004). Determinants of quality of life amongst older people in deprived neighbourhoods. *Ageing & Society, 24*(5), 793–814.
Stiglitz, J. E., Sen, A., & Fitoussi, J.-P. (2010). *Report by the commission on the measurement of economic performance and social progress.* Paris: Commission on the Measurement of Economic Performance and Social Progress.
Van der Meer, P. H. (2014). Gender, unemployment and Subjective Well-Being: Why being unemployed is worse for men than for women. *Social Indicators Research, 115*(1), 23–44.
Wang, H., Cheng, Z., & Smyth, R. (2019). Consumption and happiness. *The Journal of Development Studies, 55*(1), 120–136.
Winkelmann, R. (2009). Unemployment, social capital, and Subjective Well-Being. *Journal of Happiness Studies, 10*(4), 421–430.
Witter, R. A., Stock, W. A., Okun, M. A., & Haring, M. J. (1985). Religion and Subjective Well-Being in adulthood: A quantitative synthesis. *Review of Religious Research, 26*(4), 332–342.
Zhang, Z., & Zhang, J. (2015). Social participation and Subjective Well-Being among retirees in China. *Social Indicators Research, 123*(1), 143–160.

# 2

# Empowering the Independence of Older People with Everyday Technologies

Paolo Franco

## 1 Background

Like many developed nations, Australia faces an ageing population (Australian Bureau of Statistics, 2017). An associated challenge of such a continuing demographic shift is the pursuit of a high quality of life for this growing number of older Australians. Amongst many initiatives, to meet this challenge the Australian government seeks to develop older people's skills with everyday technologies (Be Connected, 2017). It is assumed that the adoption and consumption of smartphones, tablets and computers will enable older people to connect digitally to family and friends, shop online, be entertained and access various online welfare services—activities which promise to improve their quality of life.

P. Franco (✉)
Department of Management and Marketing,
The University of Melbourne, Melbourne, VIC, Australia
e-mail: franco.p@unimelb.edu.au



S. Awaworyi Churchill et al. (eds.), *Measuring, Understanding and Improving Wellbeing Among Older People*,
https://doi.org/10.1007/978-981-15-2353-3_2

The aim of this chapter is to contextualise these developments within the lived experiences of older people, in order to explore how their quality of life is influenced by their adoption and consumption of everyday technologies. In particular, I discuss this topic through its intersection with the concept of independence, following findings developed through an ethnography where I served as a 'tech-helper' volunteer at a retirement village in Melbourne, Australia. To achieve this aim, the chapter is structured as follows: First, I discuss the intersection between the concepts of quality of life and independence as they pertain to older people in the ageing literature. Second, I extend this discussion to the consumer literature which helps us think about the independence of older people in relation to their adoption and consumption of tech-products. Third, I describe the ethnographic fieldwork contained in this chapter. Fourth, I present two findings from the ethnography: (1) older people experience various impetuses to bring new technologies into their lives which can impact upon their independence, and (2) older people face various challenges in seeking and receiving tech-help from others. Finally, I end this chapter with a discussion of two implications for policymakers who wish to empower the independence of older people and impact upon their quality of life: (1) policies should extend their focuses beyond older people's abilities to use tech-products for their self-care needs, and (2) policies should consider and support the advantages of each source of tech-help drawn upon by older people to learn how to use and fix their tech-products.

## 2 Quality of Life and Independence for Older People

The concept of *quality of life* aims to capture something about 'the "good life" and what makes life worth living' for older people (Schwanen & Ziegler, 2011: 721). It is a subjective assessment that an older person makes about each major area of their life, such as satisfaction with their self, family life, friends, health, finances, housing situation and activities (Gabriel & Bowling, 2004). Moreover, quality of life is considered a reflection of an older person's wider well-being (Fleuret & Atkinson,

2007; Lawton, 1983) and intersects with the notion of their independence (Schwanen & Ziegler, 2011).

*Independence* is dominantly understood in Western contexts such as Australia as an older person's abilities to perform daily self-care activities such as bathing, dressing, eating and toileting which impact upon quality of life (Ball et al., 2004; Reindal, 1999). Often, independence is defined as an absence of dependence on others in order to do these activities. However, growing scholarship argues that conceptualisations of independence should be disentangled from dependence as older people might still draw help from others while at the same time still feeling that they are able to live independently (Portacolone, 2011; Secker, Hill, Villeneau, & Parkman, 2003).

In turn, scholarship has provided alternative conceptualisations which do not centre upon abilities to do daily self-care activities, but instead draw on older people's wider understandings of what independence means to them. For instance, in addition to self-care, older people consider independence as their ability to guide the direction of their life (Secker et al., 2003). That an older person has the freedom to choose the things that they do, even if this means that they require help from others to carry out these activities. This type of autonomy extends to further aspects older people consider as part of their independence. These include being able to pass time in meaningful ways (e.g. not sitting around and doing nothing) and living a lifestyle which helps them continue their sense of identity (e.g. continued pursuance of their hobbies and passions) (Ball et al., 2004).

Another strand of research highlights that independence can be considered a collective achievement of not just the older person or others involved, but also with the various non-human things in the situational environment (Schwanen & Ziegler, 2011). For example, simple material objects like handles affixed to the wall can enable an older person to use the restroom on their own (Peace, Holland, & Kellaher, 2011), and living in one's own home to 'age-in-place' enables the continuance of a desired lifestyle and identity that signals independence (Portacolone, 2011; Schwanen & Ziegler, 2011). Similarly, assistance technologies like fall alarms and mobile phones allow older people some scope to perform activities for themselves, knowing that on the off chance that they experience an emergency situation, help can be quickly contacted and be on its way (Bailey, Foran, Scanaill, & Dromey, 2011).

In sum, quality of life and independence for older people are two interrelated concepts. Independence, in particular, captures older people's abilities to carry out everyday activities for themselves, where at times they might seek out assistance. Additionally, independence strongly factors into older people's subjective quality of life assessments which concern major areas of life beyond self-care activities, and it can be considered a collective achievement done alongside various objects. In the next section, I expand upon this discussion by highlighting tech-products as a class of objects which can be involved in shaping an older person's activities (e.g. smartphones, tablets, laptops). In so doing, I argue that their adoption and consumption can have impacts upon their independence and thus the quality of life they experience.

## 3 Independence Through the Adoption and Consumption of Tech-Products

Consumer research studies which focus on older people illustrate how interactions with everyday products can shape their independence. Scholarship within this tradition provides a lens in which we can understand people's lived experiences through their acquisition, possession and use, and divestment of products (Arnould & Thompson, 2005). For instance, products can make family aware of an older relative's declining abilities to do things for themselves (Huff & Cotte, 2016). Consider an older person who experiences increasing difficulties going grocery shopping or doing their laundry. These difficulties can signal that he or she might soon require assisted living care. Similarly, tensions arise when family members such as adult children intervene in these situations (Dean, Kellie, & Mould, 2014). Simple actions such as an insistence on assisting with shopping activities or taking over the management of possessions can impinge upon an older person's feelings of independence. Such tensions may stem from the stigma that older people experience from being treated differently due to their age and the related assumptions others make about their capabilities (Tepper, 1994).

Consumer research additionally shows that hindrances to independence go beyond older people's capabilities to do daily self-care activities for themselves. For example, older people also evaluate their independence through their declining capabilities to pay bills, tend to their backyard, and to travel (Barnhart & Peñaloza, 2013). Moreover, independence can be threatened by an older person's diminishing abilities to pursue hobbies and passions such as repairing cars or collecting books (Dean et al., 2014). It is clear that the manner in which consumption activities are treated and are carried out generate meanings which inform assessments of an older person's independence.

While studies in the ageing literature dominantly examine older people's adoption of assisted living care technologies for healthcare purposes (e.g. McCreadie & Tinker, 2005; Mostaghel, 2016; Walsh & Callan, 2011; Wang, Redington, Steinmetz, & Lindeman, 2011), consumer research tends to examine the more everyday technological products which become part of their lives. Typically studied are smartphones, tablets and computers (e.g. Hough & Kobylanksi, 2009; Marchant & O'Donohoe, 2014). For simplicity, I refer to everyday products such as these in this chapter as 'tech-products'.

Many studies begin with the straightforward premise that the adoption and consumption of tech-products can improve the independence of older people. Potentials to manage physical impairments and combat social isolation through digital connections to family and friends are quickly highlighted (e.g. Hough & Kobylanksi, 2009; Nikou, 2015). However, this stance risks immediately assuming that tech-products are sure-fire solutions to various challenges to independence and that the process of learning how to use them is not without its problems. In fact, wider consumer research shows that tech-products can create as many problems as solutions in people's lives (Kozinets, 2008; Mick & Fournier, 1998). For example, tech-products can cause frustrations when they cannot be put to their uses, failing to live up to the promises that marketers make about what they enable people to do (Thompson, 1994). When experienced by an older person, these frustrations might thus be reflective of things they are not able to do for themselves—becoming further potential threats to their independence.

Indeed, consumer research shows that older people consider how tech-products might problematically impact upon their independence when thinking about whether or not to adopt them and bring them into their lives (Hough & Kobylanksi, 2009; Lee & Coughlin, 2015). For example, older consumers are commonly stereotyped as not being aware of contemporary technologies and/or being skilled in their uses (Gilly & Zeithaml, 1985; Niemelä-Nyrhinen, 2007). Thus, the adoption of a new smartphone might be seen by the older person and others to require assistance from a younger family member in order for its functions to be learned and used (Marchant & O'Donohoe, 2014). These social understandings can impinge on the older person's independence and might even become manifested as dependencies on family members in order to be able to use the tech-products in their life (Siddiqui & Turley, 2007).

What all these studies signal is a possible tension present in older people's efforts to successfully adopt and consume tech-products. That in seeking tech-products' benefits which promise improvements to their independence, older people might instead experience becoming technologically dependent on others for help in using them. These insights mirror the general ageing literature which also identifies this careful balancing act between independence and receiving help (Ball et al., 2004; Secker et al., 2003). Research suggests this balancing act stems from the perception that being able to live independently from others is a marker of social status in Western societies (Portacolone, 2011; Reindal, 1999; Schwanen & Ziegler, 2011), where an older person seeking help is interpreted as a sign of their weakness or lack of character (Secker et al., 2003). These social understandings are influences which arguably lead to older people becoming resistant towards seeking and receiving help, even if they truly need it.

Amidst this literature, the empirical research of this chapter seeks to explore this relationship between the independence of older people and the adoption and consumption of the technologies which become part of their lives. In particular, I ask two research questions: (1) *How does the adoption and consumption of tech-products shape older people's lived experience of their independence?* and (2) *What are older people's lived experiences of seeking and receiving help with their tech-products?* With this theoretical landscape outlined, I now discuss the details of the ethnography which informs the findings and policy implications contained in this chapter.

## 4 A 'Tech-Helper' Volunteer Ethnography of a Retirement Village

The research in this chapter emerged out of my wider exploration of people's lived experiences of adopting and consuming various tech-products, which involved an ethnographic component I completed within a retirement village located in Melbourne, Australia. Ethnographic methods are drawn upon in consumer research to discern patterns of consumption which contribute towards the shaping of people's lived experiences. The underlying idea is that immersion and participation in a specific cultural context enable the researcher access to such consumption patterns of members and their associated meanings as they unfold in their natural settings (Arnould, 1998; Arnould & Wallendorf, 1994). In order to be able to develop this type of understanding, the researcher must gain the trust of members and become part of their activities over a period of time. In so doing, the researcher is considered the instrument tasked with capturing things to do with the cultural context, through multiple data collection methods such as observational fieldnotes, photos and interviews (Belk, Sherry, & Wallendorf, 1988). The ultimate aim of the collection and analysis of these materials is to produce a faithful representation of how consumption impacts members' lives and how they engage with the world around them (Arnould, 1998).

Within the retirement village context, I took on the role of a volunteer by offering my technology help services to residents. I carried out these activities by holding weekly 'tech-help drop-in sessions' at the village community centre library. Residents were encouraged to bring along tech-products they wanted to learn more about or needed help with to the sessions, where I troubleshooted technical issues and coached their usage one-on-one with residents. Residents' smartphones, tablets and laptop computers were the most common technologies I encountered. To assist with less portable technologies like desktop computers and Wi-Fi routers, I made house-calls to supplement the regular drop-in sessions.

I conducted the ethnography over a period of 14 months in 2018–2019, with my collected data taking the form of audio-recorded interviews with those at the village and fieldnotes, both of which were later transcribed. I collected and analysed these materials iteratively throughout the duration of ethnography in order to develop the findings (Belk et al., 1988; Spiggle, 1994). Pseudonyms are used in this chapter for everyone I encountered during the ethnography, in order to protect their identities while I share their lived experiences through the findings sections of this chapter.

Entering into the village through a tech-helper role allowed me access to residents' everyday lived experiences with their tech-products, which was crucial to developing an understanding of their independence (Schwanen & Ziegler, 2011). It was through my successes in solving tech-problems and teaching residents various uses of contemporary technologies that I was able to gain their trust and willingness to share stories about how their lives have been impacted by their tech-products (Cayla & Arnould, 2013). Moreover, being a tech-helper volunteer placed me in a position where I could observe and be involved with residents' efforts to seek and receive tech-help, which gave me an opportunity to gauge how these experiences interplayed with their feelings of independence. As a result, themes surrounding independence naturally emerged out of the ethnographic data. To better understand this potential tension between independence and the need to seek help, further explanation of the life stage of the residents and the wider context of the village is informative.

Dissimilar to many portrayals of older people in the ageing and consumer literatures (e.g. Ball et al., 2004; Mostaghel, 2016), those at the village were for the most part able-bodied with minimal cognitive issues outside of occasional forgetfulness. The village itself is positioned as a place for retirees who wish to live a community lifestyle with access to some shared facilities such as a library, cafeteria and function hall. Moreover, the village is adorned with nineteenth-century cottages and is a short walk from train, tram and bus public transport options. These features demarcate the village from commonly studied contexts in which older people live, such as assisted living facilities or with family carers, as most residents do not have as significant caring needs and they remain mobile and active in their wider local communities.

However, residents were conscious that if their health situation and abilities were to decline that they would progress to an assisted living care facility. Thus, being part of the village could be considered a liminal life stage for residents, who for the time being were able to sustain a relatively active and independent lifestyle. For most residents, their established pathway towards future-assisted living care was, nevertheless, a far-off but lingering concern. Residents' days were filled with the minutia of a retiree lifestyle consisting of community club activities, planned outings with family and friends, and hobbies such as cooking, board games and gardening. It is within this setting that residents' experiences of their independence and the adoption and consumption of their tech-products unfolded as the following findings demonstrate.

## 5 Impetuses for Older People to Adopt and Consume New Technologies

Village residents experienced various impetuses to bring everyday tech-products like smartphones, tablets and computers into their lives. These ranged from needs to do basic things like emails and web browsing which could enable residents to manage their own affairs, to desired uses which could support their leisure activities, hobbies and passions. Additionally, tech-products on occasion suddenly appeared in residents' lives when given by family members. In these situations, residents often had little to no explanation from giving family members about how to use the tech-product they had received so they could successfully put it to use. In this section, I share examples which illustrate these observations and provide insight as to how older people's adoption and consumption of tech-products can impact upon their independence.

*Necessary Tech-Product Uses.* First and foremost, residents felt that smartphone, tablet and computer use was becoming a necessity due to life in the village being increasingly organised via email and messaging services. These uses were analogous to basic self-care activities of residents in prior research, where these tech-products enabled residents to manage their own affairs (Ball et al., 2004; Reindal, 1999). Nancy and Marie explained why emailing and messaging were necessary activities everyone should be able to do for themselves:

> If there's an emergency or I've got an invitation to dinner, I'll get a notification through my email. [People at the village] never really give phone calls because we never answer. I think it's a habit really. I mean, everybody seems to have an email. (Nancy, 82, F)

> You have to be in it now that you have to be able to send emails. No one writes letters anymore. People don't ring you. Emailing or texting is the only way you keep in touch with people these days. You have to be able to do it. (Marie, 84, F)

In turn, not being able to use such devices for email or messaging was seen as a hindrance to being able to live independently within the village, as without these abilities key information about events and activities might be missed. Jeremy expressed this sentiment about his newly purchased smartphone:

> It's a big help, you know? You have to have it nearly. If you're on your own – we're all on our own now. All these things [emails, messaging, village activities] you can't do without *that* [Jeremy points at his smartphone]. (Jeremy, 84, M)

Adopting and using tech-products enabled residents to manage their social activities within the village. Moreover, residents sought to be better able to keep connected with family and other social groups outside the village. Often these desired uses spanned beyond email. For example, many wanted to keep up with family members who regularly posted photos from family gatherings on Facebook, and others wanted to learn about other social media services like Instagram to connect with family and friends who were living or travelling overseas.

Smartphones, tablets and computers were also considered necessities to access social welfare services, which were increasingly moving online in the form of websites and apps. Several requests for tech-help involved residents needing help accessing these services when requests were made for them to fill out forms and provide documentation online by government:

> Dorothy needed some help today with this health insurance thing and something that she needs to 'opt out' of from the government. And she said that she can only do that online… (Fieldnotes, July 2018)

> Elena needed some help using the community library computers. She was going to provide some documentation that she needed to pass on to Centrelink online [Australian social welfare body] to ensure that her social welfare payments continue… She said she's been trying to do this successfully for six-months now… (Fieldnotes, March 2019)

*Meaningful Choices of Tech-Product Use.* Beyond these necessary uses where tech-products could enable residents to manage their own affairs were situations in which they could enhance other areas of their lives, such as their leisure activities, hobbies and passions. Such activities also contribute towards older people's feelings of independence as identified in prior research, as they enable residents an increased selection of meaningful ways they can choose to spend their time (Ball et al., 2004; Secker et al., 2003). For example, a few residents sought out lessons on how to listen to podcasts and use music streaming services like Spotify and Apple Music, and video streaming services like Netflix and the Australian Broadcasting Corporation's iView. All were valued for the vast catalogues of content they offered, which included music and television programs from residents' youth, and news and current affairs. A smaller selection of residents sought out help to integrate tech-products into their hobbies and passions. Consider Stuart who is a car enthusiast who relies on his satellite phone while on interstate drives, and Nancy who is a talented artist who uses her iPad and computer to help her create artworks for the village community:

> Stuart dropped by as he was about to go on a long drive to Western Australia as part of a convoy and he needed help with updating the firmware on his satellite phone [important software which enables the device to work]. It's refusing to work without the update being applied and he's not sure how to do it. He said he brings the phone just in case he and his wife get stranded in an area that doesn't have mobile phone reception and they need to call for help. The phone actually saved them before while his car broke down in rural Queensland on a previous drive… (Fieldnotes, March 2019)

> For the first time in my life, things are accessible. Doing cards and tea towel designs, everything. I did the drawings [of various cottages in the village] then photographed them [with her iPad]. I sent them to Western Australia on my computer… for someone else to print them on a coarser fabric. Yes, it's all useful equipment for doing things within the community. (Nancy, 82, F)

In both examples, the tech-products involved were essential objects which contributed towards the successful undertaking of a hobby or passion-related activity for each resident. In so doing, their uses were important to sustain identities such as car enthusiast and artist, which aided each resident's feelings of independence (Dean et al., 2014; Schwanen & Ziegler, 2011).

A final impetus for tech-adoption and consumption observed were situations where a tech-product was given to a resident by family as a gift or as a hand-me-down. These situations were different as they did not involve the older person seeking out and purchasing the technology for themselves, but rather their adoption and consumption being instigated by their sudden receipt of the tech-product. Due to this, gifts and hand-me-downs were sometimes thought of as impositions upon the resident by the giver which impinged upon their independence. Consider Josie's attempts to load music onto her iPhone, and Sally's struggles accessing her email through her computer:

> In looking at Josie's Apple Music app for her, it turned out that she's already on a family subscription and that she doesn't need to transfer music from her CDs to her iPhone. She said that her children never

explained to her how her device works when they gave it to her. It was striking that she's had the subscription to an almost unlimited library of songs and she's had no idea for months, and that she was desperate for music on her phone the whole time just to find a use for the device! (Fieldnotes, February 2019)

[Sally] said that she received the computer from her son, who's an IT professional. He's built it for her, but she said he hasn't even helped her out with this computer at all beyond setting it up – he's always 'too busy'. So, she's stuck trying to figure out how to access her email which she can't even get working on this computer... (Fieldnotes, August 2018)

Gifts and hand-me-downs from family often followed this pattern, where family members either provided little to no explanation about how to use the tech-product given, or they provided an explanation the resident could not follow and understand. When the residents I encountered at the village ended up in situations like these where they were unable to successfully use their tech-products for their necessary functions or for their potentials to enhance leisure activities, hobbies and passions, they sought out help. This was regardless of whether they purchased the tech-product for themselves or had received it as a gift or hand-me-down. Nevertheless, as I discuss in the next section, residents faced various challenges in seeking and receiving this needed technical assistance from various sources of help.

## 6 Older People's Challenges in Seeking and Receiving 'Tech-Help'

The vast majority of residents were unfamiliar with how to use contemporary tech-products like smartphones and tablets. However, some did have exposure to computers as a selection of their uses were required in their previous working lives just before they had retired. These knowledge gaps were exacerbated for residents by virtue of living in the village, as there were few opportunities to be socialised into various tech-products' uses and learn from each other, as a small handful of residents were technologically skilled. For these reasons, residents had a strong need to seek out help.

Contrary to literature which portrays older people as being reluctant to seek out help out of desires to be independent (e.g. Portacolone, 2011; Secker et al., 2003), I did not observe much hesitation by residents to seek out the technical help I provided. I believe this could be for two reasons. First, this might be a matter of the design of the ethnography, as my role in the village community as a tech-helper would predispose me to encounter residents who were happier to actively seek out tech-help. In so doing, my presence is likely to have legitimised these efforts and provided a socially sanctioned source residents could draw upon. Second, and what I believe might also be the case, is that some older people lean into the stereotype that they are not supposed to be skilled with technology (cf. Niemelä-Nyrhinen, 2007). Hence, the stereotype might have also contributed towards residents' feelings that asking for help from a younger person is appropriate and is not a sign of weakness or lack of character (cf. Secker et al., 2003). However, residents did share with me experiences of receiving help from family members, the market (e.g. salespeople and professional providers of tech-help) and others in the community which made them hesitant to return to these sources of assistance. I believe these experiences made the help I provided more attractive to the residents I encountered.

*Family Tech-Help.* Residents' first point of contact for help was usually a family member, but receiving their assistance could be complicated for a few reasons. First, living in the village meant that residents were not co-located with family members beyond a partner at best. This physical separation reduced the opportunities for in-person interaction (Epp, Schau, & Price, 2014), which impacted upon family members' abilities to assist. Receiving in-person help was crucial to residents as many did not have the skills required to operate their tech-products in order to follow directions outlined over the phone or sent via email.

Not being co-located with family and requiring in-person help was also complicated by a second challenging aspect to asking family—residents were worried that their requests for in-person help would use too much of their time. For example, Nancy shared a common sentiment amongst residents who were mindful of family members' schedules:

They're usually busy... I've actually got two grandsons who are doing their Year 12 [final year of high school in Australia] – they're studying like mad. I don't expect them to come here and sit down and help me. (Nancy, 82, F)

In situations where residents did get a chance to receive in-person help from a family member, many felt that their explanations and teachings were too fast for them to be able to follow—a third difficulty of family help. Tina expressed her frustrations in how she felt family tended to help her with her smartphone:

This is the biggest challenge for my generation is you ask a question on any technology, and they go, 'You just do it like this!' [Tina mimes tapping fast on her smartphone screen] And then they walk off! And you ask again and then they're starting to get frustrated. But if they're going 'Just like this!' [miming tapping fast again] – You've lost me at the start! (Tina, 76, F)

Brian, another village tech-helper volunteer, encountered similar stories from the residents he had encountered in the village:

It's just something that occurred to me as I watched these people, you can see that they want to try it. And of course, what the son will do, "Look Mum, it's easy. You just do... bang bang bang bang... [Brian pretends to tap furiously on a smartphone] See it's done?" And they don't know how they did it. (Brian, 70, M)[1]

Receiving help in this way hindered learning and in turn impinged on residents' independence as family were essentially operating their tech-products for them. In so doing, they were denied a chance to gain the

[1]Brian was another tech-helper in the village who was providing lessons to residents in the community's function hall during the early stages of the ethnography. I was surprised to learn that he was 70 years old and that he was very skilled with technology (I had assumed that he was much younger in his 50s when we had first met). It was clear from our interview that Brian has always had an intrinsic interest in tech-products and has kept up with the latest technologies throughout his adult life. Moreover, it was clear that Brian was passionate about helping others in his age group to experience the benefits of adopting and consuming tech-products.

skills required to do these actions for themselves, which made it difficult to keep up and follow the instructions they received. Marie emphasised the importance of getting a chance to learn by doing, which resonated across many residents' experiences of receiving tech-help:

> Instead of someone just explaining… You need to do it. See? Old people learn by doing, it's just useless talking about it. (Marie, 84, F)

*Market Tech-Help.* In order to avoid asking family and experiencing these sorts of issues, residents occasionally turned to the market, asking salespeople for in-store help or paying professional technology help service providers for home visits. Residents experienced mixed results from these sources. Salespeople were notorious amongst residents for rushing through the help they seemed to reluctantly provide. It was clear that their aim was to get older people out of retail spaces quickly:

> I've found that Telstra, they just send you on. Get me out of there to sell more of these! [Jeremy points to his smartphone] They gave me the basic things when I bought this phone. Set it going, but more or less left me to it. (Jeremy, 84, M)

> Florence couldn't connect her smartphone to her carrier and she wasn't clear about her data plan. She said that the person at the Optus store wouldn't help her and said, 'we don't give lessons at Optus.' So, the guy wouldn't even give her basic information about the phone or help her out to figure out what she's actually paying for, which is pretty [expletive] in my opinion. (Fieldnotes, February 2019)

Residents found professional tech-help service providers more welcoming in comparison. These services offered home visits to residents. Nancy and Marie both had positive experiences with the professional tech-help providers they hired:

> During the week, Nancy found her Wi-Fi went down and her iPad, laptop and iPhone could not connect to the internet at her place. She needed to get it fixed immediately. So, she decided to call up Pete [a professional tech-helper], who came over and charged her $40 and fixed up the Wi-Fi

router. He also installed the new wireless printer Nancy just bought as well. Now everything's working again and Nancy's now enjoying photo-quality print-outs of the photos that she's been taking. (Fieldnotes, August 2018)

Well I've been lucky in that I've also got a person who used to be in one of the [Apple] Mac shops and he's now set himself up in business and he's absolutely wonderful at it. So if I'm stuck, he can help me, even though he lives in Geelong, as he's here [in Melbourne] a couple of days a week. (Marie, 84, F)

Despite having positive experiences with professional providers of tech-help, residents reserved this source of help for bigger issues with their tech-products as they could be expensive to hire. Additionally, professionals were hired more to fix tech-problems for residents than to coach them in how to successfully use their devices on their own. For smaller issues and to enable learning about the uses of their tech-products, community sources of tech-help were utilised.

*Community Tech-Help.* Residents shared stories of attending technology classes provided by local libraries in the area. Many mirrored difficulties they experienced in receiving help from family and the market, which prevented them from getting the most out these classes:

I had lessons at the library down here when they first opened. Lessons on the computer and tablets. I went through all that but when I was finished, I didn't really learn much about it. When I was left on my own after, I was just lost, you know? (Jeremy, 84, M)

I think I'm best when they're taking it very slowly. Instead of going... [Alexandra makes a fast hand gesture pretending to furiously swipe her smartphone] and "that's how you do it!" I can't take that at all. (Alexandra, 77, F)

The village itself also hosted classes run by other researchers who were visiting the village during the early stages of my fieldwork. These ran across four weekly sessions that a selection of residents attended together at the village's function hall. While well-intentioned, residents still had difficulties getting the most out of these classes as Nancy explained:

> I go to the classes on Fridays – they love me there! They're very willing and helpful, but I didn't find there was anything really that *I wanted to do*, you know? (Nancy, 82, F)

Residents found that while the classes were informative for the basic operations of smartphones like calling, texting, emailing and online searching, they were not attuned to identifying things that residents *wanted to do* with their tech-products. This may be reflective of help targeted to older people overly focusing on teaching tech-products' basic functions themselves, rather than considering how these functions could fit into and enrich various parts of their lives. For instance, how the tech-product could enable meaningful ways to spend time, or how it may be involved in a hobby or passion—both important elements to independence as discussed throughout in this chapter (Ball et al., 2004; Dean et al., 2014). Residents further explained why classroom situations such as these were not ideal for their learning. The experiences they provided gave an indication as to why the consistent weekly one-on-one individual tech-help I provided over the 14-month fieldwork period was popular amongst the residents who regularly attended:

> It's the one-on-one, it's just so important! Being in a class and someone explaining… It doesn't help. There's a lot of people going "I don't get this!" all at once. It's very frustrating. (Marie, 84, F)

> You need to have an idea of where people are with it [their knowledge level]. I went in after it started and just couldn't understand anything… Since you're here once a week it's really good. It's relieving to know that you're coming next week and I can ask you for help. (Alexandra, 77, F)

> Alexandra kept saying 'if you give me too much at one time, there's no way I'm going to be able to understand it!' I think if I focus on making sure the coaching I'm giving with her smartphone is in smaller bite-sized pieces, she'll be able to pick up more from the drop-in sessions week-to-week. (Fieldnotes, January 2019)

Towards the end of the fieldwork, it had become clear that I had unintentionally stumbled into a role which had become valued by the five or so residents who regularly attended the sessions and the numerous others who sporadically dropped by. What set the sessions apart from the other sources of help residents had tried previously were their one-on-one nature and their long-term weekly regularity over the duration of 14 months. These features were advantageous as I could target my help to each resident's skill level and that together we could approach their learning step-by-step at their pace week-to-week. Moreover, the help I provided was responsive to what the residents wanted to do with their tech-products, as this naturally came from their questions. This was important to their independence as the help I provided enabled residents a wider selection of meaningful things *they could choose to do* with their tech-products and their time (Ball et al., 2004; Dean et al., 2014; Secker et al., 2003). Taken together the residents felt that the service I provided addressed a gap in how they typically received tech-help.

Overall, village residents viewed two overarching categories to their tech-product consumption activities. These categories were reflective of previous research into older people's lived experiences of independence. The first set of uses reflected necessary activities which residents considered that they should be able to do such as email and messaging, analogous to self-care activities (Ball et al., 2004; Reindal, 1999). The second set reflected additional uses which instead served to support choices of meaningful ways residents could spend their time and continue their sense of identity, such as leisure activities, hobbies and passions (Ball et al., 2004; Dean et al., 2014; Secker et al., 2003).

Moreover, village residents experienced various challenges in seeking and receiving tech-help from family members, the market and community in order to adopt and consume the tech-products in their lives. Family members were often busy and lived elsewhere, market providers were either indifferent or expensive, and community sources of help were not always attuned to their technology uses and learning needs. In the next and final section of this chapter, I conclude by offering a selection of considerations for policymakers who desire to leverage upon these ethnographic findings.

## 7 Policy Implications

The overarching message of this article is that the quality of life older people experience intersects with their independence, which can be shaped by their adoption and consumption of everyday technologies like smartphones, tablets and computers. Policies concerning older people's technological literacy which consider the various ways older people experience independence and how they seek and receive tech-help will thus be poised to better deliver quality of life outcomes. The policy implications I now highlight are grouped under two headings: (1) extend policy focus beyond self-care, and (2) consider the advantages of each source of tech-help. While each implication is a direct response to the ethnographic findings from the retirement village in Melbourne, Australia, I believe they can be informative to empower older people of various other walks of life too.

*Extend Policy Focus Beyond Self-Care.* While considering self-care needs in designing policy around technological literacy is still important, the ethnographic findings suggest that extending policy focus towards enabling older people to identify how tech-products can support meaningful ways to spend time is also warranted. In particular, leisure activities, hobbies and passions are clear areas of older people's lives in which a tech-product may find a supporting role. These activities might additionally serve to sustain and even enhance a continued sense of identity that may be important to the older person, such as a tech-product enabling a continued identity of artist, car enthusiast, collector, writer, dancer, community leader, to loving family member. Hence, the aim of teaching older people about tech-products should not merely be for their basic operations themselves, rather how these functions enable them greater choice on what they can choose to do with their time.

Similarly, going beyond self-care also means communicating to older people that independence does not mean that they must do things alone for themselves, rather, they always have the choice to seek help from others when they require it (Reindal, 1999). In this way, help is framed as a tool that an older person can draw upon to guide their life-direction as a choice, instead of something that might otherwise be perceived as a sign of weakness or lack of character (Secker et al., 2003; Tepper, 1994). Policies which take on this framing must then also consider the reasons in which an older person might choose to turn to a specific source of tech-help, as explained next.

*Consider the Advantages of Each Source of Tech-Help*. Policies should take into consideration the reasons for which an older person might choose to turn to a family member, the market or a community organisation for tech-help. Understanding these reasons can allow for policy design to support each source in their provision of help in way which is empathetic to how older people experience independence.

Family members are often the first called upon for tech-help. Their appeal can be due to the family member's close relationship to the older person, with help and technology use being another means to spend time with them (Epp et al., 2014; Marchant & O'Donohoe, 2014). Policy can be directed at family members to empower them to be able to provide more effective learning in a way that does not impinge upon their relative's independence. For example, educational materials can be provided to family members who often find themselves providing tech-help. These can be materials which outline best practices in providing tech-help to older people, such as encouraging helpers to give control of the tech-product to the older person while they are giving instructions, slowing down explanations, and to spread out their learning over a period of time into smaller and more accessible lessons. Similarly, advisory materials can be developed to tackle more difficult situations, like when tech-products are not working and need to be troubleshooted and fixed, which can require skills beyond the older person and even the tech-helper family member themselves. Moreover, these materials can address additional difficulties such as not being co-located and geographically accessible, and not having the time available to help.

In such situations where tech-products require elaborate fixes or family members are unavailable, the market might be better suited to assist. The main advantage of the market is that it can serve as a socially sanctioned way to avoid the troubles of informally asking others such as family for help (Marcoux, 2009). As such, policy might serve to encourage market providers to improve their offerings through understanding situations in which they are a preferred alternative. For example, partnerships with professional tech-help providers can be pursued, to connect them to communities of older people such as retirement villages. Bulk contracts to serve village residents might make professional help to fix tech-products more geographically accessible and less expensive. Moreover, retailers and salespeople who sell tech-products also present opportunities to offer their own specifically designed tech-help services for older people, or in the least, they should be able to give referrals to those able to provide this type of assistance.

Community sources of help such as classes run in local libraries or retirement villages were found to be more suitable for older people to learn how to use their tech-products than solving technical problems. However, classroom situations were not found to be an effective environment for learning, as each class was not able to cater to the individual learning needs and desired tech-product uses of its students. Policies might instead serve to encourage the provision of one-on-one coaching in communities. The types of commitments required for those employed or are volunteering as tech-helpers should be long term, with opportunities for help to be provided on a predictable and consistent basis—for example, on a one-hour weekly basis for more than a year, as in the ethnography. In this way, coaching relationships are able to form between older people and the employees or volunteers taking on this supporting role. This way of providing help is better able to cater to an individual older person's learning needs, as well as figuring out how their tech-products can fit more widely into desired meaningful uses of their time. The immediate challenge, however, is the potential labour intensiveness of such an approach and locating the number of volunteers it might require. Additionally, the accessibilities of communal facilities such as libraries and retirement villages might also need to be supported for such an approach to achieve success.

Overall, policymakers should consider a multi-pronged approach by engaging with family members, the market and community sources of tech-help for older people. It is across these sources of assistance that older people may pick up the skills required to not only learn and use the functions of their tech-products, but rather to find them a place in which they support an increased array of meaningful ways they can choose to spend their time. In so doing, various tech-products and their uses can contribute towards improving older people's independence and the quality of life they experience.

## References


Arnould, E. J. (1998). Daring consumer-oriented ethnography. In B. Stern (Ed.), *Representing consumers: Voices, views and visions* (pp. 85–126). London: Routledge.

Arnould, E. J., & Thompson, C. J. (2005). Consumer culture theory (CCT): Twenty years of research. *Journal of Consumer Research, 31*(4), 868–882.

Arnould, E. J., & Wallendorf, M. (1994). Market-oriented ethnography: Interpretation building and marketing strategy formulation. *Journal of Marketing Research, 31,* 484–504.

Australian Bureau of Statistics. (2017, December 20). *Media release: Census shares insights into Australia's ageing population.* Retrieved from https://www.abs.gov.au/AUSSTATS/abs@.nsf/mediareleasesbyReleaseDate/39BF03C9400F2E2DCA2581FB0019824A?OpenDocument.

Ball, M. M., Perkins, M. M., Whittington, F. J., Hollingsworth, C., King, S. V., & Combs, B. L. (2004). Independence in assisted living. *Journal of Aging Studies, 18*(4), 467–483.

Bailey, C., Foran, T. G., Scanaill, C. N., & Dromey, B. (2011). Older adults, falls and technologies for independent living: A life space approach. *Ageing & Society, 31*(5), 829–848.

Barnhart, M., & Peñaloza, L. (2013). Who are you calling old? Negotiating old age identity in the elderly consumption ensemble. *Journal of Consumer Research, 39*(6), 1133–1153.

Be Connected. (2017, October 3). *About Be Connected.* Australian Government—Department of Social Services. Retrieved from https://beconnected.esafety.gov.au/about-beconnected.

Belk, R. W., Sherry, J. F., & Wallendorf, M. (1988). A naturalistic inquiry into buyer and seller behavior at a swap meet. *Journal of Consumer Research, 14*(4), 449–470.

Cayla, J., & Arnould, E. J. (2013). Ethnographic stories for market learning. *Journal of Marketing, 77*(4), 1–16.

Dean, D., Kellie, J., & Mould, P. (2014). From pushchairs to wheelchairs: Understanding tensions in family decision making through the experiences

of adult children caring for ageing parents. *Journal of Marketing Management, 30*(15–16), 1703–1721.
Epp, A. M., Schau, H. J., & Price, L. L. (2014). The role of brands and mediating technologies in assembling long-distance family practices. *Journal of Marketing, 78*(3), 81–101.
Fleuret, S., & Atkinson, S. (2007). Wellbeing, health and geography: A critical review and research agenda. *New Zealand Geographer, 63*(2), 106–118.
Gabriel, Z., & Bowling, A. (2004). Quality of life from the perspectives of older people. *Ageing & Society, 24*(5), 675–691.
Gilly, M. C., & Zeithaml, V. A. (1985). The elderly consumer and adoption of technologies. *Journal of Consumer Research, 12*(3), 353–357.
Hough, M., & Kobylanski, A. (2009). Increasing elder consumer interactions with information technology. *Journal of Consumer Marketing, 26*(1), 39–48.
Huff, A. D., & Cotte, J. (2016). The evolving family assemblage: How senior families "do" family. *European Journal of Marketing, 50*(5/6), 892–915.
Kozinets, R. V. (2008). Technology/ideology: How ideological fields influence consumers' technology narratives. *Journal of Consumer Research, 34*(6), 865–881.
Lawton, M. P. (1983). Environment and other determinants of well-being in older people. *The Gerontologist, 23*(4), 349–357.
Lee, C., & Coughlin, J. F. (2015). Perspective: Older adults' adoption of technology: An integrated approach to identifying determinants and barriers. *Journal of Product Innovation Management, 32*(5), 747–759.
Marchant, C., & O'Donohoe, S. (2014). Edging out of the nest: Emerging adults' use of smartphones in maintaining and transforming family relationships. *Journal of Marketing Management, 30*(15–16), 1554–1576.
Marcoux, S. (2009). Escaping the gift economy. *Journal of Consumer Research, 36*(4), 671–685.
McCreadie, C., & Tinker, A. (2005). The acceptability of assistive technology to older people. *Ageing & Society, 25*(1), 91–110.
Mick, D. G., & Fournier, S. (1998). Paradoxes of technology: Consumer cognizance, emotions, and coping strategies. *Journal of Consumer Research, 25*(2), 123–143.
Mostaghel, R. (2016). Innovation and technology for the elderly: Systematic literature review. *Journal of Business Research, 69*(11), 4896–4900.
Niemelä-Nyrhinen, J. (2007). Baby boom consumers and technology: Shooting down stereotypes. *Journal of Consumer Marketing, 24*(5), 305–312.
Nikou, S. (2015). Mobile technology and forgotten consumers: The young-elderly. *International Journal of Consumer Studies, 39*(4), 294–304.

Peace, S., Holland, C., & Kellaher, L. (2011). 'Option recognition' in later life: Variations in ageing in place. *Ageing & Society, 31*(5), 734–757.

Portacolone, E. (2011). The myth of independence for older Americans living alone in the bay area of San Francisco: A critical reflection. *Ageing & Society, 31*(5), 803–828.

Reindal, S. M. (1999). Independence, dependence, interdependence: Some reflections on the subject and personal autonomy. *Disability & Society, 14*(3), 353–367.

Schwanen, T., & Ziegler, F. (2011). Wellbeing, independence and mobility: An introduction. *Ageing & Society, 31*(5), 719–733.

Secker, J., Hill, R., Villeneau, L., & Parkman, S. (2003). Promoting independence: But promoting what and how? *Ageing & Society, 23*(3), 375–391.

Siddiqui, S., & Turley, D. (2007). Media technologies: Mediated families. In G. Fitzsimons & V. Morwitz (Eds.), *Advances in consumer research* (Vol. 34, pp. 122–130). Duluth, MN: Association for Consumer Research.

Spiggle, S. (1994). Analysis and interpretation of qualitative data in consumer research. *Journal of Consumer Research, 21*(3), 491–503.

Tepper, K. (1994). The role of labeling processes in elderly consumers' responses to age segmentation cues. *Journal of Consumer Research, 20*(4), 503–519.

Thompson, C. J. (1994). Unfulfilled promises and personal confessions: A postpositivist inquiry into the idealized and experienced meanings of consumer technology. In C. T. Allen & D. R. John (Eds.), *NA—Advances in consumer research* (Vol. 21, pp. 104–108). Provo, UT: Association for Consumer Research.

Walsh, K., & Callan, A. (2011). Perceptions, preferences, and acceptance of information and communication technologies in older-adult community care services in Ireland: A case-study and ranked-care program analysis. *Ageing International, 36*(1), 102–122.

Wang, A., Redington, L., Steinmetz, V., & Lindeman, D. (2011). The ADOPT model: Accelerating diffusion of proven technologies for older adults. *Ageing International, 36*(1), 29–45.

# 3

# Investigating the Relationship Between Housing Insecurity and Wellbeing

Meg Elkins, Lisa Farrell and Jane Fry

## 1 Introduction

With an ageing population and increasing rates of homelessness in older people in most developed countries, it is important to understand the demand for housing support and its impact on the wellbeing of older people who experience housing insecurity. Homelessness relates to a situation where an individual is living without an adequate or regular

M. Elkins (✉) · L. Farrell
School of Economics, Finance and Marketing, RMIT University, Melbourne, VIC, Australia
e-mail: meg.elkins@rmit.edu.au

L. Farrell
e-mail: lisa.farrell@rmit.edu.au

J. Fry
Centre for Health Economics, Monash University, Caulfield East, VIC, Australia
e-mail: jane.fry@monash.edu


S. Awaworyi Churchill et al. (eds.), *Measuring, Understanding and Improving Wellbeing Among Older People*,
https://doi.org/10.1007/978-981-15-2353-3_3

dwelling/residence. This broad definition includes people with irregular night-time shelter, such as those in homeless shelters, domestic violence shelters, cars and sleeping on a friend's sofa or on the street. As well as obvious physical needs, a home contributes to an individual's mental health needs by providing a sense of belonging and promoting wellbeing, as such, having a secure regular dwelling is an essential, basic need. In 2017–2018, specialist homelessness agencies supported 288,000 Australians who were either currently homeless or at risk of becoming homeless.[1] This represents a homelessness rate of around 117.4 individuals per 10,000 people in the population. The actual number of homeless individuals (excluding those at risk of homelessness) is obviously smaller, with 116,427 people experiencing homelessness in Australia on Census night in 2016. Moreover, 21% of clients presenting for services in 2017–2018 were aged 45 years or older.[2]

The rise in housing insecurity in older people has significant economic and social costs. Both physical and mental health are affected by homelessness, which places a growing strain on aged care services through accommodation and healthcare needs. Data for Australia suggests that 65% of homeless people are at risk of death within five years.[3] The transition out of the labour force is a risky time for older people due to falling homeownership and inability to access superannuation or pension payments until certain ages. A growing number of older single women also experience homelessness for the first time later in life. This is often due to a lack of financial resources and assets, domestic violence or the death of a partner, which results in women being unable to sustain secure housing.

In this chapter, we examine detailed accommodation histories to identify distinct patterns in experiences (based on the number and duration of spells of homelessness, homelessness transitions and prior and subsequent accommodation arrangements) of primary and secondary homeless older people. Our analysis uses the high-quality Journeys Home data

---

[1]https://www.aihw.gov.au/reports-data/health-welfare-services/homelessness-services/overview.

[2]https://www.aihw.gov.au/reports/homelessness-services/specialist-homelessness-services-2017-18/contents/policy-framework-for-reducing-homelessness-and-service-response.

[3]Australian Government, *Living Longer, Living Better*, Aged Care Reform Report, Department of Health and Ageing, 2012.

set, which is an Australian nationally representative six-wave panel survey relating to housing stability and homelessness. Accommodation histories are captured as contiguous spells, reported to the nearest month-third over time. Identifying patterns in accommodation allows for a more accurate understanding of housing needs over time, including the extent of repeat demand or entrenched need by the same individuals. Our methodological approach allows us to answer questions about, among other things, the ease with which those experiencing primary homelessness can find night-time shelter, the stability of this shelter and whether primary homelessness is a temporary or longer-term state. Looking at housing changes in the context of housing histories allows us to understand which kinds of changes are transitory and which are likely to lead to a deep disconnect from stable housing. Using the information summarised in the accommodation histories, we then investigate the relationship between housing insecurity and wellbeing. Wellbeing tends to decrease in later life and so it is important to understand how housing insecurity might contribute to this decline. Low levels of wellbeing can lead to poor mental health and low social connections resulting in social isolation. A sense of wellbeing is important to foster a sense of independence and resilience at a time of life when the impacts of ageing can result in many changes for older people. Analysis of the detailed accommodation profiles (housing histories) and wellbeing of this vulnerable older group within our population is therefore of critical importance to a variety of stakeholders including academics, policymakers and support agencies.

## 2 Literature

There is no universal consensus on a definition of homelessness (Chamberlain, 2014; Cobb-Clark, Herault, Scutella, & Tseng, 2016). Minnery and Greenhalgh (2007) find that definitions of homelessness are dynamic and evolving, and generally suited to serving political agendas. Chamberlain and McKenzie (1992) introduced a broad cultural definition of homelessness in Australia. Chamberlain and McKenzie (2008) expanded the definition to recognise primary, secondary and tertiary levels of homelessness. Primary homelessness relates to being without conventional shelter, including sleeping rough, living in abandoned buildings, improvised dwellings, under bridges and in cars. Secondary homelessness refers to moving between different types of temporary shelter. Examples include staying with friends and family; using emergency accommodation, refuges and cheap hotels; and staying in temporary boarding house accommodation for fewer than two weeks. Tertiary homelessness involves being housed, but not in housing considered to be of an acceptable standard, including accommodation such as living in a single room or in a boarding house without a private bathroom, kitchen or secure lease. In 2012, the Australian Bureau of Statistics (ABS) expanded its use of the cultural definition adopted from Chamberlain and McKenzie (2008) and created a new definition that sought to emphasise the 'home' in homelessness. This resulted in a larger proportion of the population to be counted as homeless. The ABS currently defines homelessness as follows: "when a person does not have suitable accommodation alternatives they are considered homeless if their current living arrangement; (i) is in a dwelling that is inadequate; or (ii) has no tenure, or if their initial tenure is short and not extendable; or (iii) does not allow them to have control of, and access to space for social relations' (ABS, 2012). The ABS definition recognises primary, secondary and tertiary levels of homelessness. The choice of definition is important as it will influence findings on size of influences on, for example, durations (Cobb-Clark et al., 2016). Our study uses the Melbourne Institute definition of homelessness based on the Chamberlain and McKenzie (2008) cultural definition of primary, secondary and tertiary levels of homelessness, with additional categories for the marginally housed, those in short-term rentals and the housed.

Many studies use cross-sectional data to analyse point-in-time probabilities of being homeless or perhaps add recall information to model entry to, exit from or duration of single homelessness spells. Studies of transitions and/or durations are mostly 'point-in-time' analyses that do not distinguish between sub-groups. One exception is the taxonomy approach of Lennon, McAllister, Kuang, and Herman (2005), which identifies transient, episodic and chronic homelessness using groups differentiated by their temporal patterns in homelessness. McAllister,

Lennon, and Kuang (2011) extend the three-group typology to take account of temporal and non-temporal factors, such as individual traits like mental illness and substance abuse, and structural elements, such as mental health policies and the criminal justice system.

Longitudinal studies have shown that homelessness is a long-term phenomenon with many potential trajectories (Chamberlain & Johnson, 2013; Toro, 2007). Early studies demonstrated that, intermittently, individuals are able to find accommodation, with the likelihood of returning to homelessness depending on the quality, stability and adequacy of dwellings—although some adapt to homelessness as a state of being (May, 2000; Sosin, Piliavin, & Westerfelt, 1990). Chamberlain and Johnson (2013) refer to pathways as analytical constructs that map a typical route through homelessness. Pathways identify a personal history of those people experiencing homelessness and housing insecurity. The terms 'homelessness career' or 'trajectory pathway' are considered more neutral terms that remove the concept of a linear timeline (Fitzpatrick, Bramley, & Johnsen, 2012; Kertesz et al., 2005). The pathway approach is a holistic analytical perspective that considers a range of aspects of people's lives; in practice, homelessness is primarily part of a set of broader housing experiences (Clapham, 2005). A long-term career in homelessness is a predicament that represents a category of chronic homelessness. Pathways and trajectories have been examined by a multitude of authors. Chamberlain and Johnson (2013), Robinson (2003) and (Fiedler, 2013) all identify a multitude of pathways that differentiate the experience of homelessness, with Fiedler focusing on the elderly.

The above studies allow us to understand that homelessness experiences differ across individuals and one reason for this is that homelessness experiences are likely to be different along the life course. For example, the very young may be more likely to be living with parents (perhaps in volatile homes). Along the life course there will be differences in exposure to life events, and accumulated histories are longer for older people. Further, there are differences in the 'applicable' set of accommodation types available across the life course (i.e. foster care is irrelevant to older individuals). Such considerations suggest it is most appropriate to separately consider 'young' 'middle' and 'older' adults.

Petersen and Parsell (2015) identified three distinct pathways into homelessness for the 'older' group. The first pathway begins with conventional links to housing either from being private renters or former home-owners. For this group, it is the first time in their lives they have experienced homelessness. Typically, these people are subject to relationship breakdowns or unemployment, and/or a lack of assets and income has limited their capacity to find their own secure accommodation (Crane & Warnes, 2010; Westmore, 2011). Women with low levels of financial stability due to poorly paid, insecure work may be driving this trend (Batterham, Mallet, Yates, Kolar, & Westmore, 2013; Crane & Joly, 2014; Petersen & Parsell, 2015). The second pathway is characterised by continuous housing disruption, where homelessness is iterative and marginal and housing is substandard (Petersen & Parsell, 2015). People in this pathway have been in long-term homelessness that has been marked by continual disruption and are more likely to be living in boarding houses, caravan parks or sleeping rough. Fitzpatrick et al. (2012) find that this older group is often marked by childhood trauma and can be subject to health problems and substance abuse. Petersen and Parsell (2015) identify the third pathway as those who experience transitory accommodation; this comprises those who live as itinerant workers, house sitters or dual citizens.

Next, we turn our attention to the handful of studies that have employed the Journeys Home data set. Cobb-Clark et al. (2016) find gender, parental education and mental and physical health are characteristics associated with duration and bouts of homelessness. Scutella, Johnson, Moschion, Tseng, and Wooden (2013) find those individuals with extended periods of homelessness were more likely to have been homeless at a young age, experienced less family support during childhood and had lower levels of education and shorter work histories. Intriguingly, the study found no statistically significant correlation between mental health and extended periods of homelessness. Other studies investigate the link between youth homelessness and adult employment (Cobb-Clark & Zhu, 2017) and the relationship between substance abuse and homelessness (McVicar, Moschion, & van Ours, 2015).

Finally, we look at studies on wellbeing in later life. Wellbeing has shown to be important in later life as a protector of health maintenance.

Utilising the English Longitudinal Study of Ageing, Steptoe, Deaton, and Stone (2015) showed that wellbeing was associated with better survival rates. They report that 29.3% of people in the lowest wellbeing quartile died during the average survey follow-up period of 8.5 years compared to 9.3% of those in the highest wellbeing quartile. Indeed, Diener and Chan (2011) provide an array of evidence that suggests wellbeing is connected to longevity. It is therefore important to understand the factors that are related to wellbeing.

In this study, we look at the relationship between housing and wellbeing. To date, the literature on this topic has focused on the wellbeing of elderly people living in residential age care settings versus those living in independent living settings. In a study of housing quality, Evans, Kantrowitz, and Eshelman (2002) show that higher quality housing leads to greater attachment to a home and hence higher wellbeing. Similar findings are shown by Oswald et al. (2007) for the very old (aged 75–89 years) living independently. Studies on those living in aged care suggest that the social dimensions of communal living in old age are important determinants of wellbeing (see, e.g., Haug, Wykle, & Namazi, 1989).

This literature suggests that the negative wellbeing effects of insecure housing for the elderly are likely to be significant. Although there are papers that consider the elderly who use specific types of homeless accommodations (see Stergiopoulos & Herrmann, 2003 for the case of homeless shelters in Canada), there appears to be a paucity of studies that look at elderly people who are experiencing housing insecurity or that examine multiple accommodation types. This chapter contributes to this knowledge gap by looking at the impact of detailed accommodation histories on wellbeing for older people.

Existing studies contribute to our overall understanding of homelessness and its evidence base. However, this study seeks to examine how homelessness fits within accommodation histories as they unfold at the individual level. The focus is on simultaneously identifying patterns within and between individuals in their detailed accommodation arrangements over time, pinpointing any upward (increasingly stable) and downward (increasingly unstable) cycles using all details from calendar data in our analysis to show a complete picture of individual-level accommodation stories. These accommodation profiles are then used as a summary of an individual's housing security, and their relationship with wellbeing is examined.

## 3 Data

To date, limited longitudinal data sets focus on homelessness and housing insecurity for elderly people, in part, due to the obvious difficulties in following this group through time. The Journeys Home data set is an exception in that it provides six waves of data, where each wave is at six-month intervals (bi-annual) and the first wave was collected from September to November 2011. The survey is a national sample of individuals (clustered around 36 geographical areas across Australia) identified to be at risk of housing insecurity. The initial 62% response rate in wave 1 was 1682 individuals. Attrition is expected in longitudinal data sets and might be expected to be high in a data set that targets such a mobile population. In fact, the attrition rate in Journeys Home is low at just 16% by wave 6. This final wave of data contains some 1406 individuals. Full details of the survey methodology can be found in Wooden et al. (2012).

The data set represents a unique and rich data source for the study of housing insecurity and homelessness, in that it combines linked information from a survey of the respondents with additional information from the Australian Government's Centrelink (i.e. the income support/social security) administrative database. The Centrelink database contains payment and various personal details for all income support customers since July 2002. Centrelink indicators flag individuals who are homeless or at risk of homelessness. Wave 1 respondents were homeless (35%), at risk of homelessness (37%) or vulnerable to homelessness (or 'statistically similar' to those at risk of homelessness, 28%) (Bevitt, Chigavazira, Scutella, Tseng, & Watson, 2014).

The survey contains an accommodation 'calendar' that tracks each respondent's housing arrangements between interviews and is ideally suited to our analytical purpose. For individuals who miss responding to a wave, calendar information is recorded back to the time of the previous interview. Adopting this 'extended reference period' minimises gaps in accommodation histories but does increase the risk of recall bias. The combination of survey and administrative information makes measurement of demand for different types of accommodation somewhat less problematic than relying on administrative data alone as the data includes individuals who require assistance but do not present for services. Journeys Home is the first linked data set in Australia of this size and depth in this field of research. With six data waves available, we are uniquely placed to begin exploring what the data set tells us about individual-level patterns over time in homelessness and housing instability using the detailed accommodation calendar. For individuals characterised by housing insecurity, a lot may change in a short space of time, while for others, periods of relative stability may be observed. To capture frequent changes but still observe long-term trends, it is essential to track respondents often and over an extended period of time. Hence, the Journeys Home data presents us with a unique opportunity to consider housing patterns within this group of vulnerable people. Specifically, the diaries allow individuals to record their accommodation under several types, as follows:

1. Your own place (that you were renting, owned or were buying)
2. Your parent's home
3. The home of other relatives
4. The home of friends
5. A caravan, cabin or mobile home
6. A boarding house or rooming house or hostel
7. A hotel or motel room
8. Foster care or residential care or kin care
9. Squatting in an abandoned building
10. In emergency or crisis accommodation
11. Sleeping rough (such as the street, a park, car, tent, train station or improvised shelter)
12. A hospital, nursing home, health or other treatment facility (i.e. rehabilitation)

13. A juvenile or youth detention centre, an adult prison or a remand centre
14. Other.

Fieldwork for each wave spanned some 2.5 months, with wave 1 carried out between 2 September 2011 and 23 November 2011, and wave 6 between 1 March 2014 and 12 May 2014. As a result of the staggered fieldwork, the timing of the initial and final calendar entries varies between individuals. Rather than restrict the sequences to a shorter period common to all individuals (i.e. trimming the ends), we created a 15th category of accommodation (missing) to extend later beginnings and earlier ends to a common period.

For each accommodation change (moving event) between surveys, individuals reported the year and month they moved and whether they left at the beginning (days 1–10), middle (days 11–20) or end (days 21–31) of the month. These data were then aggregated over all waves and provided in consecutive spell format as a calendar of spells in up to 14 types of accommodation, with each spell having a corresponding start date and duration. We then transformed the accommodation data into person–period format (individuals by month-thirds) and selected a balanced panel of individuals (with usable data) in at least waves one and six for analysis. After excluding those not responding in wave 6 and/or without usable calendar information, the resulting sample size was 1249 individuals from the original 1682 wave 1 respondents.

We delineated the older age group at 40 years plus, to account for the toll of premature ageing and lower life expectancy of those who are subject to housing insecurity (Crane & Warnes, 2010; Petersen & Parsell, 2015). Table 1 shows the analytical sample composition by gender.

It is interesting to look at the analytical sample in terms of the observed frequencies by which individuals are recorded as being resident in different types of accommodation over time, see Table 2. The average

**Table 1** Age–gender profile of wave 1 respondents in the analytical sample

| Age group | Male | % | Female | % | Total | % |
|---|---|---|---|---|---|---|
| 40+ years | 217 | 59 | 152 | 41 | 369 | 100 |

**Table 2** Descriptive statistics of accommodation sequences, age 40+ years

| Accommodation type | Average months per person[a] | Percentage of individuals with at least one spell | Conditional on at least one spell | |
|---|---|---|---|---|
| | | | Average no. spells per person | Average Months per spell |
| 1. Your own place (rent own or buying) | 18.71 | 80.49 | 1.24 | 18.81 |
| 2. Your parent's home | 0.92 | 6.78 | 1.16 | 11.64 |
| 3. The home of other relatives | 1.28 | 15.18 | 1.16 | 7.27 |
| 4. The home of friends | 1.88 | 23.58 | 1.16 | 6.85 |
| 5. A caravan, cabin or mobile home | 1.24 | 9.21 | 1.21 | 11.12 |
| 6. Boarding/rooming house or hostel | 2.73 | 19.78 | 1.22 | 11.30 |
| 7. A hotel or motel room | 0.15 | 4.88 | 1.17 | 2.70 |
| 8. Foster care, residential care, kin care | 0.00 | 0.00 | 0.00 | 0.00 |
| 9. Squatting in an abandoned building | 0.09 | 1.36 | 1.00 | 6.60 |

(continued)

Table 2 (continued)

| Accommodation type | Average months per person[a] | Percentage of individuals with at least one spell | Conditional on at least one spell | |
|---|---|---|---|---|
| | | | Average no. spells per person | Average Months per spell |
| 10. Emergency or crisis accommodation | 0.61 | 10.84 | 1.13 | 4.99 |
| 11. Sleeping rough | 1.33 | 14.36 | 1.30 | 7.11 |
| 12. Hospital, nursing home, health or other treatment facility (rehabilitation) | 0.53 | 6.50 | 1.21 | 6.72 |
| 13. Juvenile/youth detention, prison or remand | 0.12 | 2.17 | 1.25 | 4.50 |
| 14. Other | 0.32 | 4.07 | 1.13 | 7.02 |

[a]Average number of months per individual for all spells
$N$ = 369 individuals; average number of accommodation types used = 1.99

number of accommodations used was 1.99, with 80.49% of participants spending time in their own home of average duration 18.71 months over the window of observation. Among the sample, 23.58% spent time living in the home of friends and 19.78% spent time in a boarding/rooming house or hostel.

In terms of wellbeing, the sample allows us to look at both life satisfaction and the Kessler (K6) psychological wellbeing score. Life satisfaction is measured on a scale of 0–10, where 0 represents 'totally dissatisfied' and 10 represents 'totally satisfied'. In our sample aged 40 years plus, the modal life satisfaction score is 8 and the average is 6.57 (Fig. 1), which is consistent with many studies of life satisfaction that show overall life satisfaction is u-shaped with age. In population-based samples, the average life satisfaction is usually around 8. Our sample reports a slightly lower score, but we have a sample aged 40 years plus so this is unsurprising.

Our second measure of wellbeing is the Kessler Psychological Distress Scale (K6), which is a six-item scale focusing on anxiety and depression with four-point Likert scale responses (Kessler et al., 2002) that has a mean score of 8.1 in our sample. This scale ranges from 0 to 24. As the score increases, so does the probability of mental illness. The scale is often dichotomised to define the threshold for clinical illness and a score of 19

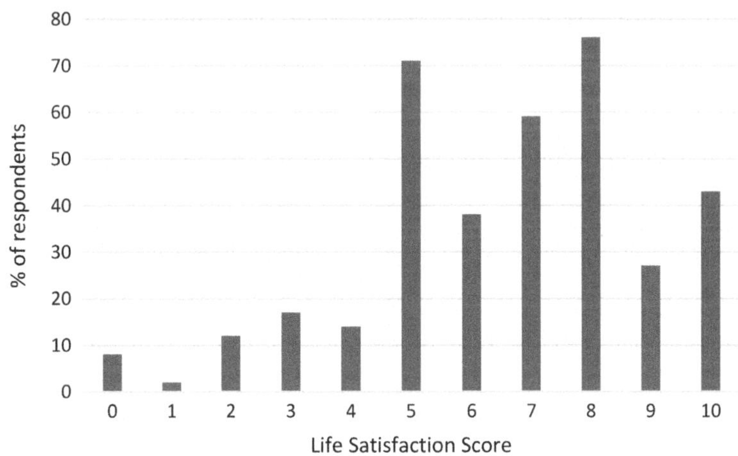


**Fig. 1** Life satisfaction

or more represents probable serious mental illness. The average score in our sample is well below this threshold. For our empirical modelling, we have reversed the Kessler scale so that an increasing score represents better mental health (higher levels of wellbeing) to allow for a more direct comparison with the modelling results on life satisfaction, which also has a scale that increases with wellbeing.

# 4 Methodology

A state of homelessness or housing insecurity comes about through a process that can, in part, be captured in housing histories. Often, however, we only look at single, discrete changes (i.e. moving from a family home to a hostel by employing event history models) (Blossfeld & Rohwer, 2002). In such a framework, the transition rate of moving from one state to another is modelled as being associated with other variables (i.e. the existence of family/domestic violence). Another approach would be to focus on the length of time that people spend in different accommodation types, but such an approach also only considers one accommodation type at a time. Since rich longitudinal data might contain a sequence of transitions where information is contained within the sequence itself, we could model each transition and/or duration contained in an individual's accommodation history. However, in many instances we are interested in the process as a whole and so want to simultaneously consider the full histories or entire accommodation profiles. Employing sequence analysis tools will allow us to identify the distinct patterns in accommodation sequences across individuals, and their correlates, providing a fuller understanding of the information contained within accommodation histories. The objective is to empirically identify a typology of sequences and identify the characteristics of the typologies themselves and the average characteristics of the individuals whose housing experiences can be captured by a given typology. Typology is a term we use to denote a group with an overall pattern in common, although this leaves room for individual variations at a more detailed level.

Assume that information collected on spells, dates, durations and transitions can be viewed/recast and analysed as a (contiguous) sequence of accommodation states linked through time or a continuous (timed) sequence of (accommodation) states for each person and time period. This implies that we can transform accommodation history information to person–period, or diary/calendar-style, data. Adopting a sequencing approach provides an overarching framework for analysis, since we can view/visualise and describe the distinct patterns and their prevalence. Moreover, sequence analysis is not subject to some of the limitations of other methods for analysing sequences with complex data structures (e.g. long and complex Markov chain models, models with multiple competing risk), sequence analysis is 'statistically agnostic' and allows very generous limits on the number of accommodation types we can simultaneously consider (see Fry & Boulton, 2013 for a full discussion). Specifically, there is no need to aggregate time periods and transition spells for analysis.[4] The sequence analysis employed here can be divided into two stages, as detailed below.

The first stage involves the detection of accommodation patterns. During this stage of analysis, we use Optimal Matching and Cluster Analysis (OMCA) for the matching and grouping of similar accommodation patterns. This technique is specifically designed for analysing information contained in 'calendar-style' data sequences. Methodology of the nature employed is explored in Cornwell (2015), who provides an excellent primer on sequence analysis techniques in the social sciences. The optimal matching process is an iterative minimisation procedure that measures the distances between every pair of sequences. This generates a distance matrix for every sequence from every other sequence. The distance matrix is obtained by considering the lowest 'cost' through which each sequence pair can be made to look identical either by insertion, deletion or substitution operations at points along the two sequences. Cluster analysis is then used to identify the number of (statistically) distinct groups (or patterns) among the sequences (the typologies). There is no necessity/imperative for OMCA to yield groups of the same or similar size; it is the similarity rather than 'commonality' of the pattern that matters. The identified typologies can then be described by

[4]In this application, we aggregate in some instances for presentation purposes and/or to preserve confidentiality due to sample size issues specific to our chosen data set.

the characteristics of the distinct sequence patterns they represent. Stata 15 and its SQ routines (Brzinsky-Fay, Kohler, & Luniak, 2006) were used for sequence analysis.[5] We then use sequence index plots of individual accommodation sequences to visualise individual trajectories and a chronograph for each typology to view prevalence of accommodation types used by different individuals over time. The sequence index plot and chronographs allow the distinct typologies to be visualised, summarised and described in terms of the accommodation profiles they represent.

The second stage of the analysis will produce tables of sequence characteristics, as well as the initial characteristics of the individuals (e.g. age, gender, education, labour force status) and changes over the course of the sequence. One of the innovative aspects of sequence analysis when compared to more traditional regression methodologies (event studies or duration analysis) is that it allows a visualisation of the data that is easy for non-specialists to understand and therefore enables the research findings to be easily communicated to policy makers and other stakeholders.

The final stage of our empirical analysis employs regression analysis where the typology identified for each individual is regressed against their subjective wellbeing. The typology is assumed to be a summary measure of their housing experiences and so captures all aspects of accommodation patterns, such as the categories of accommodation used and length of stay, which might be expected to impact on wellbeing. Specifically, we estimate:

$$\mathrm{SWB}_i = \alpha + \beta_1 T_i + \varepsilon_i \tag{1}$$

where SWB is a measure of individual subjective wellbeing. Our data allows us to capture wellbeing through a selection of variables, specifically: life satisfaction and the Kessler mental health score. As noted already, life satisfaction is measured on a scale that runs from 0 to 10. In our modelling, we will treat this scale as a continuous variable (i.e. assuming ordinality) and so estimate Eq. 1 via Ordinary Least Squares (OLS). Ferrer-I-Carbonell and Frijters (2004) present evidence that it

[5]These routines do not currently support the use of weights, so all analyses are unweighted.

makes little difference to the estimates if we assume ordinality or cardinality (i.e. estimate an ordered latent response model). The Kessler Psychological Distress Scale (K6) runs from 0 to 24 (Kessler et al., 2002) and is reversed in our modelling so that it is increasing in wellbeing. Again, the scores are treated as continuous variables in the empirical modelling and so OLS estimation is employed.

To capture the impact of housing profiles, we include the individual's housing typology, $T_i$, identified in the sequence analysis as an explanatory variable. This is a novel approach and we know of no other study to integrate sequence analysis and regression analysis in this way. The typology summarises the entire accommodation histories and so acts as an efficient variable from which we can estimate the impact of accommodation histories on an individual's current wellbeing. This allows us to look at the impact of housing stability across a period of time (waves 1–6) on current wellbeing (wave 6). In this way, we allow for the impact of an individual's current and past housing experiences as a determinant of current wellbeing. This is important as we know that current and past events impact on current wellbeing, which is especially likely to be true when we are concerned with events, like periods of homelessness, that may have lasting effects on a person's psychology.

Finally, we also estimate the models with an extended set of demographic controls known from the literature to affect wellbeing, as shown in Eq. 2, where $\bar{X}_i$ includes age, age squared, gender, marital status, income and employment status.

$$\mathrm{SWB}_i = \alpha + \beta_1 T_i + \beta_2 \bar{X}_i + \varepsilon_i \tag{2}$$

Robust standard errors are estimated for all empirical specifications—see White (1980).

## 5 Results and Discussion

This section contains stages 1 and 2 of the sequence analyses, followed by the regression analysis. We begin by presenting the sequence index plots for each of the typologies, identification of the most interesting typology and the characterisation of this typology (stage 1). We then characterise the individuals within the typology (stage 2). To retain consistency with the statistical theory we will discuss the results in terms of typologies. We note that the homelessness literature utilises the term pathway, but this term has been used with many different meanings and is often associated with studies that attempt to identify causal relationships. Here we are investigating only distinct patterns in sequence data and no attempt is made to establish causal relationships. In the interest of clarity, we will therefore discuss our findings in terms of typologies only. Further, the majority of literature to date has considered homelessness in terms of the severity of the accommodation need; here we will focus on the volatility of an individual's accommodations.

Figure 2 shows the sequences for the older individuals in our data set, where each colour represents a particular accommodation type. Four distinct typologies are identified. Typology 1 is characterised by long periods of time living in one's own home. Typology 2 is characterised by moving from different types of accommodation into one's own place. Typology 3 is the most volatile group showing a large range of, and frequent changes in, accommodation types. Typology 4 is dominated by staying at a boarding house, rooming house or hostel.

It is interesting to focus discussion on typology 2, which contains individuals who experience various less stable accommodation types but eventually finds (and seemingly secure) a place of their own. The assertion that typology 2 is worthy of detailed investigation is also supported by the chronographs shown in the second part of Fig. 2. While the sequence index plot is designed to be read horizontally, the chronographs are better thought of as vertical descriptions of the demand for different accommodation types at a given point in time. The chronograph for typology 2, shown in Fig. 2, confirms the demand for a number of different accommodation types initially, but unlike the other typologies for this older age group, the demand for different accommodation types reduces through time as individuals increasingly move into their own place. Understanding the basis for such progression could be a key to best directing policy and other efforts.

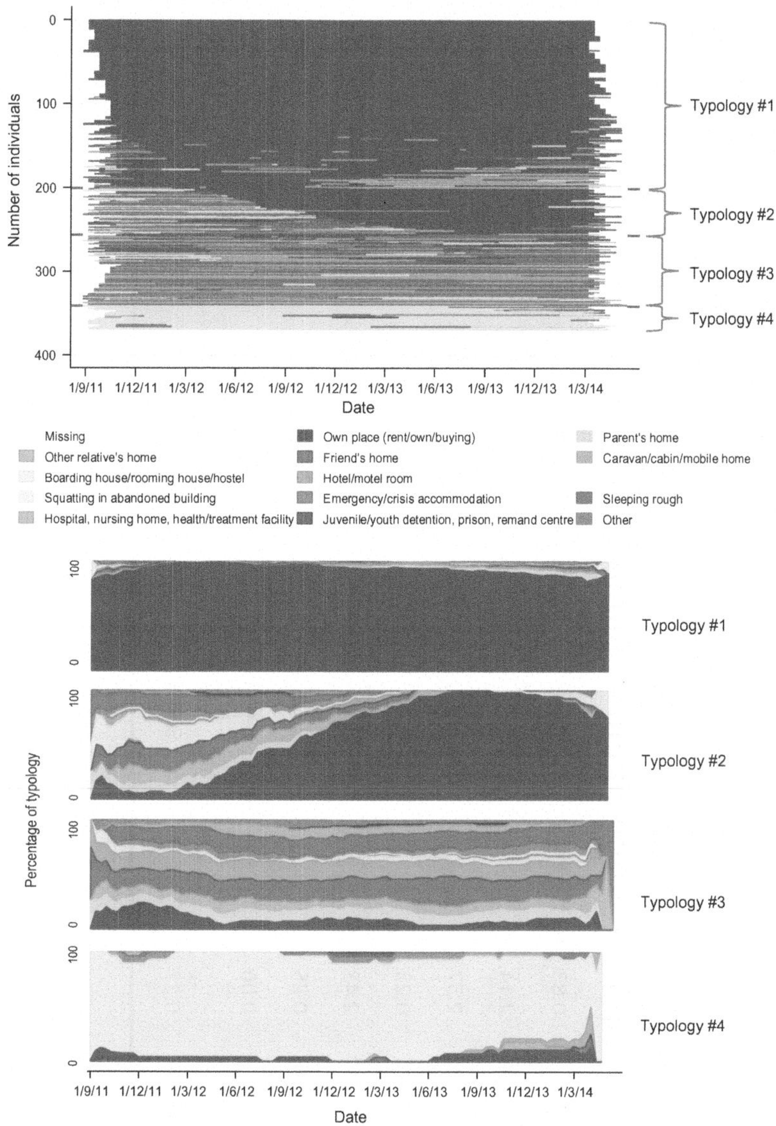


**Fig. 2** 40+ year-olds by typology (sequence index plot and chronographs)

**Table 3** Descriptive statistics of accommodation sequences, age 40+ years, typology 2

| Accommodation type | Average months per person[a] | Percentage of individuals with at least one spell | Conditional on at least one spell | |
|---|---|---|---|---|
| | | | Average no. spells per person | Average months per spell |
| 1. Your own place (rent own or buying) | 18.12 | 100.00 | 1.25 | 14.50 |
| 2. Your parent's home | 0.83 | 7.14 | 1.00 | 11.58 |
| 3. The home of other relatives | 2.14 | 26.79 | 1.40 | 5.71 |
| 4. The home of friends | 2.37 | 42.86 | 1.13 | 4.93 |
| 5. A caravan, cabin or mobile home | 0.23 | 7.14 | 1.25 | 2.53 |
| 6. Boarding/rooming house or hostel | 2.43 | 33.93 | 1.21 | 5.93 |
| 7. A hotel or motel room | 0.26 | 12.50 | 1.29 | 1.63 |
| 8. Foster care, residential care, kin care | 0.00 | 0.00 | 0.00 | 0.00 |
| 9. Squatting in an abandoned building | 0.17 | 3.57 | 1.00 | 4.83 |

| Accommodation type | Average months per person[a] | Percentage of individuals with at least one spell | Conditional on at least one spell | |
|---|---|---|---|---|
| | | | Average no. spells per person | Average months per spell |
| 10. Emergency or crisis accommodation | 0.80 | 17.86 | 1.20 | 3.75 |
| 11. Sleeping rough | 1.82 | 21.43 | 1.08 | 7.85 |
| 12. Hospital, nursing home, health or other treatment facility (rehabilitation) | 0.13 | 3.57 | 1.50 | 2.44 |
| 13. Juvenile/youth detention, prison or remand | 0.12 | 3.57 | 1.00 | 3.50 |
| 14. Other | 0.42 | 5.36 | 1.00 | 7.78 |

[a]Average number of months per individual for all spells
$N = 56$ individuals; average number of accommodation types used = 2.86

Table 3 shows the sequence characteristics for typology 2 (15% of this age group). Accommodation arrangements early in the observation window are quite varied, with 43% staying with friends; 34% using boarding houses, rooming houses or hostels; 27% staying with other relatives; and 21% sleeping rough and 18% using emergency or crisis accommodation. For each of these accommodation types, individuals average more than one spell of typically two to five months (although the average duration of a spell sleeping rough is nearly eight months), indicating there is a large amount of churning through different types of accommodation before securing a place of one's own. However, there is a definite progression from other accommodation types into one's own place and this appears to be relatively long lasting for most. As a result of this progression in arrangements, living in one's own place tends to dominate: there is an average of 1.25 spells lasting 14.5 months per spell. Examining the characteristics of individuals in this typology could be critical to assisting others to follow such trajectories in future.

Focusing on typology 2, in which individuals are increasingly moving into their own place, we now turn our attention to the characteristics of the individuals described by the typology compared to the full sample. It is important to note that the data is longitudinal, so some of these characteristics may change through time. For this reason, we report the average initial characteristics for those individuals portrayed by typology 2, and for the time-varying characteristics, we report the averages at wave 1 and then at wave 6 (see Table 4). It is possible to look at any of the information contained within the data set, but we focus on standard demographics (age, gender and education) and factors already identified in the existing literature as being correlated with housing instability (employment status, ethnic origin/immigration status, language skills and family status). For comparative purposes, the final column in Table 4 shows the averages across all typologies and allows us to perform a statistical difference of proportions t-tests to identify when typology 2 individuals differ significantly from the overall age group.

Table 4 shows the typology 2 individual descriptive statistics. Typology 2 for this age group was best summarised by accommodation sequences that involved initial churning and subsequently moving into their own place. Looking at the initial characteristics, we see that this group is more

**Table 4** Individual characteristics by typology, age 40+ years

| | | Typology 2 | | All typologies |
|---|---|---|---|---|
| *N* | | 56 | | 369 |
| **Initial characteristics** | | | | |
| Age | (Mean) | 48.80 | | 48.50 |
| Gender | % female | 32.14 | | 41.19 |
| Aboriginal or Torres Strait Islander | % ATSI | 30.36 | ** | 19.51 |
| Australian born | % Aus born | 87.50 | ** | 78.32 |
| Speaks LOTE | % speak LOTE | 21.43 | | 24.66 |
| Refugee | % refugee | 0.00 | *** | 1.90 |
| History of homelessness | % yes | 98.21 | | 95.66 |
| **Wave 1** | | | | |
| Partnership status | % partnered | 8.93 | | 10.84 |
| Divorced/separated | % div/sep | 46.43 | | 47.43 |
| Has kids U18 | % yes | 35.71 | | 44.17 |
| Has kids U18 resident | % yes | 8.93 | ** | 16.26 |
| Studying | % yes | 3.57 | | 5.42 |
| Low ed | % <y10 | 26.79 | | 25.75 |
| High ed | % Cert3/4+ | 33.93 | | 35.23 |
| Unemployed | % unemp | 14.29 | | 16.53 |
| NILF | % NILF | 64.29 | | 61.79 |
| *Homeless status at interview date* | | | | |
| Primary | % | 12.50 | ** | 4.61 |
| Secondary | % | 19.64 | ** | 10.03 |
| Tertiary | % | 30.36 | ** | 19.51 |
| Marginally housed | % | 19.64 | ** | 9.49 |
| Short-term rental | % | 1.79 | | 1.08 |

(continued)

**Table 4** (continued)

| | | Typology 2 | | All typologies |
|---|---|---|---|---|
| Long-term housed/stable | % | 16.07 | *** | 55.01 |
| *Self-assessed housing situation* | | | | |
| At risk of being homeless | % | 21.43 | | 19.51 |
| Homeless | % | 30.36 | *** | 9.21 |
| **Wave 6** | | | | |
| Partnership status | % partnered | 14.29 | | 13.82 |
| Divorced/separated | % div/sep | 41.07 | | 45.53 |
| Has kids U18 | % yes | 30.36 | | 36.86 |
| Has kids U18 resident | % yes | 7.14 | ** | 15.45 |
| Studying | % yes | 7.14 | | 8.13 |
| Low ed | % <y10 | 26.79 | | 24.66 |
| High ed | % Cert3/4+ | 35.72 | | 39.84 |
| Unemployed | % unemp | 12.50 | | 13.55 |
| NILF | % NILF | 76.79 | | 70.46 |
| *Homeless status at interview date* | | | | |
| Primary | % | 1.79 | * | 5.42 |
| Secondary | % | 7.14 | | 4.61 |
| Tertiary | % | 7.14 | ** | 15.72 |
| Marginally housed | % | 8.93 | | 9.21 |
| Short-term rental | % | 0.00 | | 0.54 |
| Long-term housed/stable | % | 75.00 | ** | 63.69 |
| *Self-assessed housing situation* | | | | |
| At risk of being homeless | % | 17.86 | | 11.11 |
| Homeless | % | 3.57 | | 3.79 |

*Notes* Testing proportions (or mean for age) for typology 2 against all typologies $*p < 0.1$; $**p < 0.05$; $***p < 0.01$. Low ed is lower than year 10; high ed is Cert III/IV or above

likely to have a history of homelessness. Given this typology represented the most insecure/unstable accommodation sequences, this is perhaps expected (some 96% of this sample have histories of homelessness prior to the window of observation). Looking at the changes in characteristics between wave 1 and wave 6, we note that typology 2 individuals are more likely to be partnered as we move through time rising to 14% in wave 6 compared to 9% in wave 1, but that the incidence of being partnered is about the same in wave 6 relative to the age group as a whole (14%). This supports the hypothesis that there is an impact of frequent changes of accommodation and types of accommodation on relationship formation. Looking further in respect to family formation, we see that at wave 1, 36% have children under the age of 18 years (although only 9% have them 'in residence'). By wave 6, there is not much change: 30% have children under 18 years, although for only 7% are the children resident.

In terms of education, we see 3.6% studying at wave 1 and 7.1% studying at wave 6 (although not necessarily the same individuals in both waves). This is about average for the group as a whole. There is not much change in study activity and therefore no change in education level for this group. However, in wave 6 it appears that this group is being left behind in terms of higher education levels (36% relative to the group as a whole at 40%).

Investigating labour force status, we find wave 1 has a high rate of being neither employed nor looking for work, which increases further by wave 6 (76%). There is not much change in unemployment, so this might indicate retirement.

Finally with respect to the individual's self-assessment of their housing situation in this typology, we find people feel they are very much living 'on the edge' in wave 1, with 21% of individuals considering themselves at risk of homelessness (relative to 20% for the age group as a whole). By wave 6, this typology still has 18% of individuals who consider themselves at risk of homelessness (relative to 11% for the entire age group).

Finally, for the 40 years plus age group, typology 2 was summarised as high demand for a variety of accommodation types at the start of the period but a transition into living in one's own home and finding relative stability by wave 6.[6] This group has a high incidence of Aboriginal and Torres Strait Islanders as well as Australian-born individuals relative to the overall age group, as well as a very low incidence of refugees.

Our study of individual accommodation arrangements revealed interesting findings. While our data is longitudinal, the time over which individuals are observed is approximately 2.5 years. By partitioning the sample into four typologies, we have been able to investigate the accommodation patterns for different groups and compare the differences in accommodation needs from an analysis of accommodation usage. It is clear from the analysis that an individual's networks of family and friendship groups are important when experiencing high levels of housing insecurity and encouraging to see that later life stages see more stable outcomes. It is important to note that the nature of our data means that we do not observe the cohort through the entire life course, so it is impossible to determine if the individuals observed as experiencing highly volatile housing patterns at the beginning of the sample had such volatile patterns prior to this.

The next stage of our analysis is novel in that it utilises the housing typologies as summary variables of the accommodation histories, in a regression analysis framework. The results are presented in Table 5. The findings suggest that housing typology 2, which was characterised by churning through family and friends, is positively correlated with life satisfaction relative to being in typology 1, which is characterised by mainly living in one's own home. This is surprising at first, but there is literature showing a positive relationship between life satisfaction and social support. Individuals who have housing support from family and friends might be feeling the psychological benefits of this support network. If we look at mental health, the picture is a little different. In this case, we see that a housing history characterised by typology 4 (relative to typology 1) increases the (reversed) Kessler mental health score, and thus, is correlated with better psychological wellbeing. Again, this finding is initially counter-intuitive. However, it could be the case that individuals who find themselves in boarding house type accommodation have

[6]From a statistical perspective, it is important to note the small sample size for typology 2 in this age group of 56 individuals.

**Table 5** Regression results

| | Life satisfaction | | | | Kessler (K6) | | | |
|---|---|---|---|---|---|---|---|---|
| | | | With controls | | | | With controls | |
| | Coefficient | *t*-stat | Coefficient | *t*-stat | Coefficient | *t*-stat | Coefficient | *t*-stat |
| Typology 2 | 0.684 | 2.12 | 0.608 | 1.96 | 1.403 | 1.73 | 0.976 | 1.22 |
| Typology 3 | 0.434 | 1.25 | 0.332 | 0.94 | 0.143 | 0.17 | −0.451 | −0.54 |
| Typology 4 | 0.029 | 0.07 | 0.028 | 0.06 | 3.331 | 3.35 | 2.976 | 2.83 |
| Age | | | 0.253 | 0.14 | | | −0.472 | −0.11 |
| Age squared | | | 0.000 | 0.08 | | | 0.002 | 0.44 |
| Female | | | −0.018 | −0.06 | | | −1.514 | −2.31 |
| Widowed | | | −1.683 | −1.59 | | | −5.675 | −2.26 |
| Divorced | | | −0.715 | −2.13 | | | −1.938 | −2.66 |
| Separated | | | −0.581 | −1.54 | | | −1.512 | −1.51 |
| Married | | | 0.851 | 1.47 | | | −2.235 | −0.74 |
| De facto | | | 0.845 | 1.71 | | | 0.769 | 0.68 |
| Income | | | 0.001 | 1.50 | | | 0.002 | 1.64 |
| Unemployed | | | −0.200 | −0.36 | | | −1.066 | −0.71 |
| Not in the labour force | | | 0.013 | 0.03 | | | −1.616 | −1.26 |
| Constant | 6.316 | 35.96 | 4.638 | 0.93 | 15.393 | 36.64 | 15.181 | 1.32 |
| $N$ | 345 | | 345 | | 363 | | 341 | |
| $R^2$ | 0.013 | | 0.090 | | 0.023 | | 0.148 | |

*Note* Omitted categories: Housing typology 1, male, single, employed

arrived there from much worse accommodation. Further, this accommodation appears to be relatively stable for many in this typology and the stability may be influencing wellbeing. It is also the case that most accommodation of this nature provides good access to allied health support and welfare support systems and the heightened wellbeing may also be reflecting these factors.

It should be noted that wellbeing is a complex construct with multiple factors affecting it. In our study, we only consider a limited model with standard demographics and housing typologies; it is therefore unsurprising that the fit of the regression models is low. Moreover, the sample size available for analysis of older people is small and the number of individuals within a given typology is also relatively small, which will affect the robustness of the findings. However, Journeys Home provides the best available data to undertake this analysis. Despite these data limitations, we find evidence that housing typologies impact on wellbeing for older Australians experiencing housing insecurity.

## 6 Concluding Remarks

Sequence analysis is a powerful tool for understanding patterns in data. Here, we employ the technique to investigate housing histories of a sample of individuals identified as being homeless or at risk of homelessness, in those aged 40 years and over. We identify four distinct patterns (typologies) in accommodation sequences of older individuals. We focus on the typology that is characterised by housing volatility followed by stability in moving into one's own place, defined over the variety of accommodations demanded and the durations of stay in each type of accommodation. The visualisations of the distinct housing sequences allow for an easy translation of the research to the widest possible audience. Further, we investigate the use of typologies as explanatory variables in a regression framework and find that they have some statistical power in understanding wellbeing of older people who experience housing insecurity. The focus of this study has been to understand longer-term housing experiences and their correlation with individual wellbeing, rather than causal relationships. Further research could investigate the associations between accommodation typologies and factors such as experience of domestic violence, substance abuse, disrupted childhood and mental health.

From a policy perspective, our analysis allows us to identify the invisible part of unmet demand for housing services for older people, since we see this age group often relies on family and friends for accommodation. So-called turn away measures only capture the 'visible' part of unmet demand and do not include the 'invisible' part associated with individuals who are in need of—but not presenting for—services. Many individuals do not present for services due to stigma (those homeless due to domestic violence are just one example group); others do not present as they know that a particular service is already over-utilised and would rather not face the disappointment of being turned away. Others are suffering ill health (both physical and mental) and are unable to present. This part of demand is not captured in administrative records of the homeless service sector. The Journeys Home data set allows us to observe in great detail the full histories of older homeless people and those at risk, and so more fully understand utilisation of a diverse set of accommodation types and the ordering in which accommodations types are utilised by older people. Housing insecurity impacts on wellbeing and we find some evidence that certain typologies are associated with different levels of life satisfaction and psychological wellbeing (mental health). These results are important since many countries are experiencing ageing populations and questioning what suitable affordable housing should look like in this sector of the market and how to protect the housing security of older people to protect their sense of wellbeing in later life. The results are also important from a modelling perspective; the inclusion of typologies in a regression framework is innovative in this chapter and the analysis suggests that sequence analysis can be integrated effectively into a statistical modelling framework.

**Acknowledgements** This chapter uses unit record data from *Journeys Home: Longitudinal Study of Factors Affecting Housing Stability* (Journeys Home). The study was initiated and is funded by the Australian Government Department of

Social Services (DSS). The Department of Employment has provided information for use in Journeys Home, which is managed by the Melbourne Institute of Applied Economic and Social Research (Melbourne Institute). The findings and views reported in this chapter, however, are those of the authors and should not be attributed to DSS, the Department of Employment or the Melbourne Institute.

## References

ABS. (2012). *Census of population and housing: Estimating homelessness.* Canberra: ABS.

Batterham, D., Mallet, S., Yates, E., Kolar, V., & Westmore, T. (2013). *Ageing out of place: The impact of gender and location on older Victorians in homelessness.* Melbourne: Hanover Welfare Services.

Bevitt, A., Chigavazira, A., Scutella, R., Tseng, Y., & Watson, N. (2014). *Journeys home user manual.* Melbourne: Melbourne Institute of Applied Economic and Social Research.

Blossfeld, H.-P., & Rohwer, G. (2002). *Techniques of event history modeling: New approaches to causal analysis* (2nd ed.). Mahwah, NJ: Lawrence Erlbaum Associates.

Brzinsky-Fay, C., Kohler, U., & Luniak, M. (2006). Sequence analysis using Stata. *Stata Journal, 6*(4), 435–460.

Chamberlain, C. (2014). *Homelessness: Re-shaping the policy agenda.* Melbourne: Australian Housing and Urban Research Institute.

Chamberlain, C., & Johnson, G. (2013). Pathways into adult homelessness. *Journal of Sociology, 49*(1), 60–77. https://doi.org/10.1177/1440783311422458.

Chamberlain, C., & McKenzie, D. (1992). Understanding contemporary homelessness: Issues of definition & meaning. *Australian Journal of Social Issues, 27*(4), 274–297.

Chamberlain, C., & McKenzie, D. (2008). *Counting the homeless 2006.* Canberra: Australian Bureau of Statistics.

Clapham, D. (2005). *The meaning of housing: A pathways approach.* Bristol: Policy Press, University of Bristol.

Cobb-Clark, D. A., Herault, N., Scutella, R., & Tseng, Y.-P. (2016). A journey home: What drives how long people are homeless? *Journal of Urban Economics, 91*(Suppl. C), 57–72. https://doi.org/10.1016/j.jue.2015.11.005.
Cobb-Clark, D. A., & Zhu, A. (2017). Childhood homelessness and adult employment: The role of education, incarceration, and welfare receipt. *Journal of Population Economics, 30*(3), 893–924. https://doi.org/10.1007/s00148-017-0634-3.
Cornwell, B. (2015). *Social sequence analysis: Methods and applications.* Cambridge: Cambridge University Press.
Crane, M., & Joly, L. (2014). Older homeless people: Increasing numbers and changing needs. *Reviews in Clinical Gerontology, 24*(4), 255–268. https://doi.org/10.1017/S095925981400015X.
Crane, M., & Warnes, A. M. (2010). Homelessness among older people and service responses. *Reviews in Clinical Gerontology, 20*(4), 354–363. https://doi.org/10.1017/S0959259810000225.
Diener, E., & Chan, M. (2011). Happy people live longer: Subjective well-being contributes to health and longevity. *Applied Psychology: Health and Well-Being, 3*(1), 1–43. https://doi.org/10.1111/j.1758-0854.2010.01045.x.
Evans, G. W., Kantrowitz, E., & Eshelman, P. (2002). Housing quality and psychological well-being among the elderly population. *The Journals of Gerontology Series B: Psychological Sciences and Social Sciences, 57*(4), P381–P383. https://doi.org/10.1093/geronb/57.4.P381.
Ferrer-I-Carbonell, A., & Frijters, P. (2004). How important is methodology for the estimates of the determinants of happiness? *Economic Journal, 114*(497), 641–659. https://doi.org/10.1111/j.1468-0297.2004.00235.x.
Fiedler, J. (2013). Home at last: Time for action on housing services and options for older people. *Parity, 26*(7), 30–32.
Fitzpatrick, S., Bramley, G., & Johnsen, S. (2012). Pathways into multiple exclusion homelessness in seven UK cities. *Urban Studies, 50*(1), 148–168. https://doi.org/10.1177/0042098012452329.
Fry, J., & Boulton, C. (2013). *Prevalence of transition pathways in Australia* (Productivity Commission Staff Working Paper). Canberra.
Haug, M. R., Wykle, M. L., & Namazi, K. H. (1989). Self-care among older adults. *Social Science and Medicine, 29*(2), 171–183. https://doi.org/10.1016/0277-9536(89)90165-2.
Kertesz, G. S., Larson, J. M., Horton, J. N., Winter, H. M., Saitz, H. R., & Samet, H. J. (2005). Homeless chronicity and health-related quality of life trajectories among adults with addictions. *Medical Care, 43*(6), 574–585. https://doi.org/10.1097/01.mlr.0000163652.91463.b4.

Kessler, R. C., Andrews, G., Colpe, L. J., Hiripi, E., Mroczek, D. K., Normand, S. L. T., … Zaslavsky, A. M. (2002). Short screening scales to monitor population prevalences and trends in non-specific psychological distress. *Psychological Medicine, 32*(6), 959–976. https://doi.org/10.1017/S0033291702006074.

Lennon, M., McAllister, W., Kuang, L., & Herman, D. (2005). *Temporality and intervention effects: Trajectory analysis of a homeless mental health program.* New York: Columbia University.

May, J. (2000). Housing histories and homeless careers: A biographical approach. *Housing Studies, 15*(4), 613–638.

McAllister, W., Lennon, M., & Kuang, L. (2011). Rethinking research on forming typologies of homelessness. *American Journal of Public Health, 101*(4), 596–601.

McVicar, D., Moschion, J., & van Ours, J. (2015). From substance use to homelessness or vice versa? *Social Science & Medicine, 136–137*, 89–98. https://doi.org/10.1016/j.socscimed.2015.05.005.

Minnery, J., & Greenhalgh, E. (2007). Approaches to homelessness policy in Europe, the United States, and Australia. *Journal of Social Issues, 63*(3), 641–655. https://doi.org/10.1111/j.1540-4560.2007.00528.x.

Oswald, F., Wahl, H.-W., Schilling, O., Nygren, C., Fange, A., Sixsmith, A., … Iwarsson, S. (2007). Relationships between housing and healthy aging in very old age. *Gerontologist, 47*(1), 96–107. https://doi.org/10.1080/11038120601151615.

Petersen, M., & Parsell, C. (2015). Homeless for the first time in later life: An Australian study. *Housing Studies, 30*(3), 368–391. https://doi.org/10.1080/02673037.2014.963522.

Robinson, C. (2003). *Understanding iterative homelessness: The case of people with mental disorders.* Melbourne: Australian Housing and Urban Research Institute.

Scutella, R., Johnson, G., Moschion, J., Tseng, Y.-P., & Wooden, M. (2013). Understanding lifetime homeless duration: Investigating wave 1 findings from the Journeys Home project. *Australian Journal of Social Issues, 48*(1), 83–110. https://doi.org/10.1002/j.1839-4655.2013.tb00272.x.

Sosin, M., Piliavin, I., & Westerfelt, H. (1990). Toward a longitudinal analysis of homelessness. *Journal of Social Issues, 46*(4), 157–174. https://doi.org/10.1111/j.1540-4560.1990.tb01804.x.

Steptoe, A., Deaton, A., & Stone, A. A. (2015). Subjective wellbeing, health, and ageing. *The Lancet, 385*(9968), 640–648. https://doi.org/10.1016/S0140-6736(13)61489-0.

Stergiopoulos, V., & Herrmann, N. (2003). Old and homeless: A review and survey of older adults who use shelters in an urban setting. *The Canadian Journal of Psychiatry, 48*(6), 374–380. https://doi.org/10.1177/070674370304800603.

Toro, P. A. (2007). Toward an international understanding of homelessness. *Journal of Social Issues, 63*(3), 461–481. https://doi.org/10.1111/j.1540-4560.2007.00519.x.

Westmore, T. (2011). Responding to the needs of the elderly homeless—Ageing in what place? *Parity, 24*(9), 33–34.

White, H. (1980). A heteroskedasticity-consistent covariance matrix estimator and a direct test for heteroskedasticity. *Econometrica, 48*(4), 817–838. https://doi.org/10.2307/1912934.

Wooden, M., Bevitt, A., Chigavazira, A., Greer, N., Johnson, G., Killackey, E., ... Watson, N. (2012). Introducing 'journeys home'. *Australian Economic Review, 45*(3), 368–378. https://doi.org/10.1111/j.1467-8462.2012.00690.x.

# 4

# Social Support and Wellbeing Among Older Australians

Samuelson Appau and Sefa Awaworyi Churchill

## 1 Introduction

We are born into groups and socialised by groups, to think and act in relation to social others across different groups. We define ourselves by groups that we belong to and those we do not belong to. Importantly, because no person is an island, we are inevitably dependent on social others in many aspects of our lives. As humans, our existence, nurturing, identity, tastes, desires, aspirations and decision making are dependent on, and heavily shaped by, social others. The inescapable human need for belongingness and the dependence of social ties is what necessitates and legitimizes the exchange of social support. Social support refers to the

S. Appau · S. Awaworyi Churchill (✉)
School of Economics, Finance and Marketing, RMIT University, Melbourne, VIC, Australia
e-mail: sefa.awaworyichurchill@rmit.edu.au

S. Appau
e-mail: samuelson.appau@rmit.edu.au


S. Awaworyi Churchill et al. (eds.), *Measuring, Understanding and Improving Wellbeing Among Older People*,
https://doi.org/10.1007/978-981-15-2353-3_4

extent and quality of a person's real and perceived dependence, exchange and integration with social others like family, friends and neighbours. Social support is proxied variably and sometimes collectively as social connection, social integration and social capital.

Not all social ties are the same, some are (emotionally and psychologically) strong and close—like family—while some are weak and distant—like work colleagues. We crave the attention and approval of other people and feel dejected without it the same way we avoid the attention of others and feel frustrated when they come our way (Granovetter, 1973). Social support may come in many forms including financial (monetary and non-monetary such as gifts), physical (labour and caregiving), sexual, emotional and psychological benefits that are given or exchanged in a social relationship. It is therefore no surprise that our sense of happiness and wellbeing is dependent on our ties to social others.

Since the notable work of French sociologist Emile Durkheim who linked the lack of social support and integration within a social group to suicide rates in the group, much research in sociology, psychology and health have further shown that a lack of social support creates social isolation and feelings of disconnection that leads to many mental and health problems. The extant research has established that people who have smaller social networks, those who lack many close relationships and those who perceive that they do not receive enough support from their social network report lower wellbeing (Kawachi & Berkman, 2001).

Epidemiological studies have shown that people with less social support tend to have higher rates of mortality, while also providing evidence that people with better social support fare better against heart diseases, infectious diseases, cancer and even death (Uchino, 2006). Social support also helps in preventing mental health problems as well as serving as a buffer against stress, depression and feelings of loneliness that negatively affect mental health and wellbeing (Cohen & Wills, 1985; Kawachi & Berkman, 2001). Thoits (2011) argues that social support may present both positive and negative effects. On the one hand, it shapes overall wellbeing by providing people with a sense of meaning, belongingness, companionship, identity and self-worth. On the other hand, social support can be associated with controlling behaviours that may negatively affect a person's wellbeing.

Time and frequency of interaction are very important in building and benefiting from social ties as is the case with family and friends (Granovetter, 1973). This is also true for even weak ties like neighbours. For example, people who have stayed longer in a neighbourhood and therefore speak frequently with their neighbours report a higher sense of wellbeing than those who have not lived in their neighbourhood for long and report lower interactions with their neighbours (Appau, Awaworyi Churchill, & Farrell, 2019).

But just as not all social ties are helpful or desired, not all social support is wanted or contributes to a person's wellbeing. For example, interactions and exchanges with ambivalent and problematic social ties like extended family members and in-laws can negatively affect physical and mental wellbeing (Rook, Luong, Sorkin, Newsom, & Krause, 2012). Some research has also found no effect of social support on subjective wellbeing (Siedlecki, Salthouse, Oishi, & Jeswani, 2014).

The preceding discussion leads us to believe that social support will be particularly valuable for the wellbeing of older people for many reasons. Older people tend to have smaller social networks and close relations due to deaths of friends and relatives, retirement from the workforce and reduced capacity to build new social connections. This leads to a prevalence of social isolation which may have implications for wellbeing. For instance, the reduced interaction with social others, shrinking social networks and the feeling of loneliness among older people have been reported to negatively impact on wellbeing (Cornwell & Waite, 2009). Older people are also more likely to develop physical problems, which could be due to the lack of social support (Uchino, 2006). Thus, we expect that social support will become more salient for the wellbeing of people as they age.

The source of the social support is also important. For instance, among older people, benefits from social support can be derived from both giving and receiving. Research suggests that among older married people, those who reported giving emotional and caregiving support to their spouse as well as friends, family and neighbours had lower mortality rates compared to those who only received the social support (Brown, Nesse,

Vinokur, & Smith, 2003). But this research focused on mortality rate as the predictive outcome, rather than wellbeing.

There is a possible connection between giving social support and the wellbeing of the giver because people in reciprocal ties gain a sense of satisfaction and meaning from giving to the relationship (Brown et al., 2003). Further, research suggests that people, especially women, with lower resources actually report lower sense of mental wellbeing from giving obligatory social support to their social connections (Kawachi & Berkman, 2001). Thus, it is also possible that givers of support may be unhappy.

The evidence on the impact of social support on wellbeing is very limited. Past research on the direct effects of social support on wellbeing of older persons has focused on measures of wellbeing such as happiness (Antonucci & Akiyama, 1987), morbidity (Bowling, 1994), life satisfaction (Yoon & Lee, 2006) and loneliness (Golden et al., 2009). Other research focuses on the impact of social support on wellbeing of older people living in small geographically defined communities such as rural areas (Yoon & Lee, 2006) and elderly communities (Centers for Disease Control and Prevention, 2005; Golden et al., 2009). However, these studies have often not used longitudinal datasets which are relevant to ensure that the wellbeing of older people is tracked through time.

This chapter seeks to contribute to this useful but scant research on the direct effect of social support on the subjective wellbeing of older persons using longitudinal data. Using data from the Household Income and Labour Dynamics in Australia (HILDA) Survey, this chapter examines the impact of social support on wellbeing of older Australians. We adopt more extensive measures of social support and wellbeing than past studies. We also consider the impact of social support on measures such as life satisfaction, depression and psychological distress, which are important indicators related to the wellbeing-related challenges commonly experienced by older people. To the best of our knowledge, no past research considers such extensive and multiple aspects of wellbeing as we do in this chapter.

# 2 Data and Variables

The data used in this study were drawn from the HILDA Survey, which is a nationally representative annual panel survey of Australian households, focused on demographic, social, economic, health and wellbeing issues. The survey commenced in 2001 with 19,914 individuals within over 7000 households and has run annually since.[1] We use Release 16 of the HILDA Survey which covers waves 1–16. However, given the focus of our study, we base our analysis on a sub-sample of the survey respondents that are above 55 years. Thus, our sample is restricted to individuals who were above 55 years when the HILDA Survey commenced in 2001 or fell into this age category at some point in subsequent surveys.[2]

## 2.1 Wellbeing

We measure wellbeing using the five-item Mental Health Inventory (MHI-5) scale, which is a subscale of the Medical Outcomes Study Short Form (SF-36) general health survey. The MHI-5 scale is based on a questionnaire of five items, whose validation has been confirmed across different samples and proven to be an effective indicator of mental or psychological wellbeing in primary care settings and population samples (see, Aaronson et al., 1998; Apolone & Mosconi, 1998; Ding, Berry, & O'Brien, 2015; Rumpf, Meyer, Hapke, & John, 2001; Yamazaki, Fukuhara, & Green, 2005). Specifically, the questionnaire asks respondents how often in the past four weeks they have: (1) been nervous; (2) felt so down in the dumps that nothing could cheer them up; (3) felt calm and peaceful; (4) felt down; and (5) been happy. Answers to each item are coded on a 1–6 scale where 1 represents 'all of the time' and 6 represents 'none of the time', except for items (3) and (5) are reverse coded, to ensure that all items on the scale correspond to better mental health. All scores across each item are then summed up, subtracting five

---

[1] See Watson and Wooden (2012) for detail description of the HILDA dataset.

[2] For individuals who fell into this age category during subsequent waves of the survey, our study focuses only on waves in which respondents met the age criteria.

and dividing by 25 to derive a 0–100 mental health scale (Ware, Snow, Kosinski, & Gandek, 2000).

## 2.2 Social Support

The measure of social support assesses a person's perception of support they receive from friends and family (see, e.g., Crosier, Butterworth, & Rodgers, 2007; Milner, Krnjacki, Butterworth, & LaMontagne, 2016). One strand of the literature has posited that perceived social support is a more accurate and preferred measure of social support given that it reflects the feeling of support that individual believe they are getting. Specifically, as social support is expected to satisfy emotional needs, a respondent may receive social support but still feel dissatisfied with the level of support. Thus, the literature has shown perceived social support to be more important than received/experienced social support in examining the effects of social support (see, e.g., Lyyra & Heikkinen, 2006; McDowell & Serovich, 2007).

Our measure of social support is based on a 10-item questionnaire where on a 1–7 scale with 1 labelled as 'strongly disagree' and 7 labelled as 'strongly agree' respondents are asked to agree or disagree to the following:

1. I enjoy the time I spend with the people that are important to me
2. I seem to have a lot of friends
3. There is someone who can always cheer me up when I am down
4. When I need someone to help me out, I can usually find someone
5. When something's on my mind, just talking with the people I know can make me feel better
6. People don't come and visit as much as I would like (reverse coded)
7. I often need help from other people but can't get it (reverse coded)
8. I don't have anyone that I can confide in (reverse coded)
9. I have no one to lean on in times of trouble (reverse coded)
10. I often feel very lonely (reverse coded).

The social support scale is created by reverse coding items 6–10 and taking the average of responses from the ten items in the scale, and thus higher scores represent higher social support while lower scores represent lower social support.

## 2.3 Covariates

Our control variables are consistent with the existing literature on the determinants of wellbeing (see, e.g., Awaworyi Churchill & Mishra, 2017; Cheng & Smyth, 2015; Helliwell & Wang, 2011). These include age (in years) and its quadratic term, employment status (dummy variables for 'employed' with 'unemployed/not in labour force' as the reference category), relationship status (dummy variables for 'separated', 'divorced', 'widowed' and 'single' with 'Married/De facto' as the reference category), income (in log), educational status (dummy variables for 'postgraduate', 'graduate diploma', 'bachelor/honours', 'diploma' and 'certificate' with 'year 12 or below' as the reference category), disability status (dummy variable for 'long-term illness/disability') and number of dependants. Our regressions also include dummy variables that control for state and time (wave) fixed effects. Table 4 presents a description and summary statistics of variables.

# 3 Econometric Framework

Our baseline estimates are based on a panel model for wellbeing as follows:

$$W_{it} = \beta_1 SS_{it} + \sum_n \beta_n X_{n,it} + \vartheta_i + \alpha_s + \mu_t + \varepsilon_{it} \qquad (1)$$

where $W$ is wellbeing of individual $i$ at time $t$ (i.e. HILDA wave) while $SS$ is the measure of social support. $X$ is a set of control variables likely to influence wellbeing. $\vartheta_i$ represents individual fixed effects, $\alpha_s$ represents state fixed effects, $\mu_t$ represents time fixed effects and $\varepsilon$ is the error term. For our baseline results, we use pooled ordinary least squares (OLS), ordered logit regressions and panel fixed effect estimators. In the wellbeing literature, some studies suggest the use of ordered logit regressions given the ordinal nature of wellbeing measures. Although Ferrer-i-Carbonell and Frijters (2004) show that findings should not be sensitive to treating measures of wellbeing as cardinal or ordinal, we report results for both pooled OLS and panel ordered logit regressions as part of the baseline model to ensure our results are robust.

We also adopt alternative estimation approaches to address endogeneity given that social support is likely to be endogenous. We adopt fixed effect two-stage least squares (2SLS) in which we instrument for social support using lagged values of ethnic diversity. Our choice of instrument is influenced by the existing literature, which suggests that social factors such as social integration, networks and support are influenced by the level of ethnic diversity in society (see, e.g., Appau et al., 2019; Awaworyi Churchill & Smyth, 2019). On the one hand, an increase in ethnic diversity in a society is likely to provide individuals with increased opportunities to interact across racial and ethnic boundaries, thus promoting social cohesion, which is an important component of social support. On the other hand, an increase in diversity is likely to make ethnic differences more visible, thus reinforcing negative stereotyping and social exclusion which could hinder social support (Farley, Steeh, Krysan, Jackson, & Reeves, 1994; Wakefield & Hudley, 2007).

We use information based on the 1991 Australian population census, which is the oldest available census from the Australian Bureau of Statistics that reports the share of ethnic groups at the state-level, to generate indices of ethnic diversity to instrument social support. We argue that the only meaningful mechanism through which historical measures of ethnic diversity are likely to influence current levels of mental health is through its effect on social factors that define social support. Further, the use of ethnic diversity indices from a previous census also provide the benefit of operating as a lag and therefore address potential issues of self-selection.

For further robustness, we supplement panel 2SLS regressions with the Lewbel (2012) 2SLS regressions. The Lewbel 2SLS approach is widely used in the literature to complement traditional 2SLS estimations or in the absence of conventional instruments (see, e.g., Ambrey & Fleming, 2014; Arcand, Berkes, & Panizza, 2015; Mallick, 2012; Millimet & Roy, 2016) and does not rely on a valid exclusion restriction but on heteroskedastic covariance restrictions to achieve identification.[3]

# 4 Results

Table 1 reports baseline results for the association between social support and wellbeing. Specifically, Columns 1, 2 and 3 report results for pooled OLS, panel ordered logit and fixed effects estimations, respectively. Across all estimation methods, we find a positive effect of social support on wellbeing. Pooled OLS results suggest that a standard deviation increase in social support is associated with an increase of 0.421 standard deviations in wellbeing. Panel ordered logit and fixed effect estimation result point to a similar relationship but with relatively weaker effect sizes. Specifically, a standard deviation increase in social support is associated with standard deviation declines of 0.051 and 0.192 in wellbeing in ordered logit and fixed effect estimations, respectively. Thus, overall, an increase in social support is associated with better wellbeing among older Australians. Comparing standardized coefficients, we also find that the effects of social support are relatively stronger compared to the effects of other covariates that are statistically significant.

## 4.1 Sensitivity to Endogeneity

Next, we examine the sensitivity of our results to endogeneity. Table 2 presents the 2SLS results. Column 1 reports findings from panel IV

[3]See Lewbel (2012) for details on how identification is achieved.

**Table 1** Social support and wellbeing (baseline results)

| Variables | (1)<br>Pooled OLS | (2)<br>Ordered logit | (3)<br>Fixed effect |
|---|---|---|---|
| Social support | 7.384*** | 0.902*** | 3.358*** |
| | (0.071) | (0.009) | (0.073) |
| | [0.421] | [0.051] | [0.192] |
| Male | 2.809*** | 0.381*** | |
| | (0.131) | (0.016) | |
| Age | 1.474*** | 0.162*** | 1.665*** |
| | (0.116) | (0.014) | (0.118) |
| Age squared | −0.865*** | −0.095*** | −1.234*** |
| | (0.081) | (0.010) | (0.084) |
| Dependants | −0.664*** | −0.102*** | −0.028 |
| | (0.178) | (0.020) | (0.249) |
| Separated | −1.398*** | −0.123*** | −2.258*** |
| | (0.404) | (0.046) | (0.529) |
| Divorced | −0.531** | −0.003 | −0.229 |
| | (0.232) | (0.027) | (0.478) |
| Widowed | 1.011*** | 0.138*** | −0.740** |
| | (0.200) | (0.024) | (0.303) |
| Single | 0.782** | 0.077** | −2.558 |
| | (0.320) | (0.039) | (1.742) |
| Income | 0.730*** | 0.077*** | 0.075 |
| | (0.092) | (0.011) | (0.094) |
| Employed | 3.449*** | 0.339*** | 1.072*** |
| | (0.160) | (0.019) | (0.180) |

| Variables | (1)<br>Pooled OLS | (2)<br>Ordered logit | (3)<br>Fixed effect |
|---|---|---|---|
| Postgraduate | 1.325*** | 0.135*** | −0.245 |
| | (0.316) | (0.038) | (2.517) |
| Graduate diploma | 2.852*** | 0.302*** | 1.611 |
| | (0.250) | (0.031) | (2.422) |
| Bachelor | 2.171*** | 0.292*** | 1.867 |
| | (0.220) | (0.027) | (2.530) |
| Diploma | 2.479*** | 0.277*** | −0.329 |
| | (0.197) | (0.025) | (2.061) |
| Certificate | 1.492*** | 0.196*** | 1.525 |
| | (0.169) | (0.021) | (1.046) |
| Illness | −6.249*** | −0.737*** | −1.403*** |
| | (0.131) | (0.016) | (0.119) |
| State fixed effect | Yes | Yes | Yes |
| Wave fixed effect | Yes | Yes | Yes |
| Individual fixed effect | No | No | Yes |
| Observations | 58,247 | 58,247 | 58,247 |
| $R^2$ | 0.269 | – | 0.050 |

Reference category for marital status is those married or in a de facto relationship, for educational status it is those whose highest education level is year 12 or below, and for employment status it is those unemployed or not in the labour force

Robust standard errors in parentheses

Standardized coefficients in brackets

***$p < 0.01$, **$p < 0.05$, *$p < 0.1$

**Table 2** Social support and wellbeing (IV results)

| Variables | (1)<br>Panel IV | (2)<br>Lewbel 2SLS |
|---|---|---|
| Social support | 10.217*** | 10.832*** |
| | (1.357) | (0.450) |
| | [0.483] | [0.618] |
| Controls? | Yes | Yes |
| State fixed effect | Yes | Yes |
| Wave fixed effect | Yes | Yes |
| Individual fixed effect | Yes | No |
| Observations | 58,247 | 58,247 |
| *First stage* | | |
| Diversity (1991) | −0.948*** | −3.877*** |
| | (0.199) | (1.152) |
| $R^2$ | 0.1091 | 0.1552 |
| *F*-statistics | 22.79 | 14.91 |
| *J P*-value | – | 0.1080 |

Robust standard errors in parentheses
Standardized coefficients in brackets
***$p < 0.01$, **$p < 0.05$, *$p < 0.1$

regressions using ethnic diversity as instrument. Column 2 reports Lewbel 2SLS results that combined our external instrument (ethnic diversity) with internally generated instruments. From Columns 1 and 2, first stage results suggest a negative effect of ethnic diversity on social support, a finding consistent with the literature.[4] Across all columns, we find that our *F* statistics are greater than 10 suggest that, at the 10% significance level, our instruments are not weakly correlated with social support (Stock & Yogo, 2005). Further, in the Lewbel 2SLS regressions, the assumption of heteroskedasticity is satisfied in our data using the Breusch and Pagan (1979) test for heteroskedasticity while the null hypothesis for the overidentifying restriction test is not rejected in regressions.

Overall, from Table 2, while 2SLS results reinforce the conclusion of a positive association between social support and wellbeing, we find evidence of an upward bias in pooled OLS and fixed effects estimates given

[4]Appau et al. (2019) find a negative effect of ethnic diversity on social integration in a UK sample.

that IV results that control for endogeneity are relatively lower in magnitude. Specifically, from Column 1, we find that a standard deviation increase in social support is associated with an increase of 0.483 standard deviations in wellbeing. While from Column 2, a standard deviation increase in social support is associated with a standard deviation decline of 0.618 in wellbeing.

## 4.2 Further Analysis

In this section, we examine the sensitivity of our results to alternative ways of measuring wellbeing. We first consider life satisfaction, a commonly used measure of subjective wellbeing, as an alternative measure of wellbeing. Life satisfaction in the HILDA Survey is based on the question: 'All things considered, how satisfied are you with your life?' Respondents report scores to this question on a scale of 0–10, where 0 is labelled as totally dissatisfied and 10 is totally satisfied. Results for the effect of social support on life satisfaction are reported in Column 1 of Table 3.

**Table 3** Robustness checks (alternative measures of wellbeing)

| Variables | (1) Life satisfaction | (2) Depression | (3) K10 distress scale | (4) K10 risk categories |
|---|---|---|---|---|
| Social support | 0.175*** | −0.025*** | −1.050*** | −0.140*** |
| | (0.007) | (0.008) | (0.045) | (0.007) |
| | [0.115] | [−0.063] | [−0.177] | [−0.174] |
| Controls? | Yes | Yes | Yes | Yes |
| State fixed effect | Yes | Yes | Yes | Yes |
| Wave fixed effect | Yes | Yes | Yes | Yes |
| Individual fixed effect | Yes | Yes | Yes | Yes |
| Observations | 58,755 | 5778 | 19,908 | 19,908 |
| $R^2$ | 0.027 | 0.011 | 0.049 | 0.039 |

Labels on top of each column represent the measure of wellbeing
Standard errors in parentheses
Standardized coefficients in brackets
$^{***}p < 0.01$, $^{**}p < 0.05$, $^{*}p < 0.1$

We find evidence of a positive association between social support and life satisfaction.

We also use measures of depression and psychological distress, which are only available in selected HILDA waves, as alternative measures of wellbeing. Waves 7 and 9 of the HILDA Survey ask respondents if they have ever been told by a doctor or nurse that they have depression or anxiety. We derive a dummy variable which equals one if respondents answer 'yes' to this question. Results for the effect of social support on depression, reported in Column 2 of Table 3, suggest a negative effect of social support on depression.

The measure of psychological distress is based on the Kessler Psychological Distress (K10) scale and is only available in waves 7, 9, 11, 13 and 15 of the HILDA Survey. The K10 is a measure of wellbeing that reflects the level of psychological fatigue, agitation, nervousness and depression. It is based on a 10-item questionnaire that has a five-level response scale, which is aggregated to generate a wellbeing scale with a minimum possible score of 10 (good wellbeing) and a maximum possible score of 50 (poor wellbeing) (ABS, 2001). We use the K10 distress scale as well as a measure of respondents' risk categories based on the K10 scale alternative measures of wellbeing. The K10 risk category variable is a 1–4 ordinal scale in which one corresponds with low risk and 4 corresponds with very high risk. Columns 3 and 4 of Table 3 report results for effects on the K10 distress scale and risk categories, respectively. These results suggest a negative association between social support and psychological distress.

## 5 Conclusion and Policy Implications

This chapter examined the direct effect of social support on the subjective wellbeing of older Australians, using data from the HILDA Survey. Our results from a sample of individuals who were above 55 years across 16 years show that social support has a positive effect on subjective wellbeing. Social support also negatively affects depression and psychological distress, which are both alternative measures of subjective wellbeing.

Overall, the results that we present in this chapter underlie the importance of social support for the subjective wellbeing of older people.

Our results also unveil a paradoxical situation. Older people really do benefit from having networks of support; people they can talk to and lean on in times of need. But as we noted earlier, older people tend to lose their social network and support over time. Thus, any policy direction or practical intervention in this regard must focus on ways to improve both the quantity and quality of social support that older people have over time.

A review of past research suggests that investing in group leisure and educational activities for older people has proven to be more effective in combating social isolation, compared to one-on-one interventions like home visitation (Cattan, White, Bond, & Learmouth, 2005). We believe that this approach will apply in our context as well. Investing in group activities for older persons will provide them with opportunities to build new social networks, engage their time and also provide them with a sense of belongingness and companionship. Social groups can be community based or connected across various geographical space through technology such as video interactive programs. Additionally, in the case of social support for older people the quality of social support is more important than quantity (i.e. several friends). Thus, efforts to sustain leisure and educational activities among groups of older people are crucial given that social ties become stronger and more valued through sustained interaction and exchange over time (Granovetter, 1973).

Volunteering could also be an important way for older people to build new and quality social connections. This is something older people can take up individually or in groups. Volunteering allows older people to be able to give social support to other people in their community and this in itself provides them with a sense of purpose, self-esteem and ultimately improves their subjective wellbeing (Appau & Awaworyi Churchill, 2018; Morrow-Howell, Hinterlong, Rozario, & Tang, 2003). Often, interventions to improve wellbeing among older people such as those combatting social isolation fail to produce demonstrable results (Morrow-Howell et al., 2003). It is therefore important that any policy or social intervention is designed with measurable outcomes that are monitored over time.

**Acknowledgements** This chapter uses unit record data from the Household, Income and Labour Dynamics in Australia (HILDA) Survey. The HILDA Project was initiated and is funded by the Australian Government Department of Social Services (DSS) and is managed by the Melbourne Institute of Applied Economic and Social Research (Melbourne Institute). The findings and views reported in this paper, however, are those of the authors and should not be attributed to either DSS or the Melbourne Institute.

## Appendix

See Table 4.

**Table 4** Description and summary statistics of variables

| Variable | Descriptions | Mean | SD |
|---|---|---|---|
| Wellbeing | Five-item Mental Health Inventory (MHI-5) scale | 76.458 | 16.958 |
| Life satisfaction | All things considered, how satisfied are you with your life? On a scale of 0–10, where 0 is labelled as totally dissatisfied and 10 is totally satisfied | 8.169 | 1.516 |
| Depression | Dummy variable if respondent has ever been told by a doctor or nurse that they have depression/anxiety? | 0.171 | 0.378 |
| K10 distress scale | Kessler Psychological Distress Scale (K10) | 14.770 | 5.783 |
| K10 risk categories | Kessler Psychological Distress Scale (K10) risk categories. 1 represents low risk, 2 moderate risk, 3 high risk and 4 very high risk | 1.443 | 0.785 |
| Social support | Social support scale | 5.325 | 0.970 |
| Age | Age of respondent | 68.219 | 8.898 |
| Age squared | Square of age/100 | 47.330 | 12.655 |
| Male | Dummy variable if respondent is male | 0.467 | 0.498 |
| Female | Dummy variable if respondent is female | 0.533 | 0.498 |
| Dependants | Number of dependents in household aged 0–24 | 0.069 | 0.365 |
| Separated | Dummy variable if respondent is separated | 0.028 | 0.165 |
| Divorced | Dummy variable if respondent is divorced | 0.097 | 0.295 |
| Widowed | Dummy variable if respondent is widowed | 0.167 | 0.373 |
| Single | Dummy variable if respondent is single | 0.044 | 0.205 |
| Married/De facto | Dummy variable if respondent is married or in a de facto relationship | 0.664 | 0.472 |
| Income | Log of household income | 10.661 | 0.850 |
| Employed | Dummy variable if respondent is employed | 0.294 | 0.455 |

(continued)

**Table 4** (continued)

| Variable | Descriptions | Mean | SD |
|---|---|---|---|
| Unemployed | Dummy variable if respondent is unemployed | 0.009 | 0.092 |
| Not in labour force | Dummy variable if respondent is not in labour force | 0.697 | 0.459 |
| Postgraduate | Dummy variable if respondent's highest education level achieved is masters or doctorate | 0.035 | 0.183 |
| Graduate diploma | Dummy variable if respondent's highest education level achieved is graduate diploma or certificate | 0.047 | 0.212 |
| Bachelor | Dummy variable if respondent's highest education level achieved is bachelor or honours | 0.084 | 0.276 |
| Diploma | Dummy variable if respondent's highest education level achieved is advanced diploma or diploma | 0.094 | 0.291 |
| Certificate | Dummy variable if respondent's highest education level achieved is certificate I, II, III or IV | 0.189 | 0.391 |
| Year 12 | Dummy variable if respondent's highest education level achieved is year 12 or below | 0.551 | 0.499 |
| Illness | Dummy variable if respondent is disabled or has a long-term illness | 0.454 | 0.498 |

# References

Aaronson, N. K., Muller, M., Cohen, P. D. A., Essink-Bot, M.-L., Fekkes, M., Sanderman, R., … Verrips, E. (1998). Translation, validation, and norming of the Dutch language version of the SF-36 health survey in community and chronic disease populations. *Journal of Clinical Epidemiology, 51*(11), 1055–1068. https://doi.org/10.1016/S0895-4356(98)00097-3.

ABS. (2001). *Information paper: Use of the Kessler Psychological Distress scale in ABS health surveys, Australia, 2001* (ABS Cat. No. 4817.0.55.001).

Ambrey, C., & Fleming, C. (2014). Public greenspace and life satisfaction in urban Australia. *Urban Studies, 51*(6), 1290–1321.

Antonucci, T. C., & Akiyama, H. (1987). An examination of sex differences in social support among older men and women. *Sex Roles, 17*(11–12), 737–749.

Apolone, G., & Mosconi, P. (1998). The Italian SF-36 health survey: Translation, validation and norming. *Journal of Clinical Epidemiology, 51*(11), 1025–1036. https://doi.org/10.1016/S0895-4356(98)00094-8.

Appau, S., & Awaworyi Churchill, S. (2018). Charity, volunteering type and subjective wellbeing. *VOLUNTAS: International Journal of Voluntary and Nonprofit Organizations, 30,* 1118–1132.

Appau, S., Awaworyi Churchill, S., & Farrell, L. (2019). Social integration and subjective wellbeing. *Applied Economics, 51*(16), 1748–1761. https://doi.org/10.1080/00036846.2018.1528340.

Arcand, J. L., Berkes, E., & Panizza, U. (2015). Too much finance? *Journal of Economic Growth, 20*(2), 105–148. https://doi.org/10.1007/s10887-015-9115-2.

Awaworyi Churchill, S., & Mishra, V. (2017). Trust, social networks and subjective wellbeing in China. *Social Indicators Research, 132*(1), 313–339. https://doi.org/10.1007/s11205-015-1220-2.

Awaworyi Churchill, S., & Smyth, R. (2019). Friendship network composition and subjective well-being. *Oxford Economic Papers, 72,* 191–215. https://doi.org/10.1093/oep/gpz019.

Bowling, A. (1994). Social networks and social support among older people and implications for emotional well-being and psychiatric morbidity. *International Review of Psychiatry, 6*(1), 41–58.

Breusch, T., & Pagan, A. (1979). A simple test for heteroscedasticity and random coefficient variation. *Econometrica, 47*(5), 1287–1294.

Brown, S. L., Nesse, R. M., Vinokur, A. D., & Smith, D. M. (2003). Providing social support may be more beneficial than receiving it: Results from a prospective study of mortality. *Psychological Science, 14*(4), 320–327.

Cattan, M., White, M., Bond, J., & Learmouth, A. (2005). Preventing social isolation and loneliness among older people: A systematic review of health promotion interventions. *Ageing & Society, 25*(1), 41–67.

Centers for Disease Control and Prevention (CDC). (2005). Social support and health-related quality of life among older adults—Missouri, 2000. *MMWR: Morbidity and Mortality Weekly Report, 54*(17), 433.

Cheng, Z., & Smyth, R. (2015). Sex and happiness. *Journal of Economic Behavior & Organization, 112,* 26–32.

Cohen, S., & Wills, T. A. (1985). Stress, social support, and the buffering hypothesis. *Psychological Bulletin, 98*(2), 310.

Cornwell, E. Y., & Waite, L. J. (2009). Social disconnectedness, perceived isolation, and health among older adults. *Journal of Health and Social Behavior, 50*(1), 31–48.

Crosier, T., Butterworth, P., & Rodgers, B. (2007). Mental health problems among single and partnered mothers. *Social Psychiatry and Psychiatric Epidemiology, 42*(1), 6–13. https://doi.org/10.1007/s00127-006-0125-4.

Ding, N., Berry, H. L., & O'Brien, L. V. (2015). One-year reciprocal relationship between community participation and mental wellbeing in Australia: A panel analysis. *Social Science and Medicine, 128,* 246–254.

Farley, R., Steeh, C., Krysan, M., Jackson, T., & Reeves, K. (1994). Stereotypes and segregation: Neighborhoods in the Detroit area. *American Journal of Sociology, 100*(3), 750–780.

Ferrer-i-Carbonell, A., & Frijters, P. (2004). How important is methodology for the estimates of the determinants of happiness? *The Economic Journal, 114*(497), 641–659. https://doi.org/10.1111/j.1468-0297.2004.00235.x.

Golden, J., Conroy, R. M., Bruce, I., Denihan, A., Greene, E., Kirby, M., & Lawlor, B. A. (2009). Loneliness, social support networks, mood and wellbeing in community-dwelling elderly. *International Journal of Geriatric Psychiatry: A Journal of the Psychiatry of Late Life and Allied Sciences, 24*(7), 694–700.

Granovetter, M. S. (1973). The strength of weak ties. *American Journal of Sociology, 78,* 1360–1380.

Helliwell, J. F., & Wang, S. (2011). Trust and well-being. *Journal of Wellbeing, 1*(1), 42–78.

Kawachi, I., & Berkman, L. F. (2001). Social ties and mental health. *Journal of Urban Health, 78*(3), 458–467.

Lewbel, A. (2012). Using heteroscedasticity to identify and estimate mismeasured and endogenous regressor models. *Journal of Business & Economic Statistics, 30*(1), 67–80. https://doi.org/10.1080/07350015.2012.643126.

Lyyra, T.-M., & Heikkinen, R.-L. (2006). Perceived social support and mortality in older people. *The Journals of Gerontology Series B: Psychological Sciences and Social Sciences, 61*(3), S147–S152.

Mallick, D. (2012). Microfinance and moneylender interest rate: Evidence from Bangladesh. *World Development, 40*(6), 1181–1189.

McDowell, T. L., & Serovich, J. (2007). The effect of perceived and actual social support on the mental health of HIV-positive persons. *AIDS Care, 19*(10), 1223–1229.

Millimet, D. L., & Roy, J. (2016). Empirical tests of the pollution haven hypothesis when environmental regulation is endogenous. *Journal of Applied Econometrics, 31*(4), 652–677. https://doi.org/10.1002/jae.2451.
Milner, A., Krnjacki, L., Butterworth, P., & LaMontagne, A. D. (2016). The role of social support in protecting mental health when employed and unemployed: A longitudinal fixed-effects analysis using 12 annual waves of the HILDA cohort. *Social Science and Medicine, 153*, 20–26.
Morrow-Howell, N., Hinterlong, J., Rozario, P. A., & Tang, F. (2003). Effects of volunteering on the well-being of older adults. *The Journals of Gerontology Series B: Psychological Sciences and Social Sciences, 58*(3), S137–S145.
Rook, K. S., Luong, G., Sorkin, D. H., Newsom, J. T., & Krause, N. (2012). Ambivalent versus problematic social ties: Implications for psychological health, functional health, and interpersonal coping. *Psychology and Aging, 27*(4), 912.
Rumpf, H.-J., Meyer, C., Hapke, U., & John, U. (2001). Screening for mental health: Validity of the MHI-5 using DSM-IV Axis I psychiatric disorders as gold standard. *Psychiatry Research, 105*(3), 243–253.
Siedlecki, K. L., Salthouse, T. A., Oishi, S., & Jeswani, S. (2014). The relationship between social support and subjective well-being across age. *Social Indicators Research, 117*(2), 561–576.
Stock, J. H., & Yogo, M. (2005). Testing for weak instruments in linear IV regression. In D. Andrews & J. Stock (Eds.), *Identification and inference for econometric models: Essays in honor of Thomas Rothenberg* (pp. 80–105). Cambridge: Cambridge University Press.
Thoits, P. A. (2011). Mechanisms linking social ties and support to physical and mental health. *Journal of Health and Social Behavior, 52*(2), 145–161.
Uchino, B. N. (2006). Social support and health: A review of physiological processes potentially underlying links to disease outcomes. *Journal of Behavioral Medicine, 29*(4), 377–387.
Wakefield, W. D., & Hudley, C. (2007). Ethnic and racial identity and adolescent well-being. *Theory into Practice, 46*(2), 147–154.
Ware, J. E., Snow, K., Kosinski, M., & Gandek, B. (2000). *SF–36 health survey: Manual and interpretation guide.* Lincoln, RI: Quality Metric Inc.
Watson, N., & Wooden, M. P. (2012). The HILDA survey: A case study in the design and development of a successful household panel survey. *Longitudinal and Life Course Studies, 3*(3), 369–381.
Yamazaki, S., Fukuhara, S., & Green, J. (2005). Usefulness of five-item and three-item Mental Health Inventories to screen for depressive symptoms in

the general population of Japan. *Health and Quality of Life Outcomes, 3*(1), 48.

Yoon, D. P., & Lee, E. K. O. (2006). The impact of religiousness, spirituality, and social support on psychological well-being among older adults in rural areas. *Journal of Gerontological Social Work, 48*(3–4), 281–298.

# 5

# Gambling and Subjective Wellbeing of Older Australians

Sefa Awaworyi Churchill and Lisa Farrell

## 1 Introduction and Background

Gambling is a social leisure activity that many people enjoy. However, for some this participation can lead to excessive consumption and addictive behaviours. The impact of gambling on subjective wellbeing has been well documented (see, Awaworyi Churchill & Farrell, 2018; Farrell, 2018; Quigley et al., 2015). There has also been much focus in the literature on this relationship at key stages in the life-course such as during youth when risky behaviours are often first experimented with and habits for adult life are formed (see, Cooper, 2002). In recent times, the liberalisation of gambling across most developed countries has seen a

S. Awaworyi Churchill (✉) · L. Farrell
School of Economics, Finance and Marketing, RMIT University, Melbourne, VIC, Australia
e-mail: sefa.awaworyichurchill@rmit.edu.au

L. Farrell
e-mail: lisa.farrell@rmit.edu.au



S. Awaworyi Churchill et al. (eds.), *Measuring, Understanding and Improving Wellbeing Among Older People*,
https://doi.org/10.1007/978-981-15-2353-3_5

rise in both participation and consumption among older people. Older people are becoming an important market segment for the industry as many countries are experiencing longer lives and so have an ageing population.

One strand of the literature has thus focused on gambling among older people. A recent meta-analysis of the literature on older people and gambling participation, Song-Iee Hong, Wang, and Cunningham-Williams (2012) identifies that the majority of the literature has focused on developed countries using a variety of instruments to measure gambling participation and mostly employed empirical analysis with a focus on negative outcomes and traditional forms of gambling. In terms of prevalence, the study reports prevalence rates of problem or pathological gambling for older adults (50+) ranging from 0.2 to 12.9%. Problem gambling in older populations has been found to be linked to both physical and mental health (Lister & Nower, 2013). In the context of Australia, where our study is based, a recent study using data from 2015 showed that compared to the Australian adult population regular gambling participants were substantially over-represented among people over the age of 50.[1] Australia is a particularly relevant country within which to undertake this study as it has an ageing population and has the highest per capita gambling expenditure in the world with average losses per adult of AU$1324 (US$958) in 2017.[2]

Gambling venues often target seniors by offering free transport, discount meals, and even providing wheelchairs and motorised scooters to heighten their mobility within the venue. Older people are more vulnerable to developing gambling problems for the following reasons. Firstly, gambling problems are often correlated with trauma and major life events. Later life is associated with the transition to retirement which has also been shown to impact on wellbeing (see Cameron & Waldegrave, 2009; Nordenmark & Stattin, 2009). Older people are more likely to experience the death of a partner or close friend which can cause severe emotional pain and feelings of loneliness (Bazargan, Bazargan,

[1] https://aifs.gov.au/agrc/publications/gambling-activity-australia/export, accessed 27 June 19.

[2] https://www.abc.net.au/news/2018-11-20/australians-worlds-biggest-gambling-losers/10495566, accessed 27 June 19.

& Akanda, 2001; Southwell, Boreham, & Laffan, 2008). Such emotions have been associated with pathways to problem gambling (Martin, Lichtenberg, & Templin, 2011).

Secondly, they often have accumulated wealth saved for their retirement, but once these are exhausted they can not easily be replaced so they are particularly vulnerable to long-term financial hardship because of excessive gambling expenditure. Moreover, the impact of these losses can spillover in the lives of adult children as evidenced in Patford (2007).

Thirdly, older people often experience social isolation and gambling venues offer them an opportunity to be in a social environment (McNeilly & Burke, 2001). They may therefore be less likely to self-identify gambling-related problems. Fourthly, older people often feel more stigmatised by addiction-related disorders and are less likely to engage in help and support-seeking behaviours.

Lastly, many older people suffer from cognitive impairments related to conditions such as Dementia and Parkinson's Disease and these can impact on their ability to make rational decisions about their gambling activities (Avanzi et al., 2006).

Despite the specific risk factors associated with gambling participation for this group of gamblers, there are studies that have reported positive impacts from exposure to gambling activities. Vander Bilt, Dodge, Pandav, Shaffer, and Ganguli (2004) recorded emotional responses (such as smiling) while individuals were engaged in the act of simulated gambling on a laptop. Respondents were offered a choice between playing slot machines, video poker, roulette, blackjack or craps. However, this study concentrates on mood enhancement, arousal and excitement generated by gambling participation rather than the longer-term effects on overall wellbeing. A related study by Dixon, Nastally, and Waterman (2010) showed that bingo participation was positively associated with happiness. However, in this case the activity took place outside of the home and in their discussion of the findings, the authors focused on social support as the explanation for this observation. Social isolation in this age group is common and activities outside of the home offer an ability to interact with others. This study highlights difficulty in identifying specific pathways and establishing causality in this field of research.

In this chapter, we examine the association between elderly gambling and subjective wellbeing in order to understand the long-term effects in later life of gambling participation. Using data from the Household, Income and Labour Dynamics in Australia (HILDA) survey, we find evidence of a negative association between gambling and subjective wellbeing for older people.

The findings from this chapter present implications for policy relating to the regulation of the betting and gaming sector in terms of its marketing to vulnerable sub-population. It will also inform addiction and support services as well as those allied health services who work with older people. This research is especially important as the baby boomers age and the proportion of the population within the 50 plus age group increases within Australia and many other developed countries.

## 2 Data and Variables

Data used in this study come from the HILDA survey. HILDA is a nationally representative panel survey which commenced in 2001 (Watson & Wooden, 2012). The survey first included a gambling module in wave 15, and thus, our study focuses on this wave. Given that our study focuses on older people, we also limit our analysis to respondents that are at 50 years old.

### 2.1 Gambling Variable

Consistent with the existing literature (Awaworyi Churchill & Farrell, 2018; Raisamo, Mäkelä, Salonen, & Lintonen, 2014), our main measures of gambling behaviour are based on the Problem Gambling Severity Index (PGSI) framework (Ferris & Wynne, 2001). The PGSI captures problematic gambling behaviour and adverse consequences of gambling experienced in the past 12 months. It is based on a nine-item questionnaire (shown in Table 6), with items that are rated on a four-point scale, where 0 represents 'never' and 3 represents 'almost always'.

PGSI scores are derived as the sum of responses from the nine-item questionnaire and thus scores range between 0 and 27 with higher scores representing more problematic gambling behaviour. We use PGSI scores as our first measure of gambling behaviour.

The second measure of gambling behaviour is a measure of gambling risk based on gambler PGSI scores. Based on PGSI scores, gamblers are categorised into four risk spectrums namely, non-problem gamblers, low-risk gamblers, moderate-risk gamblers and problem gamblers. Non-problem gamblers (or non-gamblers) are those with a PGSI score of 0 and did not engage in any problematic gambling behaviour in the past 12 months. Low-risk gamblers have PGSI scores of 1 or 2, moderate-risk gamblers have scores between 3 and 7, and problem gamblers are those with PGSI scores of 8 or above. Our second measure of gambling behaviour is therefore a four-point ordinal scale reflecting the various risk spectrums such that 1 represents non-problem gamblers, 2 represents low-risk gamblers, 3 represents medium-risk gamblers and 4 represents problem gamblers.

## 2.2 Subjective Wellbeing

Our main measure of subjective wellbeing is based on responses to a single-item question that captures overall life satisfaction. The HILDA survey asks the question: 'All things considered, how satisfied are you with your life?' Respondents report scores to this question on a scale of 0–10, in which zero is 'totally dissatisfied' and 10 is 'totally satisfied'. Questions of this sort are typically used as proxies for subjective wellbeing in the existing literature (Awaworyi Churchill & Mishra, 2017; Cummins, 1995, 2000; Pinquart & Sörensen, 2000).

In robustness checks, we examine the sensitivity of our results to alternative measures of subjective wellbeing that has been used in the literature (Awaworyi Churchill & Smyth, 2019) including the five-item Mental Health Inventory (MHI-5) scale, which is a subscale of the short form (SF-36) general health survey, and the Kessler Psychological Distress Scale (K10) to measure subjective wellbeing. The MHI-5 scale is a composite measure of subjective mental health, which is on a 0–100 scale, based on a five-item questionnaire in which respondents were asked about how often in the past four weeks they have: (1) been nervous; (2) felt so down in the dumps that nothing could cheer them up; (3) felt calm and peaceful; (4) felt down; and (5) been happy. The K10 scale is a 10–50 point scale that is derived from a 10-item questionnaire which reflects various dimensions of mental health including depression, psychological fatigue, nervousness and agitation.

### 2.3 Control Variables

In addition to measures of gambling behaviour, in all specifications, we also include a full set of variables correlated with subjective wellbeing, consistent with the existing literature (Dolan, Peasgood, & White, 2008). These include age and its quadratic term, income, marital status, educational status and employment status, among others. Table 7 provides full details on the control variables and other variables included in our analysis.

## 3 Empirical Methods

We estimate the following subjective wellbeing equation:

$$SWB_i = \alpha + \beta_1 GB_i + \sum_n \beta_n X_{n,i} + \varepsilon_i \tag{1}$$

where *SWB* is the measure of subjective wellbeing of individual $i$ while *GB* is the measure of gambling behaviour. $X$ is a set of control variables likely to influence a person's subjective wellbeing, while $\varepsilon$ is the error term. Given the ordinal nature of subjective wellbeing measures, some studies on the determinants of subjective wellbeing have used ordered logit regressions while others treat wellbeing cardinally and use ordinary least squares (OLS). However, in a methodological paper, Ferrer-i-Carbonell and Frijters (2004) show that findings are not sensitive to treating subjective wellbeing as cardinal or ordinal. To ensure robustness, we estimate Eq. (1) using OLS and ordered logit regressions.

# 4 Results

Table 1 presents results for the association between our measures of gambling behaviour and subjective wellbeing. Columns 1 and 2 present OLS results while Columns 3 and 4 present ordered logit regression results. The results suggest that gambling is associated with lower levels of subjective wellbeing. Specifically, from Column 1, we find that the coefficient on the PGSI score is negative and statistically significant at the one per cent significance level, with an effect size of 0.089. This implies a 0.089 lower subjective wellbeing (measured by life satisfaction), on a 0–10 scale, for a unit increase in PGSI score. From Column 2, the coefficient on gambling risk status is also negative and significant at the one per cent level with an effect size of 0.233. This implies a 0.233 lower life satisfaction, on a scale of 0–10, for a unit difference in risk category. From Columns 3 and 4, we find that the nature of the association between gambling behaviour and subjective wellbeing is not altered except for some marginal differences in coefficient size. Here, we find that the coefficient on the PGSI score variable is −0.107, while the coefficient on the risk status variable is −0.317. The association between gambling and wellbeing among older people is therefore not influenced by whether subjective wellbeing is modelled as cardinal or ordinal.

Table 2 presents results for the effects of various gambler categories on subjective wellbeing. The gambling risk status variable used in this chapter is an ordinal scale of gambling risk, which categorises gamblers as non-problem gamblers, low-risk gamblers, moderate-risk gamblers and problem gamblers. In Table 2, we use a dummy variable for each risk category and examine the effects of each gambler category on wellbeing. From Column 1 of Table 2, we find that compared to gamblers, on average, non-gamblers tend to have higher life satisfaction. The coefficient here is 0.304 implying a 0.304 higher life satisfaction, for a shift from a gambler category to non-gambler category. While the coefficient on the low-risk gambler dummy variable is statistically insignificant, we find that the coefficient on the medium-risk and problem gambler variables is significant at the one per cent level. From Columns 3 and 4, the coefficients on the medium-risk and problem gambler variables are −0.521 and −0.795, respectively. The results here suggest that being a

**Table 1** Gambling and life satisfaction (baseline results)

| Variables | (1) OLS | (2) OLS | (3) Ordered Logit | (4) Ordered Logit |
|---|---|---|---|---|
| PGSI score | −0.089*** | | −0.107*** | |
| | (0.018) | | (0.016) | |
| Risk status | | −0.233*** | | −0.317*** |
| | | (0.044) | | (0.048) |
| Male | −0.074** | −0.073** | −0.128*** | −0.125*** |
| | (0.037) | (0.037) | (0.047) | (0.047) |
| Age | 0.147*** | 0.149*** | 0.187*** | 0.188*** |
| | (0.023) | (0.023) | (0.030) | (0.030) |
| Age squared | −0.084*** | −0.086*** | −0.108*** | −0.109*** |
| | (0.017) | (0.017) | (0.022) | (0.022) |
| Dependants | 0.001 | 0.001 | −0.013 | −0.015 |
| | (0.031) | (0.031) | (0.039) | (0.039) |
| Separated | −0.702*** | −0.704*** | −0.795*** | −0.795*** |
| | (0.128) | (0.128) | (0.150) | (0.150) |
| Divorced | −0.360*** | −0.364*** | −0.497*** | −0.502*** |
| | (0.066) | (0.066) | (0.083) | (0.083) |
| Widowed | −0.186*** | −0.184** | −0.231** | −0.228** |
| | (0.072) | (0.072) | (0.094) | (0.094) |
| Single | −0.300*** | −0.311*** | −0.408*** | −0.413*** |
| | (0.086) | (0.088) | (0.104) | (0.104) |
| Income | 0.098*** | 0.097*** | 0.116*** | 0.115*** |
| | (0.031) | (0.031) | (0.040) | (0.040) |
| Employed | 0.077 | 0.077 | −0.084 | −0.083 |
| | (0.048) | (0.048) | (0.062) | (0.062) |
| Postgraduate | −0.137* | −0.134* | −0.227** | −0.227** |
| | (0.074) | (0.074) | (0.092) | (0.092) |
| Graduate diploma | −0.093 | −0.091 | −0.148* | −0.148* |
| | (0.068) | (0.068) | (0.089) | (0.089) |
| Bachelor | −0.154** | −0.155** | −0.225*** | −0.227*** |
| | (0.062) | (0.062) | (0.081) | (0.081) |
| Diploma | 0.066 | 0.067 | 0.046 | 0.044 |
| | (0.054) | (0.054) | (0.071) | (0.071) |
| Certificate | −0.012 | −0.011 | −0.044 | −0.044 |
| | (0.047) | (0.047) | (0.061) | (0.061) |
| Disability | −0.576*** | −0.576*** | −0.747*** | −0.746*** |
| | (0.040) | (0.040) | (0.052) | (0.052) |

(continued)

**Table 1** (continued)

| Variables | (1) OLS | (2) OLS | (3) Ordered Logit | (4) Ordered Logit |
|---|---|---|---|---|
| State fixed effect | Yes | Yes | Yes | Yes |
| Observations | 6494 | 6494 | 6494 | 6494 |
| $R^2$ | 0.102 | 0.100 | | |

Robust standard errors in parentheses
***$p < 0.01$, **$p < 0.05$, *$p < 0.1$

**Table 2** Effects by gambler category

| Variables | (1) Life satisfaction | (2) Life satisfaction | (3) Life satisfaction | (4) Life satisfaction |
|---|---|---|---|---|
| Non-gambler | 0.304*** | | | |
| | (0.069) | | | |
| Low-risk gambler | | −0.031 | | |
| | | (0.083) | | |
| Medium-risk gambler | | | −0.521*** | |
| | | | (0.113) | |
| Problem gambler | | | | −0.795*** |
| | | | | (0.257) |
| Controls | Yes | Yes | Yes | Yes |
| State fixed effect | Yes | Yes | Yes | Yes |
| Observations | 6494 | 6494 | 6494 | 6494 |
| $R^2$ | 0.098 | 0.095 | 0.098 | 0.097 |

Dependent variable is life satisfaction
Robust standard errors in parentheses
***$p < 0.01$, **$p < 0.05$, *$p < 0.1$

problem gambler is associated with more severe consequences for well-being compared to being a medium-risk gambler. Viewed together, these results suggest that as one gambles more (with higher PGSI scores or switches to higher gambling risk categories), the less satisfied they are with life.

**Table 3** Alternative measures of gambling behaviour

| Variables | (1)<br>Life satisfaction | (2)<br>Life satisfaction |
|---|---|---|
| Expenditure | −0.363 | |
| | (0.452) | |
| Activities | | −0.032* |
| | | (0.018) |
| Controls | Yes | Yes |
| State fixed effect | Yes | Yes |
| Observations | 6495 | 6495 |
| $R^2$ | 0.096 | 0.096 |

Dependent variable is life satisfaction
Robust standard errors in parentheses
***$p < 0.01$, **$p < 0.05$, *$p < 0.1$

In Table 3, we examine the robustness of our results to two alternative measures of gambling. The HILDA gambling module asked respondents about 10 gambling activities and how much, on average, is spent on each activity per month. We generate an annual expenditure variable using this information and deflate this with income to generate a gambling expenditure share, which we use as an alternative measure of gambling. We also sum up the number of gambling activities each respondent engages in to generate a second alternative measure. Table 3 reports results for the effects of these measures on life satisfaction. Our results show a statistically insignificant effect of the share of gambling expenditure but a negative and significant effect of number of activities on life satisfaction. This result suggests that the more gambling activities one engages in, the less satisfied they are with life.

In Table 4, we examine the robustness of our results to the two alternative measures of subjective wellbeing described in the data section—MHI-5 scale and the K10. Columns 1 and 2 report results for effects on the MHI-5 scale, while Columns 3 and 4 report results for effects on the K10 scale. Our results suggest a negative association between gambling and mental wellbeing, and a positive association between gambling and psychological distress. Specifically, we find that gambling behaviour (across both measures—PGSI scores and risk status) is associated with a decline in mental wellbeing and an increase in psychological distress.

**Table 4** Alternative measures of subjective wellbeing

| Variables | (1)<br>MHI-5 scale | (2)<br>MHI-5 scale | (3)<br>K10 scale | (4)<br>K10 scale |
|---|---|---|---|---|
| Gambling | −1.398*** | −4.005*** | 0.567*** | 1.665*** |
| | (0.147) | (0.453) | (0.075) | (0.193) |
| Measure of gambling | PGSI score | Risk status | PGSI score | Risk status |
| Controls | Yes | Yes | Yes | Yes |
| State fixed effect | Yes | Yes | Yes | Yes |
| Observations | 6444 | 6444 | 6409 | 6409 |
| $R^2$ | 0.117 | 0.115 | 0.144 | 0.142 |

Dependent variable in Columns 1 and 2 is the mental health inventory scale
Dependent variable in Columns 3 and 4 is the Kessler Psychological Distress Scale
The measure of gambling behaviour in Columns 1 and 3 is the PGSI score
The measure of gambling behaviour in Columns 2 and 4 is risk status
Robust standard errors in parentheses
*** $p < 0.01$, ** $p < 0.05$, * $p < 0.1$

Thus, using the MHI-5 and the K10 scales as proxies for subjective wellbeing, we find that our results are robust to the conclusion that gambling tends to reduce wellbeing.

Lastly, we extend our results to examine if results for the effects of gambling differ across age. Given that Australia's current pension eligibility age is 65 years, we use this age as a cut-off point to examine if the impact of gambling differs for older people prior to and after the pension age. Thus, we split our sample to capture two sub-groups (i.e. those up to 64 years and those 65 years and above). Table 5 presents results for the two sub-groups. We find that the effects of gambling on life satisfaction are similar across both sub-groups.

## 5 Conclusion and Policy Implications

In this chapter, we use data from the HILDA survey to examine the association between gambling and subjective wellbeing of older people. We adopt multiple measures of gambling behaviour including the PGSI, gambling risk spectrums based on PGSI scores, gambling expenditures and the number of gambling activities older people engage in. We also

Table 5 Heterogeneous effects by age

| Variables | (1) Life satisfaction | (2) Life satisfaction | (3) Life satisfaction | (4) Life satisfaction |
|---|---|---|---|---|
| PGSI score | −0.088*** | | −0.090*** | |
| | (0.022) | | (0.026) | |
| Risk status | | −0.235*** | | −0.225*** |
| | | (0.058) | | (0.064) |
| Controls | Yes | Yes | Yes | Yes |
| State fixed effect | Yes | Yes | Yes | Yes |
| Observations | 3629 | 3629 | 2865 | 2865 |
| $R^2$ | 0.100 | 0.096 | 0.068 | 0.068 |

Dependent variable is life satisfaction
Columns 1 and 2 report results for a sub-sample including ages up to 64 years
Columns 1 and 2 report results for a sub-sample including ages 65 and above
Robust standard errors in parentheses
***$p < 0.01$, **$p < 0.05$, *$p < 0.1$

examine subjective wellbeing along different dimensions including life satisfaction, the MHI-5 scale and the K10.

The results show a statistically significant association between gambling and wellbeing for older Australian. This finding is robust to the instrument used to measure wellbeing and gambling behaviours. The results suggest a need for careful monitoring of gambling associated harm in older people who are likely to be more vulnerable in society. This is particularly important as the size of the older population increases resulting from an ageing population. The findings show that any mood-enhancing benefits through social interactions or other pathways are not long term, and that the long-term impacts of gambling on overall well-being are negative.

A limitation of this chapter is that we focus on correlations rather than causality. Nevertheless, the findings carry significant policy implications. An important area worth focusing on is regulation within the gambling industry. It is important that policymakers and regulators carefully monitor the ways in which the gambling industry presents itself to older people. It is also important to recognise the opportunity to provide alternative social activities for older people. This will ensure they have various options to explore in expanding their networks rather than resorting to gambling.

A number of initiatives have been implemented in Australia to promote the social ties of older people, and these need to be encouraged. For example, the partnership between the Victorian local government and Victorian Responsible Gambling Foundation which supports the Yarra Plenty Libraries After Dark programme.[3] This programme allows libraries to stay open late on pension days to offer an alternative free venue for people to meet, have light refreshments, and free Internet access, among others, as an alternative to going to a gaming venue. It is important to offer alternative entertainment options for older people both within retirement communities and beyond, especially in the evenings when loneliness is often at its highest. Currently, the free travel and other benefits offered by gaming venues make them highly attractive to older people and habitual patterns become established that can become harmful for some individuals and for our communities in general. While regulation of the betting and gaming sector is an essential part of the solution to protecting older people from gambling harm, a more holistic approach to understanding the needs to ageing in place is likely to be important in building safe communities for an ageing population.

**Acknowledgements** This chapter uses unit record data from the Household, Income and Labour Dynamics in Australia (HILDA) Survey. The HILDA Project was initiated and is funded by the Australian Government Department of Social Services (DSS) and is managed by the Melbourne Institute of Applied Economic and Social Research (Melbourne Institute). The findings and views reported in this paper, however, are those of the authors and should not be attributed to either DSS or the Melbourne Institute.

## Appendix

See Tables 6 and 7.

[3]https://www.yprl.vic.gov.au/libraries-after-dark/, accessed 27 June 19.

Table 6 Items used in the Problem Gambling Severity Index

| | Now thinking about the last 12 months … | Never (0) | Sometimes (1) | Most of the time (2) | Almost Always (3) |
|---|---|---|---|---|---|
| 1 | Have you bet more than you could really afford to lose? | | | | |
| 2 | Have you needed to gamble with larger amounts of money to get the same feeling of excitement? | | | | |
| 3 | When you gambled, did you go back another day to try and win back the money you lost? | | | | |
| 4 | Have you borrowed money or sold anything to get money to gamble? | | | | |
| 5 | Have you felt that you might have a problem with gambling? | | | | |

(continued)

**Table 6** (continued)

| | Now thinking about the last 12 months … | Never (0) | Sometimes (1) | Most of the time (2) | Almost Always (3) |
|---|---|---|---|---|---|
| 6 | Has gambling caused you any health problems, including stress or anxiety? | | | | |
| 7 | Have people criticised your betting or told you that you had a gambling problem, regardless of whether or not you thought it was true? | | | | |
| 8 | Has your gambling caused any financial problems for you or your household? | | | | |
| 9 | Have you felt guilty about the way you gamble or what happens when you gamble? | | | | |

**Table 7** Description and summary statistics of variables

| Variable | Descriptions | Mean | SD |
|---|---|---|---|
| Life satisfaction | All things considered, how satisfied are you with your life? On a scale of 0–10, where 0 is labelled as totally dissatisfied and 10 is totally satisfied | 8.044 | 1.467 |
| Mental health | Five-item Mental Health Inventory (MHI-5) scale | 75.58 | 17.25 |
| K10 Distress Scale | Kessler Psychological Distress Scale (K10) | 15.16 | 6.112 |
| PGSI | Problem Gambling Severity Index Scores (9-item scale with maximum score of 27) | 0.287 | 1.426 |
| Risk status | 1–4 gambling risk scale based on PGSI scores. 1 means 'non-problem gambler', 2 means 'low-risk gambler', 3 means 'moderate risk gambler', 4 means 'problem gambler' | 1.126 | 0.468 |
| Non-gambler | Dummy variable if respondent is a PGSI non-problem gambler (PGSI score 0) | 0.919 | 0.273 |
| Low risk | Dummy variable if respondent is a PGSI low-risk gambler (PGSI score 1 or 2) | 0.044 | 0.206 |
| Medium risk | Dummy variable if respondent is a PGSI moderate-risk gambler (PGSI score 3–7) | 0.028 | 0.165 |
| Problem gambler | Dummy variable if respondent is a PGSI problem gambler (PGSI score 8 or above) | 0.009 | 0.093 |
| Expenditure | Gambling-related expenditure as a share of income | 0.013 | 0.041 |
| Activities | Number of gambling activities respondent participated in within the last 12 months | 0.785 | 0.990 |
| Age | Age of respondent | 64.15 | 10.22 |
| Male | Dummy variable if respondent is male | 0.466 | 0.499 |

(continued)

**Table 7** (continued)

| Variable | Descriptions | Mean | SD |
|---|---|---|---|
| Female | Dummy variable if respondent is female | 0.534 | 0.499 |
| Dependants | Number of dependents in household aged 0–24 years | 0.220 | 0.614 |
| Separated | Dummy variable if respondent is separated | 0.033 | 0.178 |
| Divorced | Dummy variable if respondent is divorced | 0.106 | 0.308 |
| Widowed | Dummy variable if respondent is widowed | 0.106 | 0.308 |
| Single | Dummy variable if respondent is single | 0.062 | 0.240 |
| Married/De facto | Dummy variable if respondent is married or in a de facto relationship | 0.694 | 0.461 |
| Income | Log of household income | 11.06 | 0.799 |
| Employed | Dummy variable if respondent is employed | 0.454 | 0.498 |
| Unemployed | Dummy variable if respondent is unemployed | 0.015 | 0.121 |
| Not in Labour Force | Dummy variable if respondent is not in labour force | 0.531 | 0.499 |
| Postgraduate | Dummy variable if respondent's highest education level achieved is masters or doctorate | 0.055 | 0.228 |
| Graduate diploma | Dummy variable if respondent's highest education level achieved is graduate diploma or certificate | 0.068 | 0.252 |
| Bachelor | Dummy variable if respondent's highest education level achieved is bachelor or honours | 0.108 | 0.310 |
| Diploma | Dummy variable if respondent's highest education level achieved is advanced diploma or diploma | 0.110 | 0.313 |

(continued)

**Table 7** (continued)

| Variable | Descriptions | Mean | SD |
|---|---|---|---|
| Certificate | Dummy variable if respondent's highest education level achieved is certificate I, II, III or IV | 0.231 | 0.421 |
| Year 12 | Dummy variable if respondent's highest education level achieved is year 12 or below | 0.428 | 0.476 |
| Disability | Dummy variable if respondent is disabled or has a long-term illness | 0.390 | 0.488 |

# References

Avanzi, M., Baratti, M., Cabrini, S., Uber, E., Brighetti, G., & Bonfà, F. (2006). Prevalence of pathological gambling in patients with Parkinson's disease. *Movement Disorders: Official Journal of the Movement Disorder Society, 21*(12), 2068–2072.

Awaworyi Churchill, S., & Farrell, L. (2018). The impact of gambling on depression: New evidence from England and Scotland. *Economic Modelling, 68,* 475–483. https://doi.org/10.1016/j.econmod.2017.08.021.

Awaworyi Churchill, S., & Mishra, V. (2017). Trust, social networks and subjective wellbeing in China. *Social Indicators Research, 132*(1), 313–339. https://doi.org/10.1007/s11205-015-1220-2.

Awaworyi Churchill, S., & Smyth, R. (2019). Transport poverty and subjective wellbeing. *Transportation Research Part A: Policy and Practice, 124,* 40–54. https://doi.org/10.1016/j.tra.2019.03.004.

Bazargan, M., Bazargan, S. H., & Akanda, M. (2001). Gambling habits among aged African Americans. *Clinical Psychologist, 22*(3–4), 51–62.

Cameron, M. P., & Waldegrave, C. (2009). Work, retirement and wellbeing among older New Zealanders. In *Enhancing wellbeing in an ageing society* (pp. 65–84). Hamilton: Population Studies Centre, University of Waikato.

Cooper, M. L. (2002). Alcohol use and risky sexual behavior among college students and youth: Evaluating the evidence. *Journal of Studies on Alcohol. Supplement, 14,* 101–117.

Cummins, R. A. (1995). On the trail of the gold standard for subjective wellbeing. *Social Indicators Research, 35*(2), 179–200.

Cummins, R. A. (2000). Personal income and subjective well-being: A review. *Journal of Happiness Studies, 1*(2), 133–158.
Dixon, M. R., Nastally, B. L., & Waterman, A. (2010). The effect of gambling activities on happiness levels of nursing home residents. *Journal of Applied Behavior Analysis, 43*(3), 531–535.
Dolan, P., Peasgood, T., & White, M. (2008). Do we really know what makes us happy? A review of the economic literature on the factors associated with subjective well-being. *Journal of Economic Psychology, 29*(1), 94–122. https://doi.org/10.1016/j.joep.2007.09.001.
Farrell, L. (2018). Understanding the relationship between subjective wellbeing and gambling behavior. *Journal of Gambling Studies, 34*(1), 55–71.
Ferrer-i-Carbonell, A., & Frijters, P. (2004). How important is methodology for the estimates of the determinants of happiness? *The Economic Journal, 114*(497), 641–659. https://doi.org/10.1111/j.1468-0297.2004.00235.x.
Ferris, J. A., & Wynne, H. J. (2001). *The Canadian problem gambling index.* Ottawa, ON: Canadian Centre on Substance Abuse.
Lister, J. J., & Nower, L. (2013). Gambling and older adults. In *The Wiley-Blackwell handbook of disordered gambling* (pp. 347–360). Oxford: Wiley-Blackwell.
Martin, F., Lichtenberg, P. A., & Templin, T. N. (2011). A longitudinal study: Casino gambling attitudes, motivations, and gambling patterns among urban elders. *Journal of Gambling Studies, 27*(2), 287–297.
McNeilly, D. P., & Burke, W. J. (2001). Gambling as a social activity of older adults. *The International Journal of Aging and Human Development, 52*(1), 19–28.
Nordenmark, M., & Stattin, M. (2009). Psychosocial wellbeing and reasons for retirement in Sweden. *Ageing & Society, 29*(3), 413–430.
Patford, J. L. (2007). Linked lives: Adult children's experiences of late onset parental gambling problems. *International Journal of Mental Health and Addiction, 5*(4), 367–380.
Pinquart, M., & Sörensen, S. (2000). Influences of socioeconomic status, social network, and competence on subjective well-being in later life: A meta-analysis. *Psychology and Aging, 15*(2), 187–224. https://doi.org/10.1037/0882-7974.15.2.187.
Quigley, L., Yakovenko, I., Hodgins, D. C., Dobson, K. S., el-Guebaly, N., Casey, D. M., … Schopflocher, D. P. (2015). Comorbid problem gambling and major depression in a community sample. *Journal of Gambling Studies, 31*(4), 1135–1152.

Raisamo, S. U., Mäkelä, P., Salonen, A. H., & Lintonen, T. P. (2014). The extent and distribution of gambling harm in Finland as assessed by the Problem Gambling Severity Index. *The European Journal of Public Health, 25*(4), 716–722.

Song-Iee Hong, S. T., Wang, C.-W., & Cunningham-Williams, R. M. (2012). Gambling behavior and problems among older adults: A systematic review of empirical studies. *The Journals of Gerontology: Series B, 67*(5), 639–652.

Southwell, J., Boreham, P., & Laffan, W. (2008). Problem gambling and the circumstances facing older people: A study of gaming machine players aged 60+ in licensed clubs. *Journal of Gambling Studies, 24,* 151–174.

Vander Bilt, J., Dodge, H. H., Pandav, R., Shaffer, H. J., & Ganguli, M. (2004). Gambling participation and social support among older adults: A longitudinal community study. *Journal of Gambling Studies, 20*(4), 373–389.

Watson, N., & Wooden, M. P. (2012). The HILDA survey: A case study in the design and development of a successful household panel survey. *Longitudinal and Life Course Studies, 3*(3), 369–381.

# 6

# Employment Types and Subjective Wellbeing: Evidence from the English Longitudinal Survey of Ageing

Samuelson Appau, Sefa Awaworyi Churchill and Lisa Farrell

## 1 Introduction

Subjective wellbeing (SWB) refers to an individual's own assessment of their happiness and satisfaction with their lives (Diener, 1994). This concept has emerged within marketing and business studies as an important measure of people's happiness, life satisfaction and quality of life (QoL) (Chen & Davey, 2008). The importance of SWB is well recognised by economists, business organisations, governments and policymakers. Thus, existing research has documented the impact of SWB on social and

S. Appau (✉) · S. Awaworyi Churchill · L. Farrell
School of Economics, Finance and Marketing, RMIT University, Melbourne, VIC, Australia
e-mail: samuelson.appau@rmit.edu.au

S. Awaworyi Churchill
e-mail: sefa.awaworyichurchill@rmit.edu.au

L. Farrell
e-mail: lisa.farrell@rmit.edu.au



S. Awaworyi Churchill et al. (eds.), *Measuring, Understanding and Improving Wellbeing Among Older People*,
https://doi.org/10.1007/978-981-15-2353-3_6

romantic relationships, physical health, consumption, employee engagement, organisational performance, and economic efficiency (Cheng & Smyth, 2015; Diener, 1994; Diener, Oishi, & Lucas, 2003; Falco, Maloney, Rijkers, & Sarrias, 2015; Hsee, Yang, Li, & Shen, 2009).

Considering the importance of SWB, a large body of literature within economics, psychology, marketing and management has focused on the determinants of SWB. Studies have examined both individual and group characteristics like education, social class, gender, religion, health, employment, income and social capital as important factors that contribute to a person's SWB (see, e.g., Awaworyi Churchill & Mishra, 2017; Diener, 1994; Diener et al., 2003; Dolan, Peasgood, & White, 2008; Easterlin, 1995; Ellison, 1991). Consumption practices like shopping, consumer-brand engagements, and green and ethical consumption (El Hedhli, Chebat, & Sirgy, 2013; Fournier, 1998) have been noted to affect SWB. Additionally, consumer engagement in the marketing process like co-creation, marketplace experiences and supporting cause-related marketing affects consumer sense of SWB (Kipnis et al., 2013; McColl-Kennedy, Hogan, Witell, & Snyder, 2017). In this regard, some scholarship like the transformative consumer research agenda has advocated for business research and practices that secures and enhances individual and social wellbeing (Davis & Pechmann, 2013).

One important strand of the literature investigates the importance of employment experience and occupation as determinants of SWB. Employees are vital to the success of businesses, and their own sense of wellbeing can affect their perceived job satisfaction, workplace performance, turnover rates and quality of service rendered to customers (e.g. Falco et al., 2015; Van Praag, Frijters, & Ferrer-i-Carbonell, 2003). But although employment occupies a significant portion of a person's time across the life course, relatively little is known about its lasting impact on wellbeing through the life course.

While the existing literature provides some evidence of the impact of employment types on SWB and QoL, its differential impacts across those active in the labour force and following the transition into retirement have not been examined. For instance, Falco et al. (2015) used longitudinal data to examine the impact of employment types on SWB.

They found that self-employed people with employees (compared to self-employed people without employees, formal salaried workers and civil workers) reported the highest levels of SWB. However, their research did not consider SWB throughout the life course. Further, they focused on a developing country with a very large informal employment sector, in the context of which it has been argued that job satisfaction is influenced by the economic motivation to earn income rather than any strong attachment to the job (Banerjee & Duflo, 2011).

In this chapter, we focus on the impact of employment types on SWB during a person's active period of employment and in retirement. The increasing casualisation of the workforce and the rise in self-employment in many developed countries have resulted in a significant change in a person's attachment to the labour market (Stone & Arthurs, 2013). Here, we will use the term *employment type* to refer to the nature of a person's employment contract (i.e. paid employee or self-employed, and permanent or temporary contract). We prefer to use the term *employment types* as opposed to *employment contracts* in recognition of the fact that the self-employed do not supply contracted labour. We demonstrate the effect of labour market attachment on SWB and QoL in a developed country context not only during the period of employment, but also during retirement.

The primary objective of this chapter then is to broaden our knowledge of the effects of employment types on SWB and QoL by examining how employment types influence wellbeing both before and after retirement. Understanding the differential impacts of employment types based on life stages is important because it provides a more holistic perspective, which can guide businesses—including employers and firms that provide services for retirees like aged care facilities—and policymakers in designing appropriate products to aid retirement planning, support wellbeing in the transition into retirement and inform on labour market policies in terms of contracting laws and regulations. Neglecting the differential impact of employment types during different stages in life implies the existing conclusions may be misleading. Our study thus puts the effects of employment types on wellbeing into perspective and provides explanations for why different effects should be expected across different life stages.

To inform our empirical investigation, we draw on social psychology theories of self-identity as an explanatory lens to posit that a person's employment type, in part, defines one's identity because *we are what we do* (Berger, 2017; Moore & Robinson, 2006; Stryker & Burke, 2000). In particular, we use the term "self-identity" to refer to a person's own global understanding of themselves, that is, their sense of self in terms of "who I am" as opposed to how others see them (Stets & Burke, 2000). Self-identity is usually defined by relatively permanent factors, such as knowledge of one's skills, talents and abilities; personality attributes; and aspects of one's occupation, or family and socioeconomic status. Additionally, identity theories have been employed in organisational studies to understand the impact of an individual's profession or job type on their engagement at work, life satisfaction and SWB (Akerlof & Kranton, 2008; Ashforth, Harrison, & Corley, 2008; Ashforth & Mael, 1989; Pratt, Rockmann, & Kaufmann, 2006). Although we do not test this empirically, we argue that the congruence between a person's self-identity and the nature of their employment will impact their SWB.

Using data from the English Longitudinal Study of Ageing (ELSA), we explore the effects of various determinants of SWB and QoL relating to employment type and retirement. It is assumed that individuals with the employment types that require deeper engagement and commitment will be likely to have self-identities that are closely tied to their employment (Berger, 2017; Carlsen, 2006; Dutton, Roberts, & Bednar, 2010; Parasuraman & Simmers, 2001) and therefore likely to experience negative impacts on their SWB and/or QoL when transitioning into retirement as a result of a loss of self-identity and the need to develop a new self-identity that is not dependent upon their employment.

Our results suggest that jobs characterised by employment types which represent deep labour market attachment (which identity theory suggests are more closely linked to a person's self-identity) are associated with higher levels of SWB and QoL. Put differently, people identify more with jobs to which they have a stronger personal investment (i.e. self-employed versus paid employees) and which are more permanent in nature (i.e. permanent versus temporary contracts). However, in retirement, withdrawal from these jobs causes a significant drop in SWB and QoL. Accordingly, our findings demonstrate that the contractual nature of our work affects our SWB and QoL, and that this effect will vary throughout a person's working life and into retirement.

We contribute to the existing literature in three ways. First, we examine the effects of retirement on SWB and QoL using longitudinal data. Second, we provide new evidence on the effects of employment type on SWB and QoL. Last, in contrast to existing studies, we consider the impact of employment types on SWB both before and after retirement. We use a cohort-based data set that examines life course SWB for people with different types of employment types, and we offer recommendations for supporting retirees' SWB and QoL based on different types of employment that they had before retirement. The next section presents a brief overview of the related literature and theoretical concepts. Section 3 explains the data and variables used in the study, while Sect. 4 provides an overview of the empirical methods. Section 5 presents our results and Sect. 6 concludes.

## 2 Related Literature and Hypotheses

When we tell other people about ourselves, we most likely include a narrative about our jobs, or what we do for a living. The phrase "do for a living" itself suggests a strong connection between life and work. Similarly, when we meet someone, we attempt to gauge their person by asking them, "What do you do?". This is perhaps because we all assume as Butler noted that "Every man's [or woman's] work, whether it be literature or music or pictures or architecture or anything else, is always a portrait of him [or her] self" (1903/1998: 7). It is almost expected that a "social résumé" of a person should include their occupation. Much research has established this connection between work and identity (e.g. Berger, 2017; Carlsen, 2006; Dutton et al., 2010; Parasuraman & Simmers, 2001).

Research suggests most people construct various identities based on the organisation they work for, their profession and the nature of their employment (Dutton et al., 2010). Some people even consider their jobs as a physical extension of their identities (Belk, 1988). This is evident in how some people decorate their workspaces and offices with pictures of family and holiday trips, and other items that represent the stories of their lives and who they are (Tian & Belk, 2005). Work-identity links are often positive for most people, and they are often relatively stable within professions, organisations and teams. Some people may experience identity conflicts and challenges when they have to change professions, organisations or workplace teams (Ashforth et al., 2008; Dutton et al., 2010; Ibarra & Barbulescu, 2010).

Certain jobs generate a stronger connection between employment and self-identity than others because they become more integral to the daily routine and social position of a person. For example, research has shown that professionals such as lawyers, engineers and doctors have a stronger job-identity connection than non-professionals or blue-collar workers (see, e.g., Berger, 2017; Jackall, 1978). This is because these professionals derive a lot of social capital and sense of self-worth from their professions, compared to non-professionals and blue-collar workers (Carlsen, 2006). Thus, they find their work to be more salient to their identities than even personal characteristics like race and gender (Hogg & Terry, 2001; Johnson, Morgeson, Ilgen, Meyer, & Lloyd, 2006).

We extend on the existing literature by looking at a range of labour market employment types to capture the effects of labour supply arrangements (as opposed to the effect of occupational class) on SWB and QoL. While there is an existing economics literature that explores the importance of employment type (see, e.g., Brown, Farrell, Harris, & Sessions [2006] and Brown, Farrell, & Sessions [2006] for studies that look at the relationship between employment types and risk-taking behaviours), this literature has not investigated the link between employment type and SWB. In this study, we use a cohort of people who are self-employed (compared to paid employees) and people with permanent jobs (compared to temporary jobs) to examine how the varying levels of the employment type-identity fit influence SWB and QoL. Where employment type-identity fit is a term used to denote the strength of the relationship between the employment type and an individual's self-identity.

The relationship between the employment, identity and SWB has become increasingly significant over the past century as many people seek work with which they can identify because they believe it is important to their happiness and SWB (Ashforth et al., 2008). Indeed, anecdotal evidence suggests that a bad day at work will mean a bad day in life, and the impact of events at work on our personal lives will depend on how much we care about and identify with our jobs. Thus, contentment with work and a strong identification with our job will result in a greater sense of SWB (see, e.g., Ashforth et al., 2008; Pratt et al., 2006). In other words, people who strongly identify with their jobs and are likely to report higher levels of job satisfaction and SWB during the period that they are working. Drawing on the literature, we posit that self-employed people, compared to paid employees, have a stronger employment type-identity fit because they have more fixed and engaging work routines incorporated into their daily lives (see, e.g., Ashforth & Mael, 1989; Blanchflower, 2000; Falco et al., 2015). On average, self-employed people work longer hours, have a higher stake in the investment and success of the business and therefore are more involved and identify more with their work role than people in paid employment. They, therefore, take more fulfilment in their work roles and the successes of the business (Parasuraman & Simmers, 2001). But this strong employment-identity fit can be both a source of happiness and stress for self-employed people because their happiness rises and wanes with the successes and failures of the business (Parasuraman & Simmers, 2001). Nonetheless, research suggests that the overall autonomy, flexibility and involvement in their jobs provide self-employed people with more life satisfaction and fulfilment than those in paid employment (Alesina, Di Tella, & MacCulloch, 2004; Blanchflower & Oswald, 2004; Falco et al., 2015). Thus, we hypothesise that:

> *H1*: People who are self-employed will report higher levels of wellbeing and quality of life than those in paid employment.

Similarly, among paid employees, those with permanent roles have a stronger employment–identity fit than those with temporary roles because work is more routinised for permanent employees (Jackall, 1978). Although the literature is inconclusive, permanent employees report relatively better physical and mental health, job satisfaction and organisational commitment than temporary employees (Bardasi & Francesconi, 2004; Forde & Slater, 2006; Rigotti & Mohr 2005; Virtanen et al., 2005). A permanent employee will more readily state his or her employment type as an identifiable occupation, whereas a temporary employee may not hold their work in the same regard ("it's just a pay check"). Permanent employment thus serves as an important identity anchor and provides economic, social and psychological security than temporary employment. It also provides the permanent employee with more stable work-life balance and social connections from the workplace and labour market, compared to temporary employees. Such normalcy and life routine provides better life satisfaction and contributes to SWB (De Cuyper et al., 2008). Based on this, we hypothesise that:

> *H2*: People with permanent employments will report higher levels of wellbeing and quality of life than those with temporary employments.

Conversely, retirement may lead to a loss of the part of our self-identity that is derived from labour market participation; it may mean a loss of this part of our self (Ashforth et al., 2008; Price, 2000). The more a person identifies with their job, the more likely they will experience lower SWB during retirement. For example, Barnes and Parry (2004) found that more British men than women have stronger attachment to their jobs and fewer non-work routines and relationships, and thus, they struggle to adapt to non-work domestic life in retirement. Thus, we expect that, although a strong employment–identity fit may lead to a higher level of SWB and QoL while a person is active in the workforce, retirement will lead to a decline in their SWB and QoL. We therefore formulate the following hypotheses:

> *H3a*: People who were self-employed will report lower levels of wellbeing and quality of life after retirement compared to people who had paid employments.
> *H3b*: People who had permanent employments will report lower levels of wellbeing and quality of life after retirement compared to people who had temporary employments.

Thus, we are interested in the impact of the employment type on SWB across the life course on an individual's SWB and QoL. It is only by understanding the integration of our working lives with the terms of our employment and our psychological wellbeing that we can better understand the welfare issues associated with transitioning from the workforce into retirement, and how these SWB and QoL impacts are patterned according to pre-retirement employment–identity relationships.

# 3 Data and Variables

The data used in this study are from the (ELSA), which is a nationally representative panel study of individuals aged 50 years and over (Marmot et al., 2017; Steptoe, Breeze, Banks, & Nazroo, 2012). The study is designed to gain a deeper understanding of the social, psychological, economic and physical aspects of ageing. ELSA commenced in 2002 with approximately 12,000 core sample members and their partners for the first wave, and the sample has been followed up every two years. Data are collected using self-completion questionnaires and computer-assisted personal interviews, with additional nurse visits every four years for the assessment of biomarkers. The survey is considered a sister study to the Health and Retirement Study in America and is also harmonised with other ageing studies around the world to facilitate international comparisons. ELSA currently has seven waves of surveys, and our study uses data from all seven waves. The data set is freely available to researchers via the UK data services and has been widely used to address various research questions (Chou, 2008; Lee, Nazroo, O'Connor, Blake, & Pendleton, 2016; McHugh, Kenny, Lawlor, Steptoe, & Kee, 2017; Netuveli, Wiggins, Hildon, Montgomery, & Blane, 2006; Pierce, Zaninotto, Steel, & Mindell, 2009; Shankar, Hamer, McMunn, & Steptoe, 2013; Torres, Lima-Costa, Marmot, & de Oliveira, 2016).

A major strength of the data, and hence of our study, is that we investigate the effect of labour market attachment on wellbeing across a range of SWB measures to ensure that the findings are general and not sensitive to the measure of SWB employed in the analysis. Our first two measures are self-reported measures of SWB, which capture an individual's evaluation of their life satisfaction (Awaworyi Churchill & Mishra, 2017; Pinquart & Sörensen, 2000). The first measure of wellbeing (*Wellbeing 1*) is based on the information provided by ELSA where, on a scale of 1–4, respondents are asked to evaluate how they feel with the way their life has turned out. Specifically, ELSA asks the question "Please say how often you feel satisfied with the way your life has turned out". In the original scale, 1 represents often and 4 represents never. However, for ease of results interpretation, we transpose this, so that 1 represents never and 4 represents often. The second measure of wellbeing (*Wellbeing 2*) is based on the ELSA question "Please say how much you agree or disagree with the following statements: I am satisfied with my life". Responses are coded, on a scale of 1–7 where 1 = strongly agree and 7 = strongly disagree. We recode this as well, such that a higher numerical score indicates the highest measure of wellbeing.

The next set of measures are based on the CASP-19 scale which has been used in the literature as a measure of qualify of life in old age (Howel, 2012; Kautonen, Kibler, & Minniti, 2017; Sexton, King-Kallimanis, Conroy, & Hickey, 2013; Sim, Bartlam, & Bernard, 2011). Developed by Hyde, Wiggins, Higgs, and Blane (2003), the CASP-19 is a 19-item scale comprising four domains: namely, control, autonomy, self-realisation and pleasure (CASP). The control domain has six items and captures aspects such as "I feel free to plan for the future" and "I can do things that I want to do". The autonomy domain has five items and includes aspects such as "I feel that I can please myself". The self-realisation and pleasure domains contain four items each, including aspects such as "I feel that life is full of opportunities" and "I enjoy the things I do", respectively. Each item on the four domains is coded on a four-point Likert-style scale such that a higher score indicates better QoL. Details of the CASP-19 scale can be found in Hyde et al. (2003). The CASP-19 scale was adopted for use in the ELSA from the second wave. We use the CASP-19 scale together with the four individual domains in our regressions.

Last, we also use another measure of wellbeing that is based on the Center for Epidemiologic Studies Depression (CES-D) scale. The CES-D scale was developed by Radloff (1977) and is a self-reported depression scale that reflects various aspects of depression, including depressed mood, and feelings of worthlessness, helplessness and hopelessness, among others. The CES-D scale is considered a reliable measure of SWB and has been widely used in the literature (Arbona, Burridge, & Olvera, 2017; Stagl et al., 2015; Steptoe & Wardle, 2012; Wolanin, Hong, Marks, Panchoo, & Gross, 2016). The ELSA measure of depression adopted for use in our analysis provides a count of the number of CES-D questions to which respondents answered "yes".

Our main explanatory variables capture retirement and employment type. Our measure of retirement is a dummy variable that is equal to one if respondents are retired and zero if otherwise. Retirement is measured based on the following ELSA question which has "retired" as one of the answers respondents choose from: "Which one of these, would you say best describes your current situation?" Based on the ELSA data, we cover two aspects of employment type. The first aspect is measured using a dummy variable that is equal to one if the respondent is self-employed and zero if they are an employee. The second aspect captures the nature of contracts held by employees. We measure this using a dummy variable that equals one if the respondent works a temp job as opposed to a permanent job.

Consistent with the SWB and QoL literature, we also control for relevant covariates that are likely to affect an individual's QoL or wellbeing. These include the respondent's age, age squared, educational and marital status, wealth, smoking status, long-standing illness, and whether they have any children (Akay, Constant, & Giulietti, 2014; Binder & Blankenberg, 2017; Bonsang & Klein, 2012; Cai & Park, 2016; Cheng & Smyth, 2015; Steptoe & Wardle, 2012). Given that we run a fixed effect model, time invariant variables are not included in the model specification. Table 5 presents a description of the variables used in our analysis and their associated summary statistics.

## 4 Method

We estimate the following QoL/wellbeing equation:

$$WB_{it} = \beta_1 R_{it} + \beta_2 J_{it} + \sum_n \beta_n X_{n,it} + \vartheta_i + \mu_t + \varepsilon_{it} \qquad (1)$$

where $WB$ is the SWB measure (i.e. life satisfaction or QoL of the $i$ th respondent at time $t$); $R$ is the measure of retirement; $J$ is a measure of employment or job type; $X$ is a vector of individual characteristics including age, age squared, educational and marital status, wealth and smoking status, among others; $\varepsilon$ is the error term; and $t$ is the time factor which corresponds to survey wave. We also include an individual fixed effect $\vartheta_i$ that captures unchanging individual influences on reported wellbeing, and a time (survey wave) fixed effect $\mu_t$ which captures shocks that are common to all individuals during each survey wave.

We also examine how the interaction between employment or job type and retirement status influences wellbeing, and thus, we augment (1) to include the interaction term $R_{it}J_{it}$ as follows;

$$WB_{it} = \beta_1 R_{it} + \beta_2 J_{it} + \beta_3 R_{it} J_{it} + \sum_n \beta_n X_{n,it} + \vartheta_i + \mu_t + \varepsilon_{it} \tag{2}$$

Lastly, while retirement and job type affects wellbeing, it is likely that wellbeing could influence retirement and job type as well. For example, suppose something changes in a person's life that lowers wellbeing (an unmeasured health event, for instance, for a family member), this change could lead one to retire. This could lead to endogeneity. However, finding appropriate instruments in survey data is a well-known issue in the empirical literature, and the use of weak instruments that do not meet exclusion restrictions is also a cause for concern. Thus, such potential endogeneity issues have often been ignored in the existing SWB literature. However, to ensure robustness to endogeneity, we adopt the Lewbel (2012) 2SLS estimation approach. This approach is commonly used in the existing literature in situations where traditional IVs are either unavailable or weak (Emran & Shilpi, 2012; Mishra & Smyth, 2015) and has recently been used in the SWB literature as well (Awaworyi Churchill & Mishra, 2017).

## 5 Results

Table 1 presents the results for the association between retirement and wellbeing. Columns 1 and 2 present the results for the effects of retirement on *Wellbeing 1* and *Wellbeing 2*, respectively. Columns 3–7 present

Table 1 Effects of retirement on wellbeing and quality of life

| Variables | (1) Wellbeing 1 | (2) Wellbeing 2 | (3) CASP-19 | (4) CASPCTL | (5) CASPAUT | (6) CASPPLE | (7) CASPSR | (8) Depression |
|---|---|---|---|---|---|---|---|---|
| Retired | 0.047*** | 0.085*** | 0.644*** | 0.069** | 0.164*** | 0.212*** | 0.309*** | −0.071*** |
| | (0.006) | (0.013) | (0.085) | (0.029) | (0.031) | (0.027) | (0.033) | (0.016) |
| Age | 0.016*** | 0.099*** | 0.825*** | 0.209*** | 0.270*** | 0.104*** | 0.248*** | −0.107*** |
| | (0.004) | (0.008) | (0.065) | (0.022) | (0.024) | (0.020) | (0.025) | (0.009) |
| Age squared | −0.017*** | −0.077*** | −0.889*** | −0.265*** | −0.254*** | −0.113*** | −0.261*** | 0.073*** |
| | (0.003) | (0.006) | (0.048) | (0.017) | (0.018) | (0.015) | (0.018) | (0.006) |
| Unemployed | −0.087*** | −0.213*** | −0.699*** | −0.182* | −0.143 | −0.132 | −0.253** | 0.140** |
| | (0.022) | (0.045) | (0.266) | (0.093) | (0.099) | (0.085) | (0.104) | (0.055) |
| Degree | −0.077*** | −0.121*** | −0.979*** | −0.422*** | −0.231*** | −0.097 | −0.264*** | 0.095** |
| | (0.017) | (0.035) | (0.219) | (0.076) | (0.081) | (0.070) | (0.085) | (0.043) |
| Below degree | −0.038** | −0.104*** | −0.868*** | −0.551*** | −0.234*** | 0.055 | −0.171** | 0.049 |
| | (0.017) | (0.034) | (0.202) | (0.070) | (0.075) | (0.064) | (0.079) | (0.041) |
| A-level | −0.011 | −0.026 | −0.621*** | −0.405*** | −0.183** | −0.078 | −0.103 | 0.010 |
| | (0.019) | (0.039) | (0.227) | (0.079) | (0.084) | (0.072) | (0.089) | (0.047) |
| O-level | −0.017 | −0.016 | −0.731*** | −0.256*** | −0.198*** | 0.012 | −0.172** | 0.020 |
| | (0.016) | (0.033) | (0.188) | (0.065) | (0.070) | (0.059) | (0.073) | (0.038) |
| Married | 0.069*** | 0.259*** | 0.261 | 0.089 | −0.345*** | 0.286*** | 0.175* | −0.247*** |
| | (0.018) | (0.037) | (0.251) | (0.087) | (0.092) | (0.078) | (0.096) | (0.043) |
| Single | 0.003 | −0.258*** | 0.325 | 0.029 | −0.243 | −0.131 | 0.514** | 0.010 |
| | (0.043) | (0.084) | (0.617) | (0.211) | (0.218) | (0.191) | (0.231) | (0.101) |

(continued)

**Table 1** (continued)

| Variables | (1) Wellbeing 1 | (2) Wellbeing 2 | (3) CASP-19 | (4) CASPCTL | (5) CASPAUT | (6) CASPPLE | (7) CASPSR | (8) Depression |
|---|---|---|---|---|---|---|---|---|
| Widowed | −0.101*** | −0.217*** | −0.022 | −0.105 | 0.461*** | −0.262*** | −0.150 | 0.551*** |
| | (0.020) | (0.041) | (0.277) | (0.096) | (0.101) | (0.086) | (0.105) | (0.047) |
| Wealth | 0.012*** | 0.031*** | 0.223*** | 0.033*** | 0.107*** | 0.031*** | 0.054*** | −0.027*** |
| | (0.002) | (0.004) | (0.023) | (0.008) | (0.009) | (0.007) | (0.009) | (0.004) |
| Illness | −0.047*** | −0.088*** | −0.719*** | −0.150*** | −0.208*** | −0.066*** | −0.272*** | 0.128*** |
| | (0.005) | (0.011) | (0.068) | (0.024) | (0.025) | (0.021) | (0.026) | (0.012) |
| Children | 0.067*** | −0.059* | −0.095 | −0.164** | −0.048 | 0.099 | 0.127 | −0.046** |
| | (0.018) | (0.036) | (0.214) | (0.073) | (0.078) | (0.066) | (0.081) | (0.020) |
| Smokes | 0.030** | 0.048* | 0.092 | 0.176*** | −0.106* | −0.002 | 0.016 | −0.134*** |
| | (0.013) | (0.028) | (0.173) | (0.060) | (0.064) | (0.055) | (0.068) | (0.032) |
| Constant | 2.869*** | 1.994*** | 24.894*** | 5.877*** | 3.349*** | 10.778*** | 4.636*** | 5.432*** |
| | (0.130) | (0.292) | (2.210) | (0.763) | (0.811) | (0.691) | (0.849) | (0.307) |
| Observations | 46,390 | 44,859 | 42,020 | 42,020 | 42,020 | 42,020 | 42,020 | 47,555 |
| $R^2$ | 0.084 | 0.085 | 0.168 | 0.159 | 0.168 | 0.058 | 0.159 | 0.109 |

Differences in number of observations are due to missing observations. However, we ensure the same sample used for regressions reported in Columns 3–7 given that they represent the CASP-19 scale and the individual components of the scale

Standard errors in parentheses

***$p < 0.01$, **$p < 0.05$, *$p < 0.1$

the results for the effects of retirement on CASP-19, CASPCTL (control), CASPAUT (autonomy), CASPPLE (pleasure) and CASPSR (self-realisation), respectively. Lastly, the results for the effects on depression are presented in Column 8. The results consistently suggest that retirement is associated with higher levels of wellbeing and QoL. Specifically, as seen in Column 1, the coefficient on the retirement dummy is 0.05, implying a 0.05 higher life satisfaction, on a scale of 1–4, if respondents are retired; and Column 2 reveals that the coefficient on the retirement dummy is 0.09, implying a 0.09 higher life satisfaction, on a scale of 1–7, if respondents are retired. Similar findings are observed for the various CASP scales, with the results suggesting higher QoL for those who are retired than those who are not. Further, the results indicate that retired people report lower levels of depression.

In Table 2, we augment the model presented in Table 1 to include the various measures of employment type. Panel 1 reports the results on the effects of employment type (i.e. whether self-employed or a paid employee). Panel 2 presents the results for the effects of permanency of job (whether temporary or permanent). From Panel 1, we observe that, on average, respondents who are self-employed tend to report higher levels of wellbeing and QoL than those with organisational employment (employees), a finding consistent with hypothesis H1. This finding is consistent across all measures of wellbeing and QoL used. The results shown in Panel 2 suggest that, on average, respondents who have temporary jobs tend to have lower levels of wellbeing than those with permanent jobs, and this is consistent with hypothesis H2. However, this finding is not robust across all measures of wellbeing and QoL. Specifically, we find statistically significant effects on *Wellbeing 1* and *Wellbeing 2* with coefficients of −0.05 and −0.25, respectively. Except for the coefficients explaining the effects on CASP-19 and the control domain of CASP-19 (CASPCTL), which are statistically significant, all other coefficients are statistically insignificant, although the signs on the coefficients are consistent with expectations.

Lastly, we examine how wellbeing changes once individuals enter retirement and withdraw from the various jobs that previously defined them. Table 3 presents the results, which include interaction terms between retirement and various employment types. Panel 1 shows the

**Table 2** Effects of job type and employment type on wellbeing and quality of life

| Variables | (1) Wellbeing 1 | (2) Wellbeing 2 | (3) CASP-19 | (4) CASPCTL | (5) CASPAUT | (6) CASPPLE | (7) CASPSR | (8) Depression |
|---|---|---|---|---|---|---|---|---|
| *Panel 1: Effects of employment type on wellbeing/quality of life* | | | | | | | | |
| Self-employed | 0.040*** | 0.033 | 0.766*** | 0.145** | 0.300*** | 0.153** | 0.276*** | −0.135*** |
| | (0.014) | (0.029) | (0.191) | (0.067) | (0.071) | (0.061) | (0.074) | (0.022) |
| Control variables? | Yes | Yes | Yes | Yes | Yes | Yes | Yes | Yes |
| Observations | 46,390 | 44,859 | 42,020 | 42,020 | 42,020 | 42,020 | 42,020 | 47,555 |
| $R^2$ | 0.084 | 0.085 | 0.169 | 0.160 | 0.168 | 0.058 | 0.160 | 0.110 |
| *Panel 2: Effects of job type on wellbeing/quality of life* | | | | | | | | |
| Temp job | −0.046** | −0.246*** | −0.430*** | −0.234** | −0.150 | −0.038 | 0.000 | −0.032 |
| | (0.020) | (0.086) | (0.077) | (0.091) | (0.103) | (0.089) | (0.111) | (0.046) |
| Control variables? | Yes | Yes | Yes | Yes | Yes | Yes | Yes | Yes |
| Observations | 19,762 | 15,315 | 15,020 | 15,020 | 15,020 | 15,020 | 15,020 | 21,503 |
| $R^2$ | 0.079 | 0.078 | 0.081 | 0.047 | 0.105 | 0.035 | 0.068 | 0.084 |

Differences in number of observations are due to missing observations. However, we ensure the same sample used for regressions reported in Columns 3–7 given that they represent the CASP-19 scale and the individual components of the scale

Panel 2 regressions are based on a sub-sample of employees only

Standard errors in parentheses

$^{***}p < 0.01$, $^{**}p < 0.05$, $^{*}p < 0.1$

**Table 3** Effects of interaction terms on wellbeing and quality of life

| Variables | (1) Wellbeing 1 | (2) Wellbeing 2 | (3) CASP-19 | (4) CASPCTL | (5) CASPAUT | (6) CASPPLE | (7) CASPSR | (8) Depression |
|---|---|---|---|---|---|---|---|---|
| *Panel 1*: | | | | | | | | |
| Self-employed | 0.045** | 0.027 | 0.816*** | 0.180* | 0.313*** | 0.149* | 0.298*** | −0.026 |
| | (0.019) | (0.040) | (0.270) | (0.094) | (0.100) | (0.086) | (0.104) | (0.047) |
| Retired | 0.051*** | 0.084*** | 0.597*** | 0.069* | 0.071* | 0.170*** | 0.274*** | −0.058*** |
| | (0.008) | (0.017) | (0.114) | (0.039) | (0.042) | (0.036) | (0.044) | (0.021) |
| Self-employed*retired | −0.117*** | −0.076*** | −0.876*** | −0.251*** | −0.357*** | −0.212*** | −0.358*** | 0.075*** |
| | (0.003) | (0.008) | (0.062) | (0.021) | (0.023) | (0.019) | (0.024) | (0.008) |
| Control variables? | Yes | Yes | Yes | Yes | Yes | Yes | Yes | Yes |
| Observations | 46,390 | 44,859 | 42,020 | 42,020 | 42,020 | 42,020 | 42,020 | 47,555 |
| $R^2$ | 0.089 | 0.082 | 0.181 | 0.193 | 0.174 | 0.090 | 0.161 | 0.119 |
| *Panel 2*: | | | | | | | | |
| Temp job | −0.053** | −0.190*** | −0.086*** | −0.273*** | −0.137 | 0.014 | 0.030 | −0.055 |
| | (0.024) | (0.022) | (0.020) | (0.105) | (0.119) | (0.103) | (0.128) | (0.054) |
| Retired | 0.062*** | 0.140*** | 1.220*** | 0.169 | 0.191 | 0.272** | 0.524*** | −0.020 |
| | (0.010) | (0.020) | (0.382) | (0.109) | (0.123) | (0.106) | (0.133) | (0.024) |
| Temp*retired | 0.106** | 0.229*** | 0.406*** | 0.285*** | 0.141*** | 0.017 | 0.058 | −0.072*** |
| | (0.003) | (0.006) | (0.153) | (0.044) | (0.049) | (0.042) | (0.053) | (0.007) |
| Control variables? | Yes | Yes | Yes | Yes | Yes | Yes | Yes | Yes |
| Observations | 19,762 | 15,315 | 15,020 | 15,020 | 15,020 | 15,020 | 15,020 | 21,503 |
| $R^2$ | 0.079 | 0.078 | 0.081 | 0.047 | 0.105 | 0.035 | 0.068 | 0.084 |

Differences in number of observations are due to missing observations. However, we ensure the same sample used for regressions reported in Columns 3–7 given that they represent the CASP-19 scale and the individual components of the scale

Panel 2 regressions are based on a sub-sample of employees only

Standard errors in parentheses

***$p < 0.01$, **$p < 0.05$, *$p < 0.1$

results for the interaction between retirement and employment contract type (self-employed = 1). Given the model specified here and the results reported in Table 3, interpretation of the interaction term can be done either with respect to employment type or with respect to retirement status. Thus, taking the derivative of the wellbeing equation with respect to employment type, and with respect to retirement, we have (3) and (4), respectively. $\beta_1$, $\beta_2$ and $\beta_3$ are drawn from Table 3, Column 1.

$$\frac{\partial WB_i}{\partial SE_i} = \beta_2 + \beta_3 R_i = 0.045 - 0.117 R_i \tag{3}$$

$$\frac{\partial WB_i}{\partial R_i} = \beta_1 + \beta_3 SE_i = 0.051 - 0.117 E_i \tag{4}$$

Accordingly, the results show that when individuals are retired ($R_i = 1$), a switch from organisational employment to self-employment is associated with a 0.072 lower individual life satisfaction, on a scale of 1–4. Similarly, when individuals are self-employed ($SE_i = 1$), a switch to retirement is associated with a 0.066 lower individual life satisfaction, on a scale of 1–4. Thus, when individuals are retired but were self-employed in the past, they tend to report lower wellbeing and QoL than those who were employees. Similar trends are observed in other columns of Table 3 as well; however, to avoid repetition, we draw on coefficients from Column 1 only.

From Panel 2, we find that the interaction between retirement and contract type (temp job = 1) is positive and significant, although not across all columns. Following a similar approach to interpretations in Panel 1, results from Panel 2, for instances where coefficients are significant, suggest that individuals who are retired but have worked on temporary contracts in the past tend to report higher levels of wellbeing than those retired who have worked in permanent positions prior to retirement. In further robustness checks not reported here, which use different estimation methods, results support this conclusion in a sample of retirees only.

## 5.1 Robustness to Endogeneity

Table 4 presents Lewbel 2SLS results. Panel 1 presents results for the effects of retirement, Panel 2 presents results for the effects of employment type (i.e. self-employed vs. employee), and Panel 3 presents results for the effects of job contract type (i.e. temp job vs. permanent job). Overidentifying restriction tests support the validity of the internally generated instruments. From the P-values reported below each table, we fail to reject the null hypothesis for the overidentifying restriction tests for each regression except for a few instances and in most of such instances, the coefficient on our explanatory variable is not significant, for instance, Column 2 of Panel 2 and Column 1 of Panel 3. Therefore, we can conclude that the internally generated instruments used are not overidentified in the first-stage regressions.

Overall, we find that our results are robust to endogeneity given that the signs on the coefficients are largely consistent with those reported for the panel fixed effect regressions. However, comparing the magnitude of the coefficients, the panel fixed effects model consistently understates the effects of retirement on wellbeing given the relatively bigger coefficients from the Lewbel 2SLS regressions. This suggests that endogeneity causes a considerable downward bias in fixed effect estimates. This is also the case for the effects of employment type (i.e. self-employed vs. employee), although this is not consistent across all columns. For the effects of job contract type (i.e. temp job vs. permanent job), we notice that some coefficients which were statistically insignificant in the fixed effect model have now gained significance while some have lost significance. However, overall, across all panels of Table 4, it is evident the overall conclusions from the fixed effect regressions remain unchanged.

# 6 Discussion and Conclusion

While a growing literature examines the impact of occupational choice on SWB and QoL, not much is known about the differential impacts of labour market attachment captured through employment contract types, which are linked to self-identity, before and after retirement. Drawing

**Table 4** Robustness check (Lewbel 2SLS results)

| Variables | (1) Wellbeing 1 | (2) Wellbeing 2 | (3) CASP-19 | (4) CASPCTL | (5) CASPAUT | (6) CASPPLE | (7) CASPSR | (8) Depression |
|---|---|---|---|---|---|---|---|---|
| *Panel 1: Effects of retirement on wellbeing/quality of life* | | | | | | | | |
| Retired | 0.070*** | 0.144*** | 0.856*** | 0.210*** | 0.182*** | 0.163*** | 0.303*** | −0.074*** |
| | (0.007) | (0.014) | (0.104) | (0.030) | (0.032) | (0.028) | (0.037) | (0.016) |
| Control variables? | Yes | Yes | Yes | Yes | Yes | Yes | Yes | Yes |
| Observations | 46,390 | 44,859 | 42,020 | 42,020 | 42,020 | 42,020 | 42,020 | 47,555 |
| $R^2$ | 0.085 | 0.084 | 0.165 | 0.156 | 0.165 | 0.057 | 0.159 | 0.107 |
| $J$-statistic ($P$-value) | 0.1620 | 0.7018 | 0.5001 | 0.1193 | 0.2227 | 0.0831 | 0.5029 | 0.1537 |
| *Panel 2: Effects of employment type on wellbeing/quality of life* | | | | | | | | |
| Self-employed | 0.022** | 0.032 | 0.902*** | 0.267*** | 0.130*** | 0.107*** | 0.400*** | −0.203*** |
| | (0.010) | (0.020) | (0.148) | (0.042) | (0.046) | (0.040) | (0.051) | (0.021) |
| Control variables? | Yes | Yes | Yes | Yes | Yes | Yes | Yes | Yes |
| Observations | 46,390 | 44,859 | 42,020 | 42,020 | 42,020 | 42,020 | 42,020 | 47,555 |
| $R^2$ | 0.079 | 0.076 | 0.075 | 0.042 | 0.100 | 0.032 | 0.065 | 0.084 |
| $J$-statistic ($P$-value) | 0.1024 | 0.0441 | 0.1043 | 0.6172 | 0.5022 | 0.1409 | 0.0873 | 0.0496 |

| Variables | (1) Wellbeing 1 | (2) Wellbeing 2 | (3) CASP-19 | (4) CASPCTL | (5) CASPAUT | (6) CASPPLE | (7) CASPSR | (8) Depression |
|---|---|---|---|---|---|---|---|---|
| *Panel 3: Effects of job type on wellbeing/quality of life* | | | | | | | | |
| Temp job | −0.008 | −0.761*** | −1.074** | 0.240 | 0.217 | −0.316** | −0.404** | 0.043 |
| | (0.031) | (0.031) | (0.545) | (0.172) | (0.186) | (0.149) | (0.194) | (0.069) |
| Control variables? | Yes | Yes | Yes | Yes | Yes | Yes | Yes | Yes |
| Observations | 19,762 | 15,315 | 15,020 | 15,211 | 15,225 | 15,251 | 15,241 | 21,503 |
| $R^2$ | 0.080 | 0.077 | 0.076 | 0.042 | 0.101 | 0.033 | 0.066 | 0.084 |
| $J$-statistic ($P$-value) | 0.0163 | 0.0563 | 0.7115 | 0.0924 | 0.0511 | 0.1864 | 0.0621 | 0.2147 |

*Notes* All regressions control for geographic regions and waves. Standard errors in parentheses, $^{***}p < 0.01$, $^{**}p < 0.05$, $^{*}p < 0.1$

on theories of social psychology, we hypothesised that labour market attachment can be linked to a person's self-identity, and thus, employment types that are more closely linked to self-identity will positively affect SWB and QoL. However, retirement may lead to a loss of this part of our identity and therefore have a negative impact on SWB and QoL.

Previous studies have found mixed results on the effect of retirement on wellbeing (Bonsang & Klein, 2012). In the present research, we contribute to this debate by showing that the effect of retirement on SWB is likely to be dependent on an individual's employment type before retirement and the degree of connection between an individual's identity and their employment type. These findings are important in modern labour markets which are characterised by rising self-employment and increasing casualisation of the workforce. Any productivity gains of these employment types need to be offset against their SWB costs (both during our working lives and into retirement) if the true economic value is to be understood. These results suggest a role for SWB support for employees in firms with large casual workforces, such that the firms creating the negative externalities (in terms of falling SWB) bear the costs of supporting their workers, as opposed to those costs being borne by the government. Our results suggest that there is a role of government in terms of the regulation of employment contracts, based on the argument that the economically optimal employment contracts offered to employees might not be socially optimal.

It is important to note that, while our empirical analysis has observed a statistically significant relationship between the nature of employment types and SWB, which is consistent with the hypotheses relating to the link between identity and labour market attachment, we have not directly proved that the mechanism is through identity. Further research is therefore needed to establish the pathway. Nevertheless, policymakers need to be aware of the links between pre-retirement labour market attachment and self-identity in order to better understand the welfare effects associated with transitioning into retirement. Retirement is shown to be welfare enhancing compared to employment but there are differential returns to retirement resulting from pre-retirement factors.

Individuals whose self-identity is less closely attached to the labour market experience the greatest increase in welfare from retirement. This indicates that differential retirement planning strategies are necessary according to the pre-retirement degree of labour market attachment. Further, it suggests that retirement planning should recognise social, emotional and mental health factors as captured by measures of SWB in addition to financial planning. Retirement is an important stage of the life course, and enhancing the welfare of retirees is essential to ensuring an equitable and functional social fabric.

## Appendix

See Table 5.

**Table 5** Description and summary statistics of variables

| Variables | Descriptions | Mean | SD |
|---|---|---|---|
| Wellbeing 1 | Four-point scale, where 1 means "never" and 4 means "often", in response to the question "Please say how often you feel satisfied with the way your life has turned out". Original scale from ELSA is transposed | 3.398 | 0.730 |
| Wellbeing 2 | Seven-point scale, where 1 means "strongly disagree" and 7 means "strongly agree", in response to "Please say how much you agree or disagree with the following statements: I am satisfied with my life". Original scale from ELSA is transposed | 5.435 | 1.345 |
| CASP-19 | CASP-19 quality of life scale | 42.116 | 8.399 |
| CASPCTL | CASP-19 control domain scale | 8.025 | 2.440 |
| CASPAUT | CASP-19 autonomy domain scale | 10.531 | 2.636 |
| CASPPLE | CASP-19 pleasure domain scale | 13.266 | 2.188 |
| CASPSR | CASP-19 self-realisation domain scale | 10.195 | 3.038 |
| Depression | Count of the number of Center for Epidemiologic Studies Depression (CES-D) scale questions that respondents answered "yes" to | 1.351 | 1.846 |
| Retired | Dummy variable equals to 1 if respondent is retired | 0.489 | 0.499 |
| Self-employed | Dummy variable equals to 1 if respondent is self-employed | 0.067 | 0.251 |
| Temp job | Dummy variable equals to 1 if respondent works as a temp | 0.041 | 0.200 |
| Age | Age of respondent | 64.956 | 9.826 |
| Age squared | Square of age/100 | 43.159 | 13.491 |
| Unemployed | Dummy variable equals to 1 if respondent is unemployed | 0.010 | 0.098 |

| Variables | Descriptions | Mean | SD |
|---|---|---|---|
| Higher education (Degree) | Dummy variable equals to 1 if respondent's highest level of education is at the tertiary level (degree) | 0.179 | 0.383 |
| Higher education (Below degree) | Dummy variable equals to 1 if respondent's highest level of education is at the tertiary level (non-degree) | 0.147 | 0.354 |
| A-level | Dummy variable equals to 1 if respondent's highest level of education is A-level | 0.081 | 0.273 |
| O-level | Dummy variable equals to 1 if respondent's highest level of education is O-level | 0.179 | 0.383 |
| Married | Dummy variable equals to 1 if respondent is married | 0.684 | 0.464 |
| Single | Dummy variable equals to 1 if respondent is single | 0.045 | 0.209 |
| Widowed | Dummy variable equals to 1 if respondent is widowed | 0.140 | 0.347 |
| Wealth | Log of respondent's wealth | 9.812 | 2.090 |
| Illness | Dummy variable equals to 1 if respondent has a long-standing illness | 0.417 | 0.493 |
| Children | Dummy variable equals to 1 if respondent has children | 0.785 | 0.410 |
| Smokes | Dummy variable equals to 1 if respondent smokes | 0.135 | 0.342 |

## References


Akay, A., Constant, A., & Giulietti, C. (2014). The impact of immigration on the well-being of natives. *Journal of Economic Behavior & Organization, 103,* 72–92. https://doi.org/10.1016/j.jebo.2014.03.024.

Akerlof, G. A., & Kranton, R. E. (2008). Identity, supervision, and work groups. *The American Economic Review, 98*(2), 212–217.

Alesina, A., Di Tella, R., & MacCulloch, R. (2004). Inequality and happiness: Are Europeans and Americans different? *Journal of Public Economics, 88,* 2009–2042.

Arbona, C., Burridge, A., & Olvera, N. (2017). The Center for Epidemiological Studies Depression Scale (CES-D): Measurement equivalence across gender groups in Hispanic college students. *Journal of Affective Disorders, 219,* 112–118.

Ashforth, B. E., Harrison, S. H., & Corley, K. G. (2008). Identification in organizations: An examination of four fundamental questions. *Journal of Management, 34*(3), 325–374.

Ashforth, B. E., & Mael, F. (1989). Social identity theory and the organization. *Academy of Management Review, 14*(1), 20–39.

Awaworyi Churchill, S., & Mishra, V. (2017). Trust, social networks and subjective wellbeing in China. *Social Indicators Research, 132*(1), 313–339. https://doi.org/10.1007/s11205-015-1220-2.

Banerjee, A. V., & Duflo, E. (2011). *Poor economics: A radical rethinking of the way to fight global poverty.* New York: Public Affairs.

Bardasi, E., & Francesconi, M. (2004). The impact of atypical employment on individual well-being: Evidence from a panel of British workers. *Social Science and Medicine, 58,* 1671–1688.

Barnes, H., & Parry, J. (2004). Renegotiating identity and relationships: Men and women's adjustments to retirement. *Ageing & Society, 24*(2), 213–233.

Belk, R. W. (1988). Possessions and the extended self. *Journal of Consumer Research, 15*(2), 139–168.

Berger, J. (2017). *Invisible influence: The hidden forces that shape behavior.* New York: Simon & Schuster.

Binder, M., & Blankenberg, A.-K. (2017). Green lifestyles and subjective well-being: More about self-image than actual behavior? *Journal of Economic Behavior & Organization, 137,* 304–323. https://doi.org/10.1016/j.jebo.2017.03.009.

Blanchflower, D. G. (2000). Self-employment in OECD countries. *Labour Economics, 7*(5), 471–505.

Blanchflower, D. G., & Oswald, A. J. (2004). Well-being over time in Britain and the USA. *Journal of Public Economics, 88,* 1359–1386.

Bonsang, E., & Klein, T. J. (2012). Retirement and subjective well-being. *Journal of Economic Behavior & Organization, 83*(3), 311–329. https://doi.org/10.1016/j.jebo.2012.06.002.

Brown, S., Farrell, L., Harris, M. N. & Sessions, J. (2006). Risk preference and employment contract type. *The Journal of the Royal Statistical Society Series A, 169*(4), 1–15.

Brown, S., Farrell, L., & Sessions, J. G. (2006). Employment contract matching: An analysis of dual earner couples and working households. *Small Business Economics, 26,* 155–172.

Butler, S. (1903/1998). *The way of all flesh.* New York: Penguin Random House.

Cai, S., & Park, A. (2016). Permanent income and subjective well-being. *Journal of Economic Behavior & Organization, 130,* 298–319. https://doi.org/10.1016/j.jebo.2016.07.016.

Carlsen, A. (2006). Organizational becoming as dialogic imagination of practice: The case of the indomitable Gauls. *Organization Science, 17*(1), 132–149.

Chen, Z., & Davey, G. (2008). Happiness and subjective wellbeing in mainland China. *Journal of Happiness Studies, 9*(4), 589–600.

Cheng, Z., & Smyth, R. (2015). Sex and happiness. *Journal of Economic Behavior & Organization, 112,* 26–32.

Chou, K.-L. (2008). Combined effect of vision and hearing impairment on depression in older adults: Evidence from the English Longitudinal Study of Ageing. *Journal of Affective Disorders, 106*(1), 191–196.

Davis, B., & Pechmann, C. (2013). Introduction to the Special Issue on transformative consumer research: Developing theory to mobilize efforts that improve consumer and societal well-being. *Journal of Business Research, 66*(8), 1168–1170.

De Cuyper, N., De Jong, J., De Witte, H., Isaksson, K., Rigotti, T., & Schalk, R. (2008). Literature review of theory and research on the psychological impact of temporary employment: Towards a conceptual model. *International Journal of Management Reviews, 10*(1), 25–51.

Diener, E. (1994). Assessing subjective well-being: Progress and opportunities. *Social Indicators Research, 31*(2), 103–157.

Diener, E., Oishi, S., & Lucas, R. E. (2003). Personality, culture, and subjective well-being: Emotional and cognitive evaluations of life. *Annual Review of Psychology, 54*(1), 403–425.

Dolan, P., Peasgood, T., & White, M. (2008). Do we really know what makes us happy? A review of the economic literature on the factors associated with subjective well-being. *Journal of Economic Psychology, 29*(1), 94–122. https://doi.org/10.1016/j.joep.2007.09.001.

Dutton, J. E., Roberts, L. M., & Bednar, J. (2010). Pathways for positive identity construction at work: Four types of positive identity and the building of social resources. *Academy of Management Review, 35*(2), 265–293.

Easterlin, R. A. (1995). Will raising the incomes of all increase the happiness of all? *Journal of Economic Behavior & Organization, 27*(1), 35–47.

El Hedhli, K., Chebat, J. C., & Sirgy, M. J. (2013). Shopping well-being at the mall: Construct, antecedents, and consequences. *Journal of Business Research, 66*(7), 856–863.

Ellison, C. G. (1991). Religious involvement and subjective well-being. *Journal of Health and Social Behavior, 32,* 80–99.

Emran, M. S., & Shilpi, F. (2012). The extent of the market and stages of agricultural specialization. *Canadian Journal of Economics/Revue canadienne d'économique, 45*(3), 1125–1153.

Falco, P., Maloney, W. F., Rijkers, B., & Sarrias, M. (2015). Heterogeneity in subjective wellbeing: An application to occupational allocation in Africa. *Journal of Economic Behavior & Organization, 111,* 137–153.

Forde, C., & Slater, G. (2006). The nature and experience of agency working in Britain: What are the challenges for human resource management. *Personnel Review, 35*(2), 141–157.

Fournier, S. (1998). Consumers and their brands: Developing relationship theory in consumer research. *Journal of Consumer Research, 24*(4), 343–373.

Hogg, M. A., & Terry, D. J. (2001). Social identity theory and organizational processes. In M. A. Hogg & D. J. Terry (Eds.), *Social identity processes in organizational contexts* (pp. 1–12). Philadelphia: Psychology Press.

Howel, D. (2012). Interpreting and evaluating the CASP-19 quality of life measure in older people. *Age and Ageing, 41*(5), 612–617. https://doi.org/10.1093/ageing/afs023.

Hsee, C. K., Yang, Y., Li, N., & Shen, L. (2009). Wealth, warmth, and well-being: Whether happiness is relative or absolute depends on whether it is about money, acquisition, or consumption. *Journal of Marketing Research, 46*(3), 396–409.

Hyde, M., Wiggins, R. D., Higgs, P., & Blane, D. B. (2003). A measure of quality of life in early old age: The theory, development and properties of a needs satisfaction model (CASP-19). *Aging & Mental Health, 7*(3), 186–194. https://doi.org/10.1080/1360786031000101157.

Ibarra, H., & Barbulescu, R. (2010). Identity as narrative: Prevalence, effectiveness, and consequences of narrative identity work in macro work role transitions. *Academy of Management Review, 35*(1), 135–154.

Jackall, R. (1978). *Workers in a labyrinth: Jobs and survival in a bank bureaucracy.* Montclair, NJ: Allanheld & Schram.

Johnson, M. D., Morgeson, F. P., Ilgen, D. R., Meyer, C. J., & Lloyd, J. W. (2006). Multiple professional identities: Examining differences in identification across work-related targets. *Journal of Applied Psychology, 91*(2), 498.

Kautonen, T., Kibler, E., & Minniti, M. (2017). Late-career entrepreneurship, income and quality of life. *Journal of Business Venturing, 32*(3), 318–333. https://doi.org/10.1016/j.jbusvent.2017.02.005.

Kipnis, E., Broderick, A. J., Demangeot, C., Adkins, N. R., Ferguson, N. S., Henderson, G. R., ... & Roy, A. (2013). Branding beyond prejudice: Navigating multicultural marketplaces for consumer well-being. *Journal of Business Research, 66*(8), 1186–1194.

Lee, D. M., Nazroo, J., O'Connor, D. B., Blake, M., & Pendleton, N. (2016). Sexual health and well-being among older men and women in England: Findings from the English Longitudinal Study of Ageing. *Archives of Sexual Behavior, 45*(1), 133–144.

Lewbel, A. (2012). Using heteroscedasticity to identify and estimate mismeasured and endogenous regressor models. *Journal of Business & Economic Statistics, 30*(1), 67–80.

Marmot, M., Oldfield, Z., Clemens, S., Blake, M., Phelps, A., Nazroo, J., ... Oskala, A. (2017). *English Longitudinal Study of Ageing: Waves 0-7, 1998-2015* [data collection] (27th ed.). UK Data Service. SN: 5050. http://doi.org/10.5255/UKDA-SN-5050-14.

McColl-Kennedy, J. R., Hogan, S. J., Witell, L., & Snyder, H. (2017). Cocreative customer practices: Effects of health care customer value cocreation practices on well-being. *Journal of Business Research, 70,* 55–66.

McHugh, J., Kenny, R., Lawlor, B., Steptoe, A., & Kee, F. (2017). The discrepancy between social isolation and loneliness as a clinically meaningful metric: Findings from the Irish and English longitudinal studies of ageing (TILDA and ELSA). *International Journal of Geriatric Psychiatry, 32*(6), 664–674.

Mishra, V., & Smyth, R. (2015). Estimating returns to schooling in urban China using conventional and heteroskedasticity-based instruments. *Economic Modelling, 47,* 166–173.

Moore, C. D., & Robinson, D. T. (2006). Selective identity preferences: Choosing from among alternative occupational identities. *Advances in group processes* (pp. 253–281). New York: Emerald Group Publishing Limited.

Netuveli, G., Wiggins, R. D., Hildon, Z., Montgomery, S. M., & Blane, D. (2006). Quality of life at older ages: Evidence from the English longitudinal study of aging (wave 1). *Journal of Epidemiology and Community Health, 60*(4), 357–363.

Parasuraman, S., & Simmers, C. A. (2001). Type of employment, work–family conflict and well-being: A comparative study. *Journal of Organizational Behavior, 22*(5), 551–568.

Pierce, M., Zaninotto, P., Steel, N., & Mindell, J. (2009). Undiagnosed diabetes: Data from the English longitudinal study of ageing. *Diabetic Medicine, 26*(7), 679–685.

Pinquart, M., & Sörensen, S. (2000). Influences of socioeconomic status, social network, and competence on subjective well-being in later life: A meta-analysis. *Psychology and Aging, 15*(2), 187–224. https://doi.org/10.1037/0882-7974.15.2.187.

Pratt, M. G., Rockmann, K. W., & Kaufmann, J. B. (2006). Constructing professional identity: The role of work and identity learning cycles in the customization of identity among medical residents. *Academy of Management Journal, 49*(2), 235–262.

Price, C. A. (2000). Women and retirement: Relinquishing professional identity. *Journal of Aging Studies, 14*(1), 81–101.

Radloff, L. S. (1977). The CES-D scale: A self-report depression scale for research in the general population. *Applied Psychological Measurement, 1*(3), 385–401.

Rigotti, T., & Mohr, G. (2005). German flexibility: Loosening the reins without losing control. In N. De Cuyper, K. Isaksson, & H. De Witte (Eds.), *Employment contracts and well-being among European workers* (pp. 75–102). Aldershot: Ashgate.

Sexton, E., King-Kallimanis, B. L., Conroy, R. M., & Hickey, A. (2013). Psychometric evaluation of the CASP-19 quality of life scale in an older Irish cohort. *Quality of Life Research, 22*(9), 2549–2559. https://doi.org/10.1007/s11136-013-0388-7.

Shankar, A., Hamer, M., McMunn, A., & Steptoe, A. (2013). Social isolation and loneliness: Relationships with cognitive function during 4 years of follow-up in the English Longitudinal Study of Ageing. *Psychosomatic Medicine, 75*(2), 161–170.

Sim, J., Bartlam, B., & Bernard, M. (2011). The CASP-19 as a measure of quality of life in old age: Evaluation of its use in a retirement community. *Quality of Life Research, 20*(7), 997–1004. https://doi.org/10.1007/s11136-010-9835-x.

Stagl, J. M., Antoni, M. H., Lechner, S. C., Bouchard, L. C., Blomberg, B. B., Glück, S., ... Carver, C. S. (2015). Randomized controlled trial of cognitive behavioral stress management in breast cancer: A brief report of effects on 5-year depressive symptoms. *Health Psychology, 34*(2), 176.

Steptoe, A., Breeze, E., Banks, J., & Nazroo, J. (2012). Cohort profile: The English Longitudinal Study of Ageing. *International Journal of Epidemiology, 42*(6), 1640–1648.

Steptoe, A., & Wardle, J. (2012). Enjoying life and living longer. *Archives of Internal Medicine, 172*(3), 273–275. https://doi.org/10.1001/archinternmed.2011.1028.

Stets, J. E., & Burke, P. J. (2000). Identity theory and social identity theory. *Social Psychology Quarterly, 63*, 224–237.

Stone, K. V. W., & Arthurs, H. (2013). *Rethinking workplace regulation: Beyond the standard contract of employment.* New York: Russell Sage Foundation.

Stryker, S., & Burke, P. J. (2000). The past, present, and future of an identity theory. *Social Psychology Quarterly, 63*, 284–297.

Tian, K., & Belk, R. W. (2005). Extended self and possessions in the workplace. *Journal of Consumer Research, 32*(2), 297–310.

Torres, J. L., Lima-Costa, M. F., Marmot, M., & de Oliveira, C. (2016). Wealth and disability in later life: The English Longitudinal Study of Ageing (ELSA). *PLOS One, 11*(11), e0166825.

Van Praag, B. M., Frijters, P., & Ferrer-i-Carbonell, A. (2003). The anatomy of subjective well-being. *Journal of Economic Behavior & Organization, 51*(1), 29–49.

Virtanen, M., Kivimäki, M., Joensuu, M., Virtanen, P., Elovainio, M., & Vahtera, J. (2005). Temporary employment and health: A review. *International Journal of Epidemiology, 34*, 610–622.

Wolanin, A., Hong, E., Marks, D., Panchoo, K., & Gross, M. (2016). Prevalence of clinically elevated depressive symptoms in college athletes and differences by gender and sport. *British Journal of Sports Medicine, 50*(3), 167–171. https://doi.org/10.1136/bjsports-2015-095756.

# 7

# Height and Health Among Older Chinese

Asadul Islam, Paul Raschky and Russell Smyth

## 1 Introduction

With rapid ageing of the population in many countries, the determinants of cognitive function and health in older age have become a major public policy priority (Maurer, 2010). Height as a marker of health and nutrition in childhood has been shown to be correlated with various outcomes later in life. Several studies document the existence of a wage-height premium (see, e.g., Case, Paxson, & Islam, 2009; Gao & Smyth, 2010; Schultz, 2002; Yamamura, Smyth, & Zhang, 2015). Case and Paxson

A. Islam · P. Raschky · R. Smyth (✉)
Department of Economics, Monash University, Caulfield, VIC, Australia
e-mail: russell.smyth@monash.edu

A. Islam
e-mail: asadul.islam@monash.edu

P. Raschky
e-mail: paul.raschky@monash.edu



S. Awaworyi Churchill et al. (eds.), *Measuring, Understanding and Improving Wellbeing Among Older People*,
https://doi.org/10.1007/978-981-15-2353-3_7

(2008a, 2011) document that height is associated with several employment outcomes later in life. In particular, based on the UK Whitehall II survey, Case and Paxson (2011) show that better childhood health—reflected in adult height—is associated with better occupational status and promotion prospects in adulthood. Deaton and Arora (2009) find that taller people report being happier in the US Gallup-Healthways Well-Being Index.

Case and Paxson (2008b) was the first study to find that the advantages of being taller follow people into old age and that for a sample of people aged 50 and above in the United States, taller people have better health along a variety of dimensions. Guven and Lee (2013, 2015) reach the same conclusion as Case and Paxson (2008b) using data from English and European surveys, while Mosca and Wright (2016) find a significant correlation between height and cognition for a sample of older people from Ireland.

Most of the literature on the relationship between height and health in old age focuses on high-income countries. There are few studies for developing countries. Exceptions for developing countries are Maurer (2010), who examines the relationship between height, education and later life cognition in Latin America and McGovern (2014), who compares the relationship between height and later-life health in six low- and middle-income countries.

There are at least three reasons why the relationship between height and health in older age is particularly relevant for developing countries (McGovern, 2014). One is that the proportion of older people in developing countries is expected to grow exponentially in coming decades. By 2050, more than 750 million people aged 60 or above are expected to live in China or India, representing over a third of the world's population in this age bracket (Chaterji et al., 2008). A second is that their ageing populations are likely to impact relatively more significantly on these economies, given that they typically have much more limited resources than high-income countries. The third is that early childhood experience of many in developing countries is likely to have been much harsher than those in developed countries, making the impact of early life circumstances on health in older age more important.

The second and third points are certainly applicable to China, in which rapid ageing has occurred at much lower levels of income than was the case in high-income countries. Exogenous shocks, such as the Great Leap Forward and Cultural Revolution impacted on the childhood and adolescence of many of those who are elderly in China now. The one-child policy in China has placed increased pressure on single children to look after ageing parents and grandparents—the so-called 1-2-4 phenomenon in which one child looks after two parents and four grandparents. The financial pressure is magnified given that while China has undertaken pension reform, the number of empty personal pension fund accounts has grown rapidly in recent years, whereby current contributions are used to fund current liabilities. According to media reports, at the end of 2014 the accumulated value of empty personal accounts was more than 3.5 trillion RMB ($US 533 billion) (China Daily, 2016).

There are several reasons why height might be associated with better health at old age (Case & Paxson, 2008b). Adult height is a proxy for a healthy environment in childhood, which affects cognitive development. Poor health and nutrition in childhood are associated with problems such as diabetes, hypertension and vascular disease, which persist into old age and make it more difficult to perform daily tasks (Brunner, 2005). Childhood environment and cognitive development affect educational achievement and occupational choice. Similarly, the choice of occupation and workplace can then have adverse effects on health and well-being later in life. In particular, blue-collar workers are at higher risk of exposure to neurotoxicants in the workplace, which have been shown to cause deterioration in health and ability to perform daily activities later in life (Schwartz et al., 2000).

We re-examine earlier findings on the relationship between height and health in older age by Case and Paxson (2008b) and others in the context of China. In so doing, we contribute to a small literature that has examined childhood circumstances on health in middle-age and old age in China. Smith, Shen, Strauss, Yang, and Zhao (2012) examine the effect of childhood health on adult health and socioeconomic status in China. Kim, Fleisher, and Sun (2017) examine the effects of the Great Leap Forward on the health of people in middle-age. Islam, Raschky, and Smyth

(2017) examine the long-run health effects of being exposed to political violence in childhood and adolescence in the Cultural Revolution. Lin and Liu (2014) examine the long-run health effects of the 1918 Taiwan influenza. These studies, however, do not specifically focus on the height-health relationship in middle and old age. The closest study to ours is Huang, Lei, Ridder, Strauss, and Zhao (2013) who examines the effect of height shrinkage on health outcomes of the elderly in China. We differ from Huang et al. (2013) in that we do not focus on height shrinkage and our identification strategy is different. Specifically, we take advantage of the fact that the Cultural Revolution represented an exogenous shock which impacted on one's height later in life.

We find that taller people have less difficulty engaging in activities of daily living (ADL) in old age, even controlling for education and self-reported childhood health among other controls. When we instrument for height using whether the person was born, or was an adolescent, in the Cultural Revolution the magnitude on the height coefficient is slightly higher, suggesting that the Ordinary Least Squares (OLS) estimates are downward biased.

## 2 Data and Methodology

We use pilot data from the China Health and Retirement Longitudinal Survey (CHARLS). CHARLS contains data from 1563 randomly selected households collected from two provinces, Zhejiang and Gansu, between July and September 2008. CHARLS sampled one person aged 45 and over, plus their spouse if one exists, in each household with an age-eligible person. Hence, overall CHARLS contains information on 2951 individuals aged 45 and older (see Zhao, Strauss, Park, & Sun, 2009). Our measure of health and well-being or quality of life is ADL, which is a composite index of the level of difficulty that the respondent has in performing a number of fairly normal and routine day-to-day activities or tasks. Specifically, we considered the degree of difficulty experienced by the respondent in performing the following 20 tasks: dressing, bathing, eating, getting in or out of bed, walking 100 metres, walking one kilometre, sitting for two hours, getting up from a chair, climbing several flights of stairs, stooping, kneeling or crouching, lifting 10 *jin* (equivalent to a heavy bag of groceries), extending one's arm, pushing or pulling large objects, urinating, doing household chores, preparing hot meals, shopping for groceries, managing money, making phone calls and taking medicine. Respondents' answers were coded: 1 = 'I do not have any difficulty in performing the task'; 2 = 'I can perform the task, but only with difficulty', 3 = 'I cannot perform the task'. Our measure of ADL is the sum of responses on all 20 tasks. Responses were normalized so that the maximum value of the composite ADL variable is 1 and the minimum value is zero. The mean value is 0.078 with a standard deviation of 0.129.

ADL was first regressed on a respondent's height, measured in centimetres, and control variables using OLS. However, adult height is an endogenous variable as it depends on environmental factors in infancy and adolescence, suggesting that OLS estimates will be biased. The most important environmental factors influencing height are the quality of the uterine environment and, in infancy (aged 1–2) and in the adolescent growth spurt, nutritional status and exposure to disease (Beard & Blaser, 2002). Epidemiological studies suggest the adolescent growth spurt in China is 10–11 for girls and 12–13 for boys (Ji, Ohsawa, & Kasai, 1995; Leung et al., 1996) 002E. The Cultural Revolution was an exogenous shock that impacted on nutritional intake of those who were born, or were in the adolescent growth spurt, in these years. Adverse effects on agricultural production meant that calorie intake was at a bare subsistence level. Despite the existence of 'barefoot doctors' in rural areas, the political campaigns and disruption to urban institutions generated an increase in epidemic disease and malnutrition in many areas. Morgan (2007) found that individuals born at the height of the Cultural Revolution (1966–1968) were much shorter as adults than those born before or after. Hence, the instrumental variables (IVs) we use for height are whether the respondent was aged 0–2 in the Cultural Revolution, 10–11 in the Cultural Revolution (if female) or 12–13 in the Cultural Revolution (if male). We also have IVs for if the person was aged 0–2 and born in rural China in the Cultural Revolution and if the respondent was born in a rural area at any time. The reason for the latter is that the quality of prenatal care, access to healthcare and nutritional intake of pregnant mothers and children is lower in rural China. Table 1 contains the list of variables, together with their definitions and descriptive statistics.

# 3 Results

Table 2 reports OLS results. We find that, on average, taller respondents have less difficulty performing everyday activities. Specifically, each additional centimetre in height is associated with 0.02 units reduction in

**Table 1** Description of variables

| Variable | Description |
|---|---|
| Height | Respondent's height in cm |
| Age | Respondent's age in years |
| Female | Dummy = 1 if respondent is female<br>0 otherwise |
| Gansu | Dummy = 1 if respondent lives in Gansu<br>0 respondent lives in Zhejiang |
| Rural | Dummy = 1 if respondent lives in rural area<br>0 respondent lives in urban area |
| Child health | Dummy = 1 if respondent reported 'excellent' or 'very good' health during childhood,<br>0 otherwise |
| Education | Highest year of education of respondent |
| Cultural revolution 0–2 years | Dummy = 1 if respondent was between born or between and 2 years old during Cultural Revolution, 0 otherwise |
| Cultural revolution 10–11 years (Female) | Dummy = 1 if respondent was between 10 and 11 years old during Cultural Revolution and female, 0 otherwise |
| Cultural revolution 12–13 years (Male) | Dummy = 1 if respondent was between 12 and 13 years old during Cultural Revolution and male, 0 otherwise |
| Born rural | Dummy = 1 if respondent was born in a rural area, 0 otherwise |

**Table 2** OLS estimates of determinants of ADL difficulty

| | | |
|---|---|---|
| Height | −0.002*** | −0.002** |
| | (0.001) | (0.001) |
| Age | 0.006*** | 0.006*** |
| | (0.001) | (0.000) |
| Female | 0.050*** | 0.051*** |
| | (0.012) | (0.011) |
| Gansu | | 0.147*** |
| | | (0.008) |
| Rural | | 0.033*** |
| | | (0.009) |
| Child health | | −0.025*** |
| | | (0.008) |
| Education | | −0.004*** |
| | | (0.001) |
| Constant | 0.099 | −0.066 |
| | (0.124) | (0.113) |
| *N* | 1946 | 1864 |

*Notes* Robust standard errors (in parentheses). ***, **, * indicate significance at the 1, 5 and 10%-level

ADL difficulty. This result holds in both column 1, when we just control for age and gender, and column 2, when we also control for the province in which the respondent lived, if he/she lived in a rural area, education and childhood health. Of the other variables, we find that age and being female is associated with greater ADL difficulty, while those who self-reported having better childhood health and the better educated have less ADL difficulty. The results for education are consistent with previous research suggesting that the better educated have better cognitive skills at older ages (see, e.g., Huang & Zhou, 2013). While we do not report them, it is worth noting that the results are qualitatively similar if estimates are derived using Tobit, rather than OLS.

The results for the IV estimates are presented in Table 3. The first stage estimates and the validity of the IVs, reported at the bottom of Table 3, suggest that these IVs are appropriate instruments for height. The second stage estimates, reported at the top of Table 3, indicate that taller people have less difficulty performing everyday activities at older ages. The magnitude of the coefficient on height in the IV estimates is slightly

**Table 3** IV estimates of determinants of ADL difficulty

| | |
|---|---|
| *Second stage estimates* | |
| Height | −0.013* |
| | (0.007) |
| Age | 0.004*** |
| | (0.001) |
| Female | −0.074 |
| | (0.074) |
| Gansu | 0.149*** |
| | (0.009) |
| Rural | 0.013 |
| | (0.016) |
| Child health | −0.023** |
| | (0.009) |
| Education | −0.002 |
| | (0.002) |
| Constant | 1.972* |
| | (1.193) |
| *First stage estimates* | |
| Cultural revolution | −1.947** |
| 0–2 years | (0.825) |
| Cultural revolution | −0.862* |
| 10–11 years, female | (0.503) |
| Cultural revolution | −1.036* |
| 12–13 years, male | (0.551) |
| Cultural revolution | −1.022 |
| 0–2 years * Born rural | (2.003)** |
| Born rural | −1.438 |
| | (0.679) |
| Angrist-Pischke Test a | 0.003 |
| Kleibergen-Paap statistic a | 0.007 |
| Hansen Test a | 0.544 |
| *N* | 1864 |

*Notes* Robust standard errors (in parentheses). a p-values. ***, **, * indicate significance at the 1, 5 and 10%-level

higher than in the OLS estimates. Of the other variables, age and self-reported child health continue to be significant with the expected signs, but education, gender, the rural-urban and province dummies become insignificant. The results for height are consistent with previous results for high-income countries reported in Case and Paxson (2008b), Guven and Lee (2013, 2015) and Mosca and Wright (2016) for Europe and the United States and for low- and middle-income countries reported in Maurer (2010) and McGovern (2014). Our findings strongly suggest that early life experiences, as proxied by adult height, have consequences for well-being at older ages.

## 4 Conclusion

The results reported here suggest that height is associated with better health and quality of life in terms of performing a range of routine daily activities in old age, even after we control for education and self-reported health in childhood. Our findings contribute to our understanding of the relationship between childhood circumstance and cognitive function in old age, which, to this point, has mainly centred on high-income countries. Our results also add to the China-specific literature on the effect of exogenous shocks, such as the Great Leap Forward and Cultural Revolution on health later in life and, more generally, economic and epidemiological studies of the effects of specific shocks to health in utero and in early childhood on cognitive and physical health later in life. This literature has focused on shocks due to disease (Almond, 2006), famine (Neelsen & Stratmann, 2011), civil war (Akresh, Bhalotra, Leone, & Osili, 2012), World War II (Kesternich, Siflinger, Smith, & Winter, 2014) and economic downturn (Cutler, Miller, & Norton, 2007). Our findings are consistent with the general tenor of such studies that exogenous shocks can have persistent long-term effects on health that continue well into adult life.

Our results support the Barker (1990) hypothesis that chronic health problems in old age, including cognitive decline, can be traced to the womb and shocks in utero are correlated with declining mental and physical health in old age. Because height in adulthood is determined by environmental factors aged 0-2 and in the adolescent growth spurt, the results reported here have implications for investment in health human capital in the womb, infancy and adolescence. Specifically, the findings suggest that investing in health and nutrition in these critical times can improve the health and quality of life of people in old age, which is potentially a very important result given China's ageing population.

## References


Akresh, R., Bhalotra, S., Leone, M., & Osili, U. O. (2012). War and stature: Growing up during the Nigerian civil war. *American Economic Review, 102*(3), 273–277.

Almond, D. (2006). Is the 1918 influenza pandemic over? Long-term effects of *in utero* influenza exposure in the post 1940 US population. *Journal of Political Economy, 114,* 672–712.

Barker, D. J. P. (1990). The fetal and infant origins of adult disease: The womb may be more important than the home. *British Medical Journal, 301,* 1111.

Beard, A. S., & Blaser, M. J. (2002). The ecology of height: The effect of microbial transmission on human height. *Perspectives in Biology and Medicine, 45*(4), 475–499.

Brunner, E. J. (2005). Social and biological determinants of cognitive aging. *Neurobiology of Aging, 26*(1), 17–20.

Case, A., & Paxson, C. (2008a). Stature and status: Height, ability and labor market outcomes. *Journal of Political Economy, 116*(3), 499–532.

Case, A., & Paxson, C. (2008b). Height, health and cognitive function at older ages. *American Economic Review Papers and Proceedings, 98*(2), 463–467.

Case, A., & Paxson, C. (2011). The long reach of childhood health and circumstance: Evidence from the Whitehall II study. *Economic Journal, 121,* F183–F204.

Case, A., Paxson, C., & Islam, M. (2009). Making sense of the labor market height premium: Evidence from the British household panel survey. *Economics Letters, 102*(3), 174–176.

Chatterji, S., Kowal, P., Mathers, C., Maidoo, N., Verdes, E., Smith, J. P., et al. (2008). The health of aging populations in China and India. *Health Affairs, 27*(4), 1052–1063.

*China Daily*. (2016, January 8). Empty personal pension accounts. *China Daily,* p. 8.

Cutler, D., Miller, G. & Norton, D. M. (2007). Evidence on early life income and late life health from America's dust bowl era. *Proceedings of the National Academy of Science, 104*(33), 13244–13249.

Deaton, A., & Arora, R. (2009). Life at the top: The benefits of height. *Economics & Human Biology, 7*(2), 133–136.

Gao, W., & Smyth, R. (2010). Health human capital, height and wages in China. *Journal of Development Studies, 46*(3), 466–484.

Guven, C., & Lee, W. S. (2013). Height and cognitive function at older ages: Is height a useful summary measure of early childhood experiences? *Health Economics, 22*, 224–236.

Guven, C., & Lee, W. S. (2015). Height, aging and cognitive abilities across Europe. *Economics & Human Biology, 16*, 16–29.

Huang, W., Lei, X., Ridder, G., Strauss, J., & Zhao, Y. (2013). Health, height shrinkage and SES in older ages: Evidence from China. *American Economic Journal: Applied Economics, 5*(2), 86–121.

Huang, W., & Zhou, Y. (2013). Effects of education on cognition at older age: Evidence from China's great famine. *Social Science and Medicine, 98*, 54–62.

Islam, A., Raschky, P. A., & Smyth, R. (2017). The long-term health effects of mass political violence: Evidence from China's cultural revolution. *Social Indicators Research, 132*(1), 257–272.

Ji, C. Y., Ohsawa, S., & Kasai, N. (1995). Secular changes in the stature, weight and age at maximum growth increments of urban Chinese girls from the 1950s to 1985. *American Journal of Human Biology, 7*(4), 473–484.

Kesternich, I., Siflinger, B., Smith, J. P., & Winter, J. K. (2014). The effects of World War II on economic and health outcomes across Europe. *Review of Economics and Statistics, 96*(1), 103–118.

Kim, S., Fleisher, B., & Sun, J. Y. (2017). The long-term health effects of fetal malnutrition: Evidence from the 1959–1961 China great leap forward famine. *Health Economics, 26*, 1264–1277.

Leung, S. S. F., Lau, J. T. F., Xu, Y. Y., Tse, L. Y., Huen, K. F., Wong, G. W. K., … Leung, N. K. (1996). Secular changes in standing height, sitting height and sexual maturation of Chinese—The hong kong growth study. *Annals of Human Biology*, 23(4), 297–306.

Lin, M. J., & Liu, E. M. (2014). Does in *utero* exposure to illness matter? The 1918 influenza epidemic in Taiwan as a natural experiment. *Journal of Health Economics, 37*, 152–163.

Maurer, J. (2010). Height, education and later-life cognition in Latin America and the Caribbean. *Economics & Human Biology, 8*, 168–176.

McGovern, M. E. (2014). Comparing the relationship between stature and later life health in six low and middle-income countries. *Journal of the Economics of Ageing, 4*, 128–148.

Morgan, S. (2007). *Stature and famine in China: The welfare of the survivors of the great leap forward famine.* http://papers.ssrn.com/sol3/papers.cfm?abstract_id=1083059.

Mosca, I., & Wright, R. E. (2016). Height and cognition at older ages: Irish evidence. *Economics Letters, 149,* 98–101.

Neelsen, S., & Stratmann, T. (2011). Effects of prenatal and early life malnutrition: Evidence from the Greek Famine. *Journal of Health Economics, 30,* 479–488.

Schultz, T. P. (2002). Wage gains associated with height as a form of health human capital. *American Economic Review, 92*(2), 349–353.

Schwartz, B. S., Stewart, W. F., Bolla, K. I., Simon, D., Bandeen-Roche, K., Gordon, B., ... Todd, A. C. (2000). Past adult lead exposure is associated with longitudinal decline in cognitive function. *Neurology, 55*(8), 1144–1150.

Smith, J. P., Shen, Y., Strauss, J., Yang, Z., & Zhao, Y. (2012). The effects of childhood health on adult health and SES in China. *Economic Development and Cultural Change, 61*(1), 127–156.

Yamamura, E., Smyth, R., & Zhang, Y. (2015). Decomposing the effect of height on income in China: The role of market and political channels. *Economics & Human Biology, 19,* 62–74.

Zhao, Y., Strauss, J., Park, A., & Sun, Y. (2009). *China health and retirement longitudinal study, Pilot User's Guide.* National School of Development, Peking University.

# 8

# Ethnic Diversity, Prejudice and Wellbeing Among Older Chinese

Esenam Agyekumhene, Dillys Amega, Samuelson Appau, Sefa Awaworyi Churchill and Janet Ocloo

## 1 Introduction

A relatively large body of literature explores the determinants of wellbeing. This literature focuses on a wide range of determinants including factors such as trust and social capital, income and education, among

E. Agyekumhene (✉)
Femme Foundation, Accra, Ghana

D. Amega
Living Waters Hospital, Ejisu, Ghana

S. Appau · S. Awaworyi Churchill
School of Economics, Finance and Marketing, RMIT University, Melbourne, VIC, Australia
e-mail: samuelson.appau@rmit.edu.au

S. Awaworyi Churchill
e-mail: sefa.awaworyichurchill@rmit.edu.au

J. Ocloo
Korle Bu Teaching Hospital, Accra, Ghana



S. Awaworyi Churchill et al. (eds.), *Measuring, Understanding and Improving Wellbeing Among Older People*,
https://doi.org/10.1007/978-981-15-2353-3_8

others (see, e.g., Bjørnskov, 2003; Elgar et al., 2011; Helliwell, 2003; Helliwell & Putnam, 2004; Helliwell & Wang, 2011). Despite the vast literature that focuses on the determinants of wellbeing, not much has been done on the association between ethnic diversity and wellbeing.

The existing literature in the area of race and ethnicity has mostly focused on the variations in mental health services uptake as well as how wellbeing and mental health vary between various ethnic groups. For instance, research has shown that in most developed countries, ethnic minorities tend to access mental health services less than ethnic majorities relative to their respective population sizes. Similarly, evidence suggests that ethnic minorities are more likely to experience stress, depression, mental health problems and lower life satisfaction and wellbeing compared to the general population (Bartram, 2011; Bobowik, Basabe, & Páez, 2015; Fazel, Wheeler, & Danesh, 2005; Safi, 2009; Verkuyten, 2008). Discussions from this strand of literature indicate that ethnic minorities are often over-represented in deprived communities and thus suffer from lower life satisfaction and conditions that hinder wellbeing.

These studies have improved our understanding of why levels of life satisfaction and mental wellbeing vary among different ethnic groups. However, they do not explain whether, and how, living in ethnically diverse (or homogenous) communities influence wellbeing. In this chapter, we attempt to contribute to the literature on the impact of ethnic diversity on life satisfaction using a sample of older people from China. We also explore the important role of discrimination, an element which is more pronounced in ethnically heterogeneous areas, on subjective wellbeing.[1]

A relatively large body of literature exclusively from the field of public health, psychology and epidemiology focuses on the effects of discrimination on various health outcomes (see, e.g., Paradies, 2006; Williams, Neighbors, & Jackson, 2003). On the other hand, majority of studies examining the implications of discrimination in economics focus on its impact on labour market outcomes (see, e.g., Åslund & Rooth, 2005;

[1]While we use the term discrimination across the manuscript, our measures of what we call discrimination actually capture discriminatory attitudes or prejudicial opinions. However, the findings are still relevant for policy given that opinions about discrimination are likely to be manifested.

Davila & Mora, 2005; Kaushal, Kaestner, & Reimers, 2007). However, the impact of discrimination on subjective wellbeing is relatively under-explored, and where explored, is in the case of developed countries, especially the United States (see, e.g., Branscombe, Schmitt, & Harvey, 1999; Foster, 2000). Other studies in this area attempt to examine the effect of employee or workplace discrimination on wellbeing at the workplace (see, e.g., Goldman, Gutek, Stein, & Lewis, 2006; Gutek, Cohen, & Tsui, 1996).

Overall, in the existing literature on the association between discrimination and health, it is hypothesized that discrimination can induce both psychological and physiological issues which can be detrimental to health. Discrimination has also been associated with the reception of poorer health care due to discrimination on the part of healthcare providers (Johnston & Lordan, 2012). Given the association between an individual's health and his or her assessment of overall life satisfaction, we expect discrimination to affect wellbeing.

With regard to the association between ethnic diversity and wellbeing, our study is related to those conducted by Betz and Simpson (2013) and Akay, Constant, and Giulietti (2014), and similar to Longhi (2014) who examine the impact of cultural diversity on wellbeing using British data. Betz and Simpson (2013) and Akay et al. (2014) explore the impact of migration on wellbeing using data on European countries. Migration is a global phenomenon, which creates societies where individuals from diverse ethnic backgrounds cohabit in the same neighbourhood, and thus is largely correlated with ethnic diversity. However, rather than exploring the implication of immigration, which is argued to promote ethnic diversity, we explore the direct effects of ethnic diversity on wellbeing. Furthermore, unlike the previous studies that have used data from developed countries, more precisely European countries, we explore a new perspective on the effects of ethnic diversity on subjective wellbeing using data from China.

The focus on China thus responds to the call for further studies on the determinants of wellbeing in developing countries. Evidence presented for China in this context may offer additional insights to other countries with similar cultural backgrounds, demographics and socio-economic conditions. We also focus on a single country, China, to allow for a more detailed analysis of the geography and demography of China and how this affects the association between ethnic diversity and wellbeing. It has been argued that findings could be flawed given that life satisfaction might not have comparable meaning across different countries (Helliwell, 2003), and thus, the use of data for a single country mitigates some existing concerns regarding the use of life satisfaction indicators in cross-country studies.

Furthermore, as the most populous country in the world, and the second-largest economy by GDP, China makes for an interesting sample characterized by a unique socio-economic and institutional context, and it is surprising that very little is known about the determinants of wellbeing in the Chinese context (Yip et al., 2007). Also, contrary to observations in other transition and developing economies, China has experienced significant economic development although this growth occurred in an economic and institutional environment that defies conventional economic theories (Boisot & Child, 1996; Li, 2004; Li, S., Li, S., & Zhang, 2000; Nee, 1992; Walder, 1995; Wang, Zeng, Wei, & Zhang, 2012). Therefore, by observing social patterns and how these might affect wellbeing, this study aims to provide some insights into the phenomenon of high growth in China. With a relatively slower pace of social transformation in this country (Yip et al., 2007), it is worthwhile examining the extent to which these patterns of social transformation in terms of ethnic diversity and discrimination affect the wellbeing of its population.

Specifically, evidence provided for China would give a unique perspective on the determinants of wellbeing for several reasons. First, discrimination in China not only is a social issue but is also rooted in institutional barriers imposed by the government on migrants via such systems as the *Hukou*. Thus, beyond unpleasant social encounters faced by individuals which can be classified as discriminating, China presents a unique case of institutional discrimination which is discussed extensively in the literature (see, e.g., Afridi, Li, & Ren, 2015; Chen, 2013; Huang, 2001; Liu, 2005; Zhigang & Shunfeng, 2006).

We also focus on a sample of older people in China which is timely and relevant for policy, given issues associated with China's ageing population. With decreasing birth rates in China, the country is faced with an increasingly serious case of an ageing society. It is thus important to understand what factors influence the wellbeing of the older population to ensure the right policies are implemented.

The remainder of the chapter is structured as follows. Section 2 presents information on the data and variables used in our analysis as well as the empirical specification. Section 3 presents the empirical results and robustness checks to verify the robustness of our results, and lastly, Sect. 4 presents some discussions and conclusions.

# 2 Data, Variables and Methodology

## 2.1 Data

Data for this study are collected from the World Values Survey (WVS) for China. The WVS is a non-profit organization comprising of a network of social scientists around the world. Surveys conducted by the WVS aim at investigating sociocultural and political change, and thus, survey questions attempt to capture such phenomena as culture, ethnicity and diversity, gender issues, religion and religiosity, politics, insecurity, national identity and subjective wellbeing, among others. Since the 1980s, the WVS has carried out nationally representative surveys involving about 100 countries across the globe. Data are freely available for non-profit purposes and can be retrieved from the WVS website http://www.worldvaluessurvey.org.

Since 1981, the WVS has conducted six waves of surveys with the sixth wave released in 2014. Based on data availability, we draw on five waves of data (waves 2–6) for China and examine the relationships of interest. Except for our measure of ethnic diversity, all other variables are drawn from the WVS data set. We restrict our sample to respondents that are at least 50 years old given that we aim to focus only on older people.

### 2.1.1 Wellbeing

While there is no precise definition for wellbeing in the literature, existing literature focuses on subjective life satisfaction as a measure of wellbeing (see, e.g., Helliwell, 2003; Helliwell & Wang, 2011; Longhi, 2014; Portela, Neira, & del Mar Salinas-Jiménez, 2013). Subjective life satisfaction is the result of the evaluation of one's own life. This measure is often associated with an individual's long-term opportunities and goals. The WVS asks the question: "All things considered, how satisfied are you with your life as a whole these days? 1 means you are 'completely dissatisfied' and 10 means you are 'completely satisfied' where would you put your satisfaction with life as a whole?"

### 2.1.2 Ethnic Diversity

Ethnic diversity generally refers to the representation of different social categories, based on race or ethnicity, in a society. Alesina and Zhuravskaya (2011), in their seminal work, developed a measure of ethnic diversity for a cross section of countries using a Herfindahl-type fractionalization formula. Indices computed are both national level and subnational level indices. For China, indices of ethnic fractionalization, *F*, are computed for 28 provinces as follows:

$$F_j = 1 - \sum\nolimits_{e=1}^{N} s_{ej}^2$$

where $s_{ej}$ is the share of ethnic group $e$ in a province. $F_j$ is the measure of ethnic diversity which measures the probability that two randomly selected individuals in a Chinese province are from different ethnic groups. For details on the index construction process, see Alesina and Zhuravskaya (2011).

For WVS data, we identify the province in which each respondent resides and merge individual-level data with province-level indices of ethnic fractionalization. Indices of ethnic fractionalization are argued to be relatively stable overtime, as ethnic composition or the share of each ethnic group in a population is persistent overtime, usually over a 30-year period (Alesina, Devleeschauwer, Easterly, Kurlat, & Wacziarg, 2003). Thus, merging ethnic fractionalization indices with survey data collected between 1990 and 2014 does not pose much problem. This practice is also consistent with the ethnic diversity literature (see, e.g., Alesina et al., 2003; Alesina & Zhuravskaya, 2011; Easterly & Levine, 1997).

### 2.1.3 Discrimination

Discrimination is generally defined as pertaining to the unjust or prejudicial treatment of different categories of people, especially on the grounds of race, age, religion or sex. In this chapter, we create several measures of discrimination drawn from the various questions asked by the WVS relating to various expectations of individuals with regard to others who are fundamentally "different". We attempt to capture three main dimensions of discrimination and thus focus on survey questions relating to labour market discrimination, discrimination on the basis of race and discrimination on the basis of religion. Our first two measures of discrimination capture labour market discrimination. For the first measure (*discrimination 1*), respondents are coded as discriminating if they agree when jobs are scarce, men should have more rights to a job than women. For our second measure of discrimination (*discrimination 2*), respondents are coded as discriminating if they agree when jobs are scarce, locals should be given priority over immigrants.

Our third and fourth measures of discrimination capture discrimination that is based on race. For *discrimination 3*, respondents are coded as discriminating if they would not like to have people of different race as neighbours, and *discrimination 4* if respondents would not like to have immigrants as neighbours. Lastly, *discrimination 5* attempts to capture religious discrimination. Thus, respondents are coded as discriminating if they would not like to have people of different religion as neighbours. We also take the average of all five measures of discrimination to form one overall measure of discrimination.

### 2.1.4 Other Control Variables

Our choice of control variables is consistent with the existing literature on the determinants of subjective wellbeing. Specifically, we control for demographic variables and socio-economic characteristics of the Chinese population such as gender, age, income, marital status and employment status.

We also control for the level of freedom or control perceived by respondents (*freedom*). Our measure of *freedom* is coded based on the WVS question: "how much freedom of choice and control do you have over your life?", where 1 means "no choice and control at all" and 10 means "a great deal of choice and control". We also control for the financial freedom of respondents (*money*), and thus, we use the WVS question which attempts to capture if respondents have gone in the past without money to afford basic needs. We also capture the importance of religion to respondents. Other control variables included dummy variables which represent respondents' fear or worry of civil war and terrorist attack, as well as unsafe feelings associated with crime. Table 1 presents a description and summary statistics of all variables.

## 2.2 Empirical Model

Our main aim is to examine the effect of ethnic diversity and discrimination on subjective wellbeing, conditional on demographic variables and other relevant covariates. To this end, we estimate the following equation:

$$SWB_i = \alpha + \sum_m \gamma_m \boldsymbol{K}_{m,i} + \sum_n \beta_n X_{n,i} + \varepsilon_i$$

where $i$ indexes the individuals, $SWB$ is the measure of subjective wellbeing, $\boldsymbol{K}_m$ is a vector of our main explanatory variables (i.e. ethnic diversity and discrimination), $X_n$ is a set of control variables described earlier, $\gamma_m$ and $\beta_n$ are parameters to be estimated, and $\varepsilon$ is the random error term.

**Table 1** Descriptive and summary statistics

| Variable | Description | Mean | S.D. |
|---|---|---|---|
| Wellbeing | All things considered, how satisfied are you with your life as a whole these days? 1 means you are "completely dissatisfied" and 10 means you are "completely satisfied" where would you put your satisfaction with your life as a whole? | 6.91 | 2.31 |
| Ethnic diversity | Province-level index of ethnic fractionalization | 0.11 | 0.15 |
| Discrimination | Average of all discrimination measures | 0.36 | 0.19 |
| Discrimination 1 | Dummy variable equals to 1 if respondent agrees when jobs are scarce, men should have more rights to a job than women | 0.42 | 0.49 |
| Discrimination 2 | Dummy variable equals to 1 if respondent agrees when jobs are scarce, locals should be given priority over immigrants | 0.66 | 0.47 |
| Discrimination 3 | Dummy variable equals to 1 if respondent would not like to have people of different race as neighbours | 0.17 | 0.35 |
| Discrimination 4 | Dummy variable equals to 1 if respondent would not like to have immigrant as neighbours | 0.19 | 0.37 |
| Discrimination 5 | Dummy variable equals to 1 if respondent would not like to have people of different religion as neighbours | 0.07 | 0.26 |
| Income | Scale of income | 4.16 | 1.92 |
| Male | Dummy variable equals to 1 if respondent is male | 0.54 | 0.49 |
| Married | Dummy variable equals to 1 if respondent is married | 0.83 | 0.38 |
| Unemployed | Dummy variable equals to 1 if respondent is unemployed | 0.03 | 0.16 |
| Age | Age of respondent | 58.98 | 6.76 |
| Age squared | Square of age/100 | 35.24 | 8.26 |
| Freedom | How much freedom of choice and control do you have over your life? scale where 1 means "no choice at all" and 10 means "a great deal of choice" | 7.06 | 2.31 |
| Dependence | Dummy variable equals to 1 if respondent depend on friends, family or relatives as information source | 0.86 | 0.35 |

(continued)

**Table 1** (continued)

| Variable | Description | Mean | S.D. |
|---|---|---|---|
| Money | Dummy variable equals to 1 if respondent has in the past gone without money | 0.81 | 0.38 |
| Unsafe | Dummy variable equals to 1 if respondent has in the past felt unsafe from crime | 0.78 | 0.38 |
| Help | Dummy variable equals to 1 if It is important for respondent to help people nearby | 0.97 | 0.13 |
| Religion | Dummy variable equals to 1 if religion is important to respondent | 0.13 | 0.32 |
| Job loss | Dummy variable equals to 1 if respondent worries about losing his/her job or not finding a job | 0.19 | 0.39 |
| Terrorism | Dummy variable equals to 1 if respondent worries about a terrorist attack | 0.12 | 0.32 |
| Civil war | Dummy variable equals to 1 if respondent worries about a civil war | 0.11 | 0.33 |

# 3 Empirical Results

Table 2 presents results for the association between ethnic diversity and subjective wellbeing, as well as discrimination and subjective wellbeing. Results in column 1 show that ethnic diversity exerts a significant negative effect on subjective wellbeing among older Chinese. More specifically, on a life satisfaction scale ranging from 0 to 10, we find that a 1% increase in the degree of ethnic diversity results in a 0.005 decrease in individual life satisfaction. In terms of standard deviations, a standard deviation increase in ethnic diversity is associated with a decline of 0.03 standard deviations in individual life satisfaction. Column 2 likewise shows that the discrimination index (measured as the average of all 5 discrimination measures) also exerts a significant negative effect on subjective wellbeing among older Chinese. Comparing standardized coefficients, the effect of discrimination appears to be relatively stronger with a standardized coefficient of 0.17.

Columns 3–7 report on the association between our various measures of discrimination and subjective wellbeing. We can see that in four of the five measures of discrimination tested, the results point to a negative effect of discrimination on wellbeing. Specifically, the coefficients on discrimination from column 4 are *not* statistically significant, which shows that the exercise of discrimination by giving priority to locals over immigrants when jobs are scarce does not influence one's level of subjective wellbeing. However, from column 3, we observe that on a scale of 1–10, SWB declines due to discrimination for those who exhibit a gender bias against women in the labour market.

Further, from columns 5 and 6, we can see that SWB declines due to discrimination along racial lines and discrimination against immigrant neighbours, respectively. Similarly, from column 7, results show that SWB declines due to discrimination along religious lines, specifically, when people do not share the same faith as respondents. On a scale of 1–10, the change in SWB caused by these discrimination variables ranges between a narrow band of 0.19 and 0.65 units, or 0.09 and 0.17 standard deviations. In other words, the magnitude of the predicted declines in SWBs is no smaller than 0.19 units and no larger than 0.65 units due to discrimination along these lines.

**Table 2** Ethnic diversity, discrimination and wellbeing (OLS robust regressions)

| Variables | (1) | (2) | (3) | (4) | (5) | (6) | (7) |
|---|---|---|---|---|---|---|---|
| Ethnic diversity | −0.005* | | | | | | |
| | (0.002) | | | | | | |
| | [−0.03] | | | | | | |
| | | −0.65*** | −0.19** | −0.17 | −0.24* | −0.34*** | −0.35* |
| | | (0.24) | (0.09) | (0.16) | (0.13) | (0.12) | (0.19) |
| | | [−0.17] | [−0.09] | [−0.01] | [−0.12] | [−0.14] | [−0.14] |
| Income | 0.17*** | 0.18*** | 0.18*** | 0.18*** | 0.18*** | 0.18*** | 0.18*** |
| | (0.03) | (0.03) | (0.03) | (0.03) | (0.03) | (0.03) | (0.03) |
| Male | −0.13 | −0.08 | −0.07 | −0.08 | −0.09 | −0.10 | −0.08 |
| | (0.10) | (0.09) | (0.09) | (0.09) | (0.09) | (0.09) | (0.09) |
| Married | 0.22 | 0.16 | 0.15 | 0.15 | 0.15 | 0.15 | 0.14 |
| | (0.16) | (0.15) | (0.15) | (0.15) | (0.15) | (0.15) | (0.15) |
| Unemployed | −0.21 | −0.19 | −0.17 | −0.17 | −0.17 | −0.20 | −0.16 |
| | (0.34) | (0.33) | (0.33) | (0.32) | (0.33) | (0.33) | (0.33) |
| Age | −0.09*** | −0.08*** | −0.08*** | −0.08*** | −0.08*** | −0.08*** | −0.08*** |
| | (0.01) | (0.01) | (0.01) | (0.01) | (0.01) | (0.01) | (0.01) |
| Age squared | 0.10*** | 0.09*** | 0.09*** | 0.09*** | 0.09*** | 0.09*** | 0.09*** |
| | (0.01) | (0.01) | (0.01) | (0.01) | (0.01) | (0.01) | (0.01) |
| Freedom | 0.42*** | 0.42*** | 0.42*** | 0.42*** | 0.41*** | 0.42*** | 0.41*** |
| | (0.03) | (0.02) | (0.02) | (0.02) | (0.02) | (0.02) | (0.02) |
| Dependence | 0.26 | 0.31** | 0.28* | 0.31** | 0.29* | 0.29** | 0.30** |
| | (0.16) | (0.15) | (0.15) | (0.15) | (0.15) | (0.15) | (0.15) |
| Money | −0.46** | −0.47*** | −0.48*** | −0.47*** | −0.47*** | −0.47*** | −0.47*** |
| | (0.20) | (0.18) | (0.18) | (0.18) | (0.18) | (0.18) | (0.18) |
| Unsafe | −0.18 | −0.17 | −0.18 | −0.18 | −0.16 | −0.19 | −0.18 |
| | (0.19) | (0.18) | (0.18) | (0.18) | (0.18) | (0.18) | (0.18) |

| Variables | (1) | (2) | (3) | (4) | (5) | (6) | (7) |
|---|---|---|---|---|---|---|---|
| Help | −0.41 | −0.32 | −0.29 | −0.28 | −0.35 | −0.33 | −0.25 |
| | (0.30) | (0.28) | (0.28) | (0.27) | (0.28) | (0.28) | (0.28) |
| Religion | −0.05 | −0.08 | −0.07 | −0.08 | −0.06 | −0.07 | −0.07 |
| | (0.15) | (0.14) | (0.14) | (0.14) | (0.14) | (0.14) | (0.14) |
| Job loss | −0.16 | −0.16 | −0.15 | −0.16 | −0.15 | −0.17 | −0.15 |
| | (0.15) | (0.14) | (0.15) | (0.15) | (0.15) | (0.14) | (0.15) |
| Terrorism | −0.06 | −0.06 | −0.04 | −0.05 | −0.05 | −0.06 | −0.02 |
| | (0.26) | (0.26) | (0.26) | (0.26) | (0.26) | (0.26) | (0.26) |
| Civil war | 0.37 | 0.25 | 0.25 | 0.24 | 0.25 | 0.26 | 0.23 |
| | (0.26) | (0.26) | (0.26) | (0.26) | (0.25) | (0.25) | (0.26) |
| Constant | 7.51** | 6.18** | 6.20** | 5.95** | 6.41** | 6.13** | 5.99** |
| | (3.27) | (2.89) | (2.89) | (2.90) | (2.92) | (2.89) | (2.89) |
| Waves dummies | Yes | Yes | Yes | Yes | Yes | Yes | Yes |
| Province dummies | Yes | Yes | Yes | Yes | Yes | Yes | Yes |
| Observations | 1702 | 1970 | 1970 | 1970 | 1970 | 1970 | 1970 |
| $R^2$ | 0.22 | 0.22 | 0.22 | 0.22 | 0.22 | 0.22 | 0.22 |

Dependent variable is wellbeing
Robust standard errors in parentheses
Standardized coefficients in brackets
$^{***}p < 0.01$, $^{**}p < 0.05$, $^{*}p < 0.1$

Examining the standardized coefficients and comparing the effects of ethnic diversity and discrimination to the effects of other control variables, we find that ethnic diversity's effects on subjective wellbeing are relatively weaker compared to the effects of most control variables although discrimination's effect is relatively stronger. For instance, in the case of older Chinese, a factor such as income appears to be a stronger determinant of subjective wellbeing than ethnic diversity while discrimination tends to influence wellbeing more strongly than income.

## 3.1 Robustness Checks

Given the ordinal nature of the measure of wellbeing used in the literature, some studies adopt the ordered logit estimation technique instead of the OLS. Thus, the existing literature on the determinants of wellbeing often adopts one of two methods (OLS or the ordered logit method). To supplement OLS estimations, we also run ordered logit regressions to ensure that results are robust to estimation methods. Table 3 presents results for ordered logit regressions. Ordered logit regressions results are identical to OLS results except for minor variations in coefficient sizes which are not unexpected. Overall, compared to ordered logit regressions, OLS results report relatively stronger effects of discrimination on wellbeing, and this is also the case for the effect of ethnic diversity.

Furthermore, given arguments suggesting reverse causality between discrimination and wellbeing, it becomes imperative that we address any endogeneity bias in our estimation. As we have established, discrimination affects wellbeing. However, it is likely that people's level of life satisfaction or wellbeing can also affect their ability or attitude to discriminate, and so causality may run the other way as well. On the other hand, ethnic diversity has been argued to be exogenous, and thus, in the literature indices of fractionalization are often not considered endogenous (see, e.g., Alesina & Zhuravskaya, 2011; Easterly & Levine, 1997). To ensure accuracy and reliability of our estimates, we employ instrumental variable (IV) techniques and re-estimate our equations accordingly. Econometrically, we will require IVs which are correlated with the discrimination variable but uncorrelated with the wellbeing variable and the

**Table 3** Ethnic diversity, discrimination and wellbeing (ordered logit regressions)

| Variables | (1) | (2) | (3) | (4) | (5) | (6) | (7) |
|---|---|---|---|---|---|---|---|
| Ethnic diversity | −0.003* | | | | | | |
| | (0.001) | | | | | | |
| | [−0.02] | | | | | | |
| Discrimination | | −0.61*** | −0.16** | −0.16* | −0.16 | −0.37*** | −0.15* |
| | | (0.21) | (0.08) | (0.08) | (0.12) | (0.11) | (0.08) |
| | | [−0.13] | [−0.08] | [−0.06] | [−0.02] | [−0.10] | [−0.05] |
| Income | 0.13*** | 0.13*** | 0.14*** | 0.13*** | 0.14*** | 0.13*** | 0.14*** |
| | (0.02) | (0.02) | (0.02) | (0.02) | (0.02) | (0.02) | (0.02) |
| Male | −0.11 | −0.08 | −0.06 | −0.08 | −0.08 | −0.09 | −0.08 |
| | (0.09) | (0.08) | (0.08) | (0.08) | (0.08) | (0.08) | (0.08) |
| Married | 0.20 | 0.15 | 0.14 | 0.15 | 0.14 | 0.14 | 0.15 |
| | (0.14) | (0.12) | (0.12) | (0.12) | (0.12) | (0.12) | (0.12) |
| Unemployed | −0.05 | −0.03 | −0.02 | −0.01 | −0.02 | −0.06 | −0.02 |
| | (0.26) | (0.27) | (0.27) | (0.27) | (0.27) | (0.28) | (0.27) |
| Age | −0.11 | −0.07 | −0.07 | −0.06 | −0.08 | −0.07 | −0.06 |
| | (0.10) | (0.08) | (0.08) | (0.08) | (0.08) | (0.08) | (0.08) |
| Age squared | −0.08*** | −0.07*** | −0.07*** | −0.07*** | −0.07*** | −0.07*** | −0.07*** |
| | (0.01) | (0.01) | (0.01) | (0.01) | (0.01) | (0.01) | (0.01) |
| Freedom | 0.09*** | 0.08*** | 0.08*** | 0.08*** | 0.08*** | 0.08*** | 0.08*** |
| | (0.01) | (0.01) | (0.01) | (0.01) | (0.01) | (0.01) | (0.01) |
| Dependence | 0.13 | 0.20 | 0.17 | 0.19 | 0.18 | 0.18 | 0.20 |
| | (0.15) | (0.13) | (0.13) | (0.13) | (0.13) | (0.13) | (0.13) |
| Money | −0.34* | −0.40*** | −0.41*** | −0.40*** | −0.40*** | −0.40*** | −0.40*** |
| | (0.18) | (0.14) | (0.15) | (0.15) | (0.15) | (0.14) | (0.14) |
| Unsafe | −0.16 | −0.15 | −0.15 | −0.15 | −0.15 | −0.17 | −0.15 |
| | (0.18) | (0.15) | (0.15) | (0.15) | (0.15) | (0.15) | (0.15) |

(continued)

**Table 3** (continued)

| Variables | (1) | (2) | (3) | (4) | (5) | (6) | (7) |
|---|---|---|---|---|---|---|---|
| Help | −0.24 | −0.14 | −0.12 | −0.10 | −0.15 | −0.17 | −0.12 |
| | (0.26) | (0.26) | (0.26) | (0.26) | (0.26) | (0.27) | (0.26) |
| Religion | −0.14 | −0.15 | −0.14 | −0.15 | −0.14 | −0.15 | −0.13 |
| | (0.13) | (0.12) | (0.12) | (0.12) | (0.12) | (0.12) | (0.12) |
| Job loss | −0.13 | −0.14 | −0.13 | −0.14 | −0.13 | −0.15 | −0.13 |
| | (0.15) | (0.12) | (0.12) | (0.12) | (0.12) | (0.12) | (0.12) |
| Terrorism | −0.14 | −0.13 | −0.11 | −0.12 | −0.12 | −0.14 | −0.13 |
| | (0.28) | (0.22) | (0.22) | (0.22) | (0.22) | (0.22) | (0.22) |
| Civil war | 0.45 | 0.33 | 0.32 | 0.31 | 0.32 | 0.34 | 0.32 |
| | (0.28) | (0.22) | (0.22) | (0.22) | (0.22) | (0.22) | (0.22) |
| Waves dummies | Yes | Yes | Yes | Yes | Yes | Yes | Yes |
| Province dummies | Yes | Yes | Yes | Yes | Yes | Yes | Yes |
| Observations | 1702 | 1970 | 1970 | 1970 | 1970 | 1970 | 1970 |
| $R^2$ | 0.22 | 0.22 | 0.22 | 0.22 | 0.22 | 0.22 | 0.22 |

Dependent variable is wellbeing
Robust standard errors in parentheses
Standardized coefficients in brackets
$^{***}p < 0.01$, $^{**}p < 0.05$, $^{*}p < 0.1$

error term. However, we do not have such variables in our data set, and thus, we adopt the Lewbel 2SLS approach (Lewbel, 2012) which deals with endogeneity in the absence of conventional IVs.

From Table 4, we find that Lewbel 2SLS results are consistent with OLS results which show a negative effect of discrimination on wellbeing. However, the 2SLS estimates appear relatively stronger than those from the OLS regressions, which then implies that OLS estimates have underestimated the effects of discrimination on wellbeing. Put differently, there is a downward bias associated with OLS estimates which we attribute to endogeneity bias. Specifically, the OLS results report a standardized coefficient of −0.17 that explains the strongest effect of discrimination on wellbeing (column 2). The 2SLS regressions, however, show a standardized coefficient of 0.22 (column 2). Nonetheless, the existing conclusions on the direction of association between discrimination and subjective wellbeing remain unchanged.

## 4 Discussions and Conclusion

This study sought to examine the effects of ethnic diversity and discrimination on the subjective wellbeing of Older Chinese. We provide evidence on the effects of ethnic diversity on subjective wellbeing, as well as on the effects of discrimination on subjective wellbeing.

The importance of wellbeing cuts across various areas, and governments and policymakers are increasingly identifying the need of wellbeing in policy decisions (Waldron, 2010). Accordingly, it is important to identify whether society and its characteristics affect the life satisfaction or wellbeing of individuals, especially older individuals in the wake of an ageing society where we have increasing number of older people. We therefore explore the effect of ethnic diversity and discrimination on the subjective wellbeing of older people using data from China.

The main findings of this study demonstrate that both discrimination and ethnic diversity negatively influence subjective wellbeing. Ethnic diversity has the potential to negatively influence social capital, and given the large body of literature which shows a positive association between social capital and wellbeing, it is sufficient to say that social

**Table 4** Discrimination and wellbeing (Lewbel 2SLS regressions)

| Variables | (1) | (2) | (3) | (4) | (5) | (6) |
|---|---|---|---|---|---|---|
| Discrimination | −0.99*** | −0.34*** | −0.68*** | −0.26 | −0.73*** | −0.34* |
| | (0.15) | (0.08) | (0.16) | (0.17) | (0.14) | (0.18) |
| | [−0.22] | [−0.10] | [−0.16] | [−0.04] | [−0.19] | [−0.09] |
| Control variables? | Yes | Yes | Yes | Yes | Yes | Yes |
| Waves dummies | Yes | Yes | Yes | Yes | Yes | Yes |
| Province dummies | Yes | Yes | Yes | Yes | Yes | Yes |
| Observations | 1970 | 1970 | 1970 | 1970 | 1970 | 1970 |
| $R^2$ | 0.28 | 0.23 | 0.28 | 0.28 | 0.28 | 0.28 |

Dependent variable is wellbeing
Robust standard errors in parentheses
Standardized coefficients in brackets
$^{***}p < 0.01$, $^{**}p < 0.05$, $^{*}p < 0.1$

capital is a major channel of influence that can explain our results. To examine if this is the case for older Chinese, consistent with the existing literature, we adopt trust as our measure of social capital (see, e.g., Leigh, 2006).

We measure trust using the standard "generalized trust" question developed by the WVS. The WVS asks the question: "*Generally speaking, would you say that most people can be trusted or that you cannot be too careful in dealing with people*?" Consistent with the existing literature, we code respondents who agree that "*most people can be trusted*" as trusting. From Table 5, results show a negative association between ethnic diversity and trust. Specifically, from column 1, results show that a standard deviation increase in ethnic diversity is associated with a decline of 0.13 standard deviations in generalized trust. Thus, ethnic diversity is associated with lower trust in China, a finding consistent with existing literature that has considered a sample for developed countries (see, e.g., Leigh, 2006). Accordingly, we argue that ethnic diversity leads to a decline in social capital (measured by trust), and this negatively affects wellbeing.

We also argue that the negative effect of ethnic diversity on wellbeing could be explained via its effect on discrimination. As we have established, discrimination negatively influences wellbeing. However, we also hypothesize that ethnic diversity promotes discrimination. From Table 5, columns 2–7, results largely show that ethnic diversity promotes discrimination, and this is consistent across various measures of discrimination. From column 2, where we use the mean value of all discrimination measures, results show that ethnic diversity is positively associated with discrimination. Here, a standard deviation increase in ethnic diversity is associated with an increase of 0.09 standard deviations in discrimination. Results across other columns also show a positive association between ethnic diversity and discrimination. Thus, an increase in ethnic diversity leads to an increase in discrimination. Consequently, our analyses show and support the idea that the adverse effects of ethnic diversity on wellbeing are not only direct but also indirect through effects on factors such as discrimination and social capital.

Findings regarding the effects of discrimination on wellbeing mainly tie in with an existing strand of the literature in psychology. For instance,

**Table 5** Ethnic diversity, discrimination and trust (logit regressions)

| Variables | (1) | (2) | (3) | (4) | (5) | (6) | (7) |
|---|---|---|---|---|---|---|---|
| Ethnic diversity | −0.08*** | 0.13** | 0.05** | 0.08 | 0.15** | 0.19** | 0.15** |
| | (0.02) | (0.07) | (0.02) | (0.06) | (0.06) | (0.08) | (0.07) |
| | [−0.13] | [0.09] | [0.04] | [0.03] | [0.10] | [0.12] | [0.09] |
| Control variables? | Yes | Yes | Yes | Yes | Yes | Yes | Yes |
| Waves dummies | Yes | Yes | Yes | Yes | Yes | Yes | Yes |
| Province dummies | Yes | Yes | Yes | Yes | Yes | Yes | Yes |
| Observations | 1700 | 1702 | 1702 | 1702 | 1702 | 1702 | 1702 |

Dependent variable: Column 1 = Trust, Columns 2–7 = Discrimination
Robust standard errors in parentheses
Standardized coefficients in brackets
$^{***}p < 0.01$, $^{**}p < 0.05$, $^{*}p < 0.1$

Baumeister and Leary (1995) demonstrate that people inherently have the need to belong, and this need contributes to their survival and satisfaction. Therefore, discrimination, which includes the exclusion of certain categories of people, can directly affect and hinder the fulfilment of the inherent need to belong. Additionally, discrimination can also generate animosity and hostility in a social setting, especially when victims of discrimination attempt to retaliate, or a more common scenario where some individuals who discriminate become physically hostile (Branscombe et al., 1999; Stangor et al., 2003). This level of animosity and hostility can negatively influence wellbeing.

With regard to the effects of our control variables, some of our results are consistent with previous studies showing a positive association of wellbeing with income, feeling of control and freedom, and a negative association of wellbeing with age (Helliwell & Wang, 2011; Kessler, Mickelson, & Williams, 1999; Lachman & Weaver, 1998). Interestingly, income appears to be a stronger determinant of subjective wellbeing than ethnic diversity but not discrimination. The stronger effect of income compared to ethnic diversity is contrary to existing research that argues against income as a stronger determinant of wellbeing compared to social constructs such as social capital, specifically trust (see, e.g., Bjørnskov, 2003). We argue that this observation could be explained by economic and demographic factors. Existing research that shows a weaker effect of income on wellbeing uses a sample for developed countries, and this is expected given that income would not lead to more life satisfaction once high levels of income have been attained (Easterlin, 1995). However, in the case of a developing country, income can be associated with higher levels of satisfaction as income aids in the provision of basic needs. Accordingly, higher income would be prioritized and therefore would be a stronger determinant compared to social constructs such as ethnic diversity.

In summary, contrary to existing literature which often focuses on the determinant of wellbeing for developed countries, we use a sample for China (a developing country) and examine the effects of ethnic diversity and discrimination on the wellbeing of older people. Our results show that both ethnic diversity and discrimination negatively influence subjective wellbeing. Our evidence also shows that ethnic diversity is associated with lower trust in China and also promotes discrimination. Further research may consider comparing the effect of discrimination and ethnic diversity on wellbeing across various demographic groups, as this could shed more light to the relationship of interest.

## References

Afridi, F., Li, S. X., & Ren, Y. (2015). Social identity and inequality: The impact of China's hukou system. *Journal of Public Economics, 123,* 17–29.

Akay, A., Constant, A., & Giulietti, C. (2014). The impact of immigration on the well-being of natives. *Journal of Economic Behavior & Organization, 103,* 72–92.

Alesina, A., & Zhuravskaya, E. (2011). Segregation and the quality of government in a cross section of countries. *American Economic Review, 101*(5), 1872–1911. https://doi.org/10.1257/aer.101.5.1872.

Alesina, A., Devleeschauwer, A., Easterly, W., Kurlat, S., & Wacziarg, R. (2003). Fractionalization. *Journal of Economic Growth, 8*(2), 155–194.

Åslund, O., & Rooth, D.-O. (2005). Shifts in attitudes and labor market discrimination: Swedish experiences after 9-11. *Journal of Population Economics, 18*(4), 603–629.

Bartram, D. (2011). Economic migration and happiness: Comparing immigrants' and natives' happiness gains from income. *Social Indicators Research, 103*(1), 57–76.

Baumeister, R. F., & Leary, M. R. (1995). The need to belong: Desire for interpersonal attachments as a fundamental human motivation. *Psychological Bulletin, 117*(3), 497.

Betz, W., & Simpson, N. B. (2013). The effects of international migration on the well-being of native populations in Europe. *IZA Journal of Migration, 2*(1), 1–21.

Bjørnskov, C. (2003). The happy few: Cross-country evidence on social capital and life satisfaction. *Kyklos, 56*(1), 3–16. https://doi.org/10.1111/1467-6435.00207.

Bobowik, M., Basabe, N., & Páez, D. (2015). The bright side of migration: Hedonic, psychological, and social well-being in immigrants in Spain.

*Social Science Research, 51,* 189–204. https://doi.org/10.1016/j.ssresearch.2014.09.011.

Boisot, M., & Child, J. (1996). From fiefs to clans and network capitalism: Explaining China's emerging economic order. *Administrative Science Quarterly, 41*(4), 600–628. https://doi.org/10.2307/2393869.

Branscombe, N. R., Schmitt, M. T., & Harvey, R. D. (1999). Perceiving pervasive discrimination among African Americans: Implications for group identification and well-being. *Journal of Personality and Social Psychology, 77*(1), 135.

Chen, J. (2013). Perceived discrimination and subjective well-being among rural-to-urban migrants in China. *Journal of Social Welfare, 40,* 131.

Davila, A., & Mora, M. T. (2005). Changes in the earnings of Arab men in the US between 2000 and 2002. *Journal of Population Economics, 18*(4), 587–601.

Easterlin, R. A. (1995). Will raising the incomes of all increase the happiness of all? *Journal of Economic Behavior & Organization, 27*(1), 35–47.

Easterly, W., & Levine, R. (1997). Africa's growth tragedy: Policies and ethnic divisions. *The Quarterly Journal of Economics, 112*(4), 1203–1250.

Elgar, F. J., Davis, C. G., Wohl, M. J., Trites, S. J., Zelenski, J. M., & Martin, M. S. (2011). Social capital, health and life satisfaction in 50 countries. *Health & Place, 17*(5), 1044–1053. https://doi.org/10.1016/j.healthplace.2011.06.010.

Fazel, M., Wheeler, J., & Danesh, J. (2005). Prevalence of serious mental disorder in 7000 refugees resettled in western countries: A systematic review. *The Lancet, 365*(9467), 1309–1314.

Foster, M. D. (2000). Positive and negative responses to personal discrimination: Does coping make a difference? *The Journal of Social Psychology, 140*(1), 93–106.

Goldman, B. M., Gutek, B. A., Stein, J. H., & Lewis, K. (2006). Employment discrimination in organizations: Antecedents and consequences. *Journal of Management, 32*(6), 786–830.

Gutek, B. A., Cohen, A. G., & Tsui, A. (1996). Reactions to perceived sex discrimination. *Human Relations, 49*(6), 791–813.

Helliwell, J. F. (2003). How's life? Combining individual and national variables to explain subjective well-being. *Economic Modelling, 20*(2), 331–360.

Helliwell, J. F., & Putnam, R. D. (2004). The social context of well-being. *Philosophical Transactions of the Royal Society, 359,* 1435–1446.

Helliwell, J. F., & Wang, S. (2011). Trust and wellbeing. *International Journal of Wellbeing, 1*(1), 42–78.

Huang, Y. (2001). Gender, hukou, and the occupational attainment of female migrants in China (1985–1990). *Environment and Planning A, 33*(2), 257–280.

Johnston, D. W., & Lordan, G. (2012). Discrimination makes me sick! An examination of the discrimination–health relationship. *Journal of Health Economics, 31*(1), 99–111. https://doi.org/10.1016/j.jhealeco.2011.12.002.

Kaushal, N., Kaestner, R., & Reimers, C. (2007). Labor market effects of September 11th on Arab and Muslim residents of the United States. *Journal of Human Resources, 42*(2), 275–308.

Kessler, R. C., Mickelson, K. D., & Williams, D. R. (1999). The prevalence, distribution, and mental health correlates of perceived discrimination in the United States. *Journal of Health and Social Behavior, 40,* 208–230.

Lachman, M. E., & Weaver, S. L. (1998). The sense of control as a moderator of social class differences in health and well-being. *Journal of Personality and Social Psychology, 74*(3), 763.

Leigh, A. (2006). Trust, inequality and ethnic heterogeneity. *Economic Record, 82*(258), 268–280. https://doi.org/10.1111/j.1475-4932.2006.00339.x.

Lewbel, A. (2012). Using heteroscedasticity to identify and estimate mismeasured and endogenous regressor models. *Journal of Business & Economic Statistics, 30*(1), 67–80.

Li, S. (2004). The puzzle of firm performance in China: An institutional explanation. *Economics of Planning, 37*(1), 47–68.

Li, S., Li, S., & Zhang, W. (2000). The road to capitalism: Competition and institutional change in China. *Journal of Comparative Economics, 28*(2), 269–292.

Liu, Z. (2005). Institution and inequality: The hukou system in China. *Journal of Comparative Economics, 33*(1), 133–157.

Longhi, S. (2014). Cultural diversity and subjective well-being. *IZA Journal of Migration, 3*(1), 1–19.

Nee, V. (1992). Organizational dynamics of market transition: Hybrid forms, property rights, and mixed economy in China. *Administrative Science Quarterly, 37*(1), 1–27. https://doi.org/10.2307/2393531.

Paradies, Y. (2006). A systematic review of empirical research on self-reported racism and health. *International Journal of Epidemiology, 35*(4), 888–901.

Portela, M., Neira, I., & del Mar Salinas-Jiménez, M. (2013). Social capital and subjective wellbeing in Europe: A new approach on social capital. *Social Indicators Research, 114*(2), 493–511.

Safi, M. (2009). Immigrants' life satisfaction in Europe: Between assimilation and discrimination. *European Sociological Review, 26*(2), 159–176.

Stangor, C., Swim, J. K., Sechrist, G. B., Decoster, J., Van Allen, K. L., & Ottenbreit, A. (2003). Ask, answer, and announce: Three stages in perceiving and responding to discrimination. *European Review of Social Psychology, 14*(1), 277–311.

Verkuyten, M. (2008). Life satisfaction among ethnic minorities: The role of discrimination and group identification. *Social Indicators Research, 89*(3), 391–404.

Walder, A. G. (1995). Local governments as industrial firms: An organizational analysis of China's transitional economy. *American Journal of Sociology, 101*(2), 263–301. https://doi.org/10.2307/2782429.

Waldron, S. (2010). Measuring subjective wellbeing in the UK (*UK Office for National Statistics Working Paper September 2010*).

Wang, Z.-H., Zeng, H.-L., Wei, Y.-M., & Zhang, Y.-X. (2012). Regional total factor energy efficiency: An empirical analysis of industrial sector in China. *Applied Energy, 97,* 115–123. https://doi.org/10.1016/j.apenergy.2011.12.071.

Williams, D. R., Neighbors, H. W., & Jackson, J. S. (2003). Racial/ethnic discrimination and health: Findings from community studies. *American Journal of Public Health, 93*(2), 200–208. https://doi.org/10.2105/AJPH.93.2.200.

Yip, W., Subramanian, S. V., Mitchell, A. D., Lee, D. T. S., Wang, J., & Kawachi, I. (2007). Does social capital enhance health and well-being? Evidence from rural China. *Social Science and Medicine, 64*(1), 35–49. https://doi.org/10.1016/j.socscimed.2006.08.027.

Zhigang, L., & Shunfeng, S. (2006). Rural–urban migration and wage determination: The case of Tianjin, China. *China Economic Review, 17*(3), 337–345.

# 9

# Witchcraft Accusations and the Social Exclusion of the Elderly in Northern Ghana: Understanding How Cultural Discourses and Practices Affect the Wellbeing of the Elderly

Matthew Gmalifo Mabefam and Samuelson Appau

## 1 Introduction

In popular discourse and academic discussion alike, it is sometimes suggested that old age in various African and other 'non-Western' societies does not carry the negative connotations of 'decrepit', 'decaying', 'worn out' and 'senile'. The term 'old', it is claimed, engenders positive feelings. Old age is regarded as a stage of life in which people reach their full potential, since they have acquired wisdom and experience and are able to guide the young to success in life. The old are therefore respected

M. G. Mabefam (✉)
Department of Anthropology and Development Studies, University of Melbourne, Parkville, VIC, Australia
e-mail: matthewgmalifo.mabefam@unimelb.edu.au

S. Appau
School of Economics, Finance and Marketing, RMIT University, Melbourne, VIC, Australia
e-mail: samuelson.appau@rmit.edu.au



S. Awaworyi Churchill et al. (eds.), *Measuring, Understanding and Improving Wellbeing Among Older People*,
https://doi.org/10.1007/978-981-15-2353-3_9

> and honoured, and enjoy considerable social and political power. (Van der Geest, 2002: 438)

The above quote underscores the critical role cultural discourse plays in determining what it means to be ‘old’ and how those of ‘old age’ are perceived and treated in any culture. In Ghana, this quote can be said to be true in one breadth and not true in another. First, to what extent is Van der Geest right?

In many communities in Ghana, the elderly are considered the wisest people, are revered and held in high esteem. They perform inimitable roles in ensuring that the transference and continuation of cultural practices are protected and hence are seen as the embodiment of the cultural texts of societies. This gives the elderly culturally legitimate power to manage, inform, teach or otherwise control cultural information that informs discourses and socialization in their communities. For example, during festive occasions such as funerals, naming, marriage and ceremonies, the elderly are often called upon to take charge in dispensing the appropriate rituals and rites of passage that need to be followed. The Ghanaian culture also prescribes a reciprocal duty of care between the elderly and their families as well as communities (Crampton, 2013). Most Ghanaians accept that they have a responsibility to take care of their elderly parents when they are in need, like their parents took care of them when they were young and needy (Crampton, 2013). For many local Ghanaians, even after death, the elderly pass on as ancestors on whom the living call for protection, counsel and guidance. To be old is an indication that one has lived a worthy and fulfilled life and is therefore worth celebrating. In this regard, therefore, Van der Geest (2002) is right that old age, with all its commensurate cultural and symbolic capital, is a milieu of happiness and veneration. But this is only half the story.

Despite the veneration and support for the elderly, the other side of the coin reveals that in many other cases, the elderly are also looked down upon by a certain section of their communities (Crampton, 2013: 199; Van der Geest, 2002: 437). Thus, the veneration and care they receive are paradoxically accompanied by resentment and mistreatment by their own families and communities. This paradox seemed apparent to Van der Geest too when she wrote of an informant, ‘at the start he [the informant] pointed out that old people are respected and loved, then he suggested that people dislike them and resent their age'. Why this paradox within the same cultural discourse, and why the resentment of the elderly? The purpose of this chapter is to problematize one source of resentment towards the elderly—witchcraft—and its consequence on their wellbeing. As we show later, many in Ghana believe that witchcraft—the possession of evil spiritual capabilities believed to be often misused to harm others—is mostly possessed and used by the elderly (women) against other people. It is this ageism and feminization of witchcraft that we specifically problematize here. Based on ethnographic data from northern Ghana, we examine the role of witchcraft and how it contributes to the maltreatment of the elderly by banishing them from their natal and marital homes.

For the field research that informed this chapter, the first author stayed in Gnani community in northern Ghana, one of the communities where accused witches who have been banished from their communities reside. There are currently six witch camps in northern Ghana. A witch camp serves three basic purposes: (1) verification of people accused of witchcraft to confirm their innocence or guilt, (2) cleansing of the powers of confirmed witches, and (3) providing residence for confirmed and cleansed witches. First, when a person is accused of witchcraft, such accusations need to be verified in a witch camp, and after which the accused could be cleared of the accusation or found guilty. A person accused of witchcraft is presumed to be a witch until he/she goes through a ceremony conducted to confirm or refute an allegation against an accused. Verification is currently done in all the witch camp communities in northern Ghana.

If a person is confirmed to be a witch, he or she is spiritually cleansed by going through a ritual undertaken by the shrine priest. The spiritually cleansed witch is then allowed to return home after performing the ritual, if they choose to. However, the available evidence showed that most accused and spiritually cleansed witches were compelled to or preferred to stay in the camps rather than return home. ActionAid Ghana (2008) found that spiritually cleansed witches in the camp stayed because they risked being killed, lynched and discriminated against if they returned to their community. Every person living in any of the witch camps as an alleged witch initially went there (first and foremost) to find out whether he/she had the powers of a witch.

For the ethnographic data collection, the first author stayed in the Ghanaian witch camp for ten months (May 2016–February 2017) and interviewed 68 people, involving many face-to-face individual interviews and two focus group discussions. The research participants were diverse including government, NGO, officials and local leadership as well as accused witches (both men and women). In the following sections, we delve into the phenomenon of witchcraft in Ghana and Africa and how it mostly affects the elderly. This is followed by our findings where we unpack the influencing factors and the effects of witchcraft accusation against the elderly on their wellbeing. We conclude with the paradox of regulating and controlling witchcraft beliefs and practices.

## 2 Witchcraft in Ghana and Africa

Like other belief systems, the prevalence of witchcraft and its concomitant effects have attracted sustained scholarship over decades. Within different periods, people accused of witchcraft have been persecuted, convicted and possibly evicted and excluded from their natal or marital societies (see Baba, 2013; Comaroff & Comaroff, 2000, 1999; Mabefam, 2019; Monter, 2010; Wolfe, 1997). For example, in early Europe, it has been estimated that between 35,000 and 100,000 accused witches were executed between 1450 and 1750 (Gaskill, 2010; Monter, 2010; Wolfe, 1997). The cruelty of such persecutions—a scar on the history of humanity—is continuously revisited by scholars across many academic disciplines including history, anthropology, sociology and theology. The continued relevance of these studies betrays the persistence of the rather inhuman treatments meted out to the mostly elderly people who have been accused as witches.

A review of extensive body of scholarship on witchcraft shows that there is no single meaning of witchcraft. It is therefore important that witchcraft is understood in the specific context in which it arises. For example, while Evans-Pritchard (1937) argues that various practices and symbolism are associated with witchcraft, the essential component is that it is 'lived' and embedded in every aspect of life; it is not necessarily objectified and discussed. In his famous account, *Witchcraft, Oracles and Magic Among the Azande*, he reports that witchcraft is ubiquitous among the Azande people of Sudan and acts as an explanatory cause for misfortune. Like in Azande society, in Ghana, we found that witchcraft is discursively prevalent in the everyday life; it is something everyone seems to have a deep sense of knowledge about. Conversations around it are quite frequent.

Despite witchcraft being studied widely in Africa, the notion that it is aligned to a lack of development or that it is non-modern has been articulated by some scholars (Parrinder, 1958). Nonetheless, some recent scholarship has challenged the non-modern or primitive idea of witchcraft, as missionaries and colonialists have portrayed it (see Comaroff & Comaroff, 1999, 2000; Geschiere, 1997; Onyinah, 2002). For example, Onyinah (2002) discounts the idea of primitivism associated with witchcraft and even describes Parrinder, a professor of comparative religion at King's College, London, and a Methodist minister, as 'a false prophet' who in 1958 proclaimed that witchcraft was backward and superstitious and would fade away with 'enlightened religion, education, medicine and better social and racial conditions' among Africans (p. 108). Parrinder's proposition was not an isolated case but followed an established scholarly trajectory that constructed societies in Africa as backward and unable to rationalize things through scientific modes of explanation (see Mair, 1969: 335). We suppose Parrinder meant that if Africans assimilate Christianity, formal education, modern medicine, and improved social conditions and other elements, then witchcraft would disappear.

However, from the colonial period until contemporary times, the available evidence shows that most of the population in African societies have converted to Christianity, have experienced formal education, used biomedical medicine and have seen advances in their general development. Yet, the belief in and the practice of witchcraft do not appear to have decreased. An example presented by Onyinah discounts Parrinder's proposition, finding that 100% of participants surveyed in 1999, and who had a first degree, asserted that witchcraft existed (2002: 118).

According to Byrne (2011: 1), witchcraft belief is 'ingrained in popular mentality and informs and underscores social, political and cultural beliefs and practices'. In addition, Mavhungu (2012: 1) adds that 'even as Africa is increasingly urbanizing and Africans are embracing modern day technological advancement, there is a prevailing common belief across the continent that there are people who can secretly use supernatural power to harm others or help themselves at the expense of others…'. These ongoing discussions ensure that those concerned with witchcraft have an impetus to rethink what it means and how it affects people, especially within development practices

In Ghana, as in many other societies, witchcraft beliefs and practices are an important aspect of social and spiritual life. Witchcraft is embedded in everyday life and each individual is confronted daily by it in one way or another. Although there is no empirical evidence of the prevalence of witchcraft in Ghana, ActionAid Ghana (2008) has estimated that about 90% of Ghanaians believe that witchcraft exists and perceive it to have affected their lives in some way. Despite growing public debate and an emergent, although small, class that proclaims they do not believe in it, or are at least beginning to challenge this belief (see Onyinah, 2002: 118), for most people, witchcraft is an all-encompassing aspect of life.

In the Ghanaian societies, witchcraft is socially constructed. It is not a neutral term and thus comes with connotations of the constructor, the religious leanings, the culture and the environment within which both the accuser and accused are located. All religious people in Ghana commonly see witchcraft is malicious in nature, *whether real or imagined.* The harmful effects of witchcraft therefore have to be matched with powerful religious practices that can prevent such harm (Schubert and Mabefam), forthcoming. Thus, many churches in Ghana see it as moral obligation to 'deal' with accused witches in a way that brings justice to their victims, and save others from potential witchcraft attack.

# 3 Old and Wicked: Witchcraft Accusations Against the Elderly

> In Ghana, older women may be marginalized, abused, and even killed as witches. Media accounts imply this is common practice, mainly through stories of "witches camps" to which the accused may flee. (Crampton, 2013: 199)

Similar to other contexts in Africa, the elderly are mostly accused of witchcraft in Ghana.

The issue of age being used as a mark of accusing people of witchcraft in Africa is well documented (see Eboiyehi, 2017; HelpAge International, 2010; Machangu, 2015; Miguel, 2005). For example, Miguel (2005) found that 3072 accused witches were killed in Sukumaland, Tanzania, from 1970 to 1988. Out of these, about 80% of the victims were elderly women. Miguel argues that elderly women serve as scapegoats for the communities in Tanzania and are rejected in times of economic crisis and natural disasters. They are accused of being responsible for such acts. Machangu's (2015) study in the Fipa of Sumbawanga district of Tanzania between 1961 and 2010 found that the area was among the five top areas noted for the killing of elderly women based on witchcraft accusations. This is probably why Crampton (2013: 199) labelled witchcraft as an 'old woman's problem'.

In Ghana, several studies have found that accused witches are often elderly, who are marginalized, abused and even killed (Crampton, 2013; Van der Geest, 2002). Our fieldwork in Gnani witch camp showed that majority of people who were accused and banished from their communities and now residing in Gnani were also mostly elderly women. This chapter discusses the prevalence of witchcraft accusation against the elderly in Ghana as a problematic cultural discourse and examines its consequence on the wellbeing of the elderly. In our research, we were interested in examining the source of witchcraft allegation, confrontation and final eviction from the community to understand if there were any systematic trends in the accusation practices.

Based on our ethnographic data, in the following sections, we discuss three emerging themes towards the chapter's objectives. First, we examine witchcraft accusation as rooted in violence and structural tensions in Ghanaian society, resulting from economic polarities and intergenerational contestations of power. Secondly, we discuss witchcraft confirmation and its role in the social displacement of people accused of witchcraft. Thirdly, we unpack the paradoxical role of witch camps and the paradoxical negotiation of status and identity by the displaced elderly person living in the witch camps. We conclude with discussions on the politics of witchcraft accusation in Ghana.

## 4 Witchcraft Accusations as Manifestations of Structural Tensions

### 4.1 Poverty and Economic Polarities

A key explanation for the persistence of witchcraft is economic inequality. In contexts of economic crisis or inequality, often older people are mostly accused of using witchcraft to unduly amass wealth and/or using witchcraft destroy the wealth of others (Ashforth, 1998; Comaroff & Comaroff, 1999; Geschiere, 1997; Jensen & Buur, 2004). In our research, we found that it was mostly poor older women who are more likely to be accused of using witchcraft to destroy the wealth of more successful people in the community. This is because those who are relatively successful fear that the poor are jealous and envious of them. Thus, poor old people—who are social failures because the elderly are culturally expected to have acquired more material wealth over time—are deeply suspected to be more likely to use their spiritual knowledge as witchcraft to destroy the wealth of relatively younger successful people in the community. They, therefore, also resort to using witchcraft accusation to remove the poor elderly from their community. Thus, as an extension of prior research, we argue that economically motivated accusations against the elderly are a cultural rebuke against their poverty, relative to their lived opportunities.

But this has a serious impact on the economic and material wellbeing of the already poor elderly women who are accused of witchcraft as they are forcefully removed from their communities without being allowed to take along any of their possessions. They also lose access to land or any other property they had in the community. Although it might be too simplistic to assert that poverty is the main cause of witchcraft in Ghana, we identified that the majority of people found in the witch camps are very poor, deprived of possessions or property that they may have acquired throughout their lives in their natal communities prior to their accusation and banishment.

## 4.2 Inter-Generational Contestations of Power

The cultural and symbolic capital possessed by the elderly makes them repositories of power in their communities that they exercise over others. And this power can be contested where the subjects of the power desire same power or resent that power. As Comaroff and Comaroff (1999) have eloquently articulated, in the post-colonial polity in sub-Saharan Africa, colonial legacies set in motion a contestation of power between tradition and modernity in which the modern—the discursive moniker of colonial and post-colonial rhetoric—has sought to usurp power from tradition. Here, the old ways and structures of tradition, embodied by the elderly, are posited as antithetical to that which is modern, young and new.

In our research, we found that such contestations of power are also manifest in what we observed as trends of the youth in the community accusing the elderly of witchcraft and displacing them physically from their homes and symbolically from their abodes of power. We found that although accusers could be anyone in the community, the youth were main actors, often denoted as 'they' by the accused witches in interviews. We often hear statements such as these from the accused witches: 'the child was sick, and *they* said I was the cause of it', 'someone died, and *they* said it was me', among others. On the one hand, the use of *they* here in reference to the youth mob that carry out accusation and eviction reveals the necessary collectivization of individuals that motivates and legitimizes a successful contestation of power. On the other hand, it also reveals the successful de-identification and de-personalization of agency that is intended and results from collective mob actions of usurpation and subversion (Thompson, 1971; see also de Certeau, 1984). Here, *they* is everyone and no one.

The case of N-yajah, an elderly man [75] accused and although present in the community but socially excluded, is an important case for a useful illustration. For a long time, it was rumoured in the community that he was a wizard, but no one had gathered courage to accuse and evict him from the community. This is because he held an important position in the community. He was the eldest (Unikpel) of his community and had many sons to support him, thus potentially discouraging any individual to accuse their father as a wizard. Eventually, a very successful young man who was N-yajah's extended family member died suddenly and it was alleged that N-yajah's witchcraft was responsible. There was a lot of tension in the community, but no one attempted to confront N-yajah. As other relatives from the other communities attended the funeral and rumours of the allegation against N-yajah spread, the youth held a meeting and decided that they needed to confront N-yajah. The youth discussed that if *they* did it as a group, it would be difficult for any one of them to be held to account for it through further bewitching by N-yajah, thus burying individual responsibility and agency in the collective.

Since it was difficult for them to confront him as a result of his position and power, *they* mobilized the community and insisted they had to take all every male household head in the community to a witch camp for verification to determine who had used witchcraft to cause the young man's death. *They* hired a car and conveyed all the household heads to the Gnani witch camp community. After the verification ceremony, N-yajah was confirmed as a wizard but refused to stay in the camp. This created a sour relationship between him and other members of the community who have socially excluded him. Apart from his children and wife, the rest of the community has cut links with him and refuse to interact with him since his return to the community. Whenever he joins other members of the community who might be seated together at any point, they leave one after the other until he is left seated alone. This experience is horrible and isolating for someone who once was seen as the most powerful and respected person in the community due to his age and position.

The actions of the youth were because *they* constantly felt that they are the major targets of such malicious attacks from witches and hence could not be aloof. Through such self-victimization, the youth erect a boundary between the elderly as the oppressors and *they* as the oppressed, moralizing their collective action to contest and remove the oppression. Regardless of the truth in this perception, it is deeply felt and hence everywhere in the northern Ghana, the youth have always played a key role in banishing, committing violence or threat of violence towards accused witches. The consequences of these are severe for the elderly. They lose their social connections and as well living in constant fear. They probably do not know when next there will be any form of violence towards them.

## 5 Witchcraft Confirmation and the Violence of Social Displacement

> When we got home (to mean when they returned home after the verification ritual in Gnani), he [the accuser] told the community that I was confirmed as a witch. The youth in the village started insulting, backbiting and shaming me. My son, who was the assemblyman (opinion leader) of the community, did not take it kindly with the youth. My son was preparing to visit another village when the youth threatened to kill him. When he entered his room to dress up for the journey, the youth mobilized themselves and surrounded him. They said they wanted to kill my son and kill me too. This was because he was very protective of me. How can someone be in his house and you surround the house to kill him? Will anyone in his/her right senses allow himself to be killed under such a circumstance? My son thought it was a joke. But before he realized, they wanted to kill him. One came with a cutlass and the other with a pestle. It was at that time that my son took his gun and started shooting at them. He killed two of the young men and wounded the third one. My home village was not safe for me and hence why I returned to the camp. (Wapu [age-70], 2016)

As we can surmise from the above narrative vignette provided by an accused elderly woman [70 years], the journey to the witch camp is not a kind removal of the accused from their communities, but a violent displacement. In the absence of the state's protection or any effective regulatory control, the accused person—and their family—experiences a painful transition that opens them up to violence, abuse, conflict and even death, as we can see from the above narrative.

It appears that regardless of the outcome of the verification ritual, accused persons are earmarked for social displacement and violence. In this particular case, although the accused claimed that she is not a witch and that the verification ritual supported her claim, the accuser who accompanied her to the camp provided a contrary claim. Due to the perception that witches are malicious, people are more likely to believe the narrative of the accuser more than the accused after the ritual. We cannot also discount the imbalance of the probability in this community to accept a young man's accusation against an elderly woman's denial. This is because the accused (elderly woman) is already seen as a threat to the survival of people in the community and thus any attempt to remove the person from the community will be celebrated.

Witchcraft confrontations in most instances have the potential threat of violence or violence itself occurring. Though the accused witch was not killed in this instance, she lives within fear for her life, that of her son and trauma after witnessing the casualties in the community as a result of her accusation and confrontation. At the time of fieldwork, her son had been charged with murder and was in jail. The criminal department of the Ghana Police Service told us that they were handling the case purely as a criminal one. The inherent issue of violence towards accused witches and others was common in the narratives of other accused witches.

Similar evidence of the tragic experience that deeply shatters the physical, psychological and emotional wellbeing of the elderly accused of witchcraft has been noted elsewhere in Africa. For example, in some places, elderly people accused of witchcraft are gruesomely murdered by angry mobs (Comaroff & Comaroff, 1999, 2000; Mavhungu, 2012). Others, according to local narratives, have their powers exorcized by Christian pastors, Islamic imams or fetish/shrine priests by going through shameful practices. While the acts of mob injustice usually take place within the community or its peripherals, exorcism as a way of neutralizing a witch's powers can take place either in the same community or at a distance, after which the person is made to return home (see Onyinah, 2002; Parish, 1999).

Furthermore, accusing and removing people from their communities as accused witches deny them the opportunity to be socially, economically and politically connected with resources in their home communities. Eviction is for life and any attempt to return home is done at great risk. The place of self in relationship to the larger society, especially people the accused have known, become truncated leading to loneliness, abandonment, with both psychological and physical ramifications both from themselves and people who depended on them. Their sense of entitlement to their property is always curtailed leading them to a more impoverished lifestyle in already poor areas of Ghana.

## 6 The Paradox of Witch Camps and the Continued Negotiation of Status and Identity After Displacement

### 6.1 The Paradox of Witch Camps

When elderly people are accused of witchcraft and displaced from their homes, status, identity and social ties in their communities, they find a home in witch camps like the one in Gnani. Each of the seven witch camps has a unique history. But for this chapter, we focus on that of Gnani where our study was based. The Gnani community is one of the oldest communities in the Yendi municipality. According to some authors, the Gnani witch camp started as a spiritual village meant to protect people in the community and its environs (ActionAid, 2008; Baba, 2013; Tayo, 2010). Stephen Tayo (2010) reported that the first settlers of the community, Jabaal, through *tiboar* (the process of divination) found there was a powerful fetish symbolized by a stone and laid in the bush. However, because most of these accounts were oral, it is difficult to learn the exact dates. Jabaal took the opportunity to locate the stone which had these spiritual powers of protection. Jabaal built a room around the stone and it became a shrine that people visited for testing and verification of whether they possessed the spirit of witchcraft.

However, the place became a witch camp when two old women, who were accused of witchcraft by their community members, were ostracized and sent to the shrine built by Jabaal in Gnani, never to return. Initially, the Uwadaan (shrine priest) was scared about the arrival of the two old women into his house at night, but he accommodated them for the night anyway. The next morning, he enquired about their mission. They told him that they were chased out of their communities because of witchcraft allegations. He quickly took them to the shrine, made a sacrifice, prepared some concoctions for them to drink, satisfied that they had been spiritually pacified and later asked them to stay if they had no place to go. This process is necessary because for the accused witches to be allowed to stay, the community must be assured that they are clean and cannot harm them. Residing in Gnani without undertaking these rituals meant that harm would be possible if they were actually witches.

According to Tayo (2010), in no time, people heard about the generosity of the Uwadaan and the new life of the two accused witches. Following their experience, others who were accused of witchcraft in their communities, for fear of being violated and/or called for verification and purification, fled to Gnani for refuge. Their communities rejected them no matter the outcome. The accused witches found Gnani accommodating and so remained there. During my interaction with the Uwadaan, he did acknowledge that they do not force people to stay in the camp after the pacifications are completed. However, because of the expulsion of accused witches from their home communities, almost all those accused of witchcraft preferred to stay. The first author spoke with the only Dagomba man living in the community as an accused wizard and he told him that he 'preferred to live in Gnani because you do not run into trouble with anyone there. You live a peaceful life with your neighbours in Gnani. No one accuses you of being a witch'. This among other reasons may account for why indigenes dislike the name 'witch camp' as a place of abuse and suffering. They think rather that they are offering a welfare service, a second chance at belonging, to people banished from their own communities.

But despite its very important function as place where displaced accused witches can restart life, the very existence of witch camps is in itself a paradox for two related reasons. First, the very existence of a place for accused witches to reside provides both legitimation and structure for the displacement of the elderly on the bases of witchcraft. We cannot say for sure that in the absence of the witch camps, displacement would stop, or the accusations would end. On the contrary, it is very much possible that the displacement would persist, and displaced elderly people might be caught in a limbo, living under worse circumstances. But the presence of the witch camps also plays a key role in the structuration of the violence of witchcraft accusation and displacement by providing a structural endpoint for the practice.

Secondly, we found that accused witches are not allowed to reside in the witch camp until certain rituals are performed to purify them of the witchcraft if they were found guilty or prevent them from acquiring one if they did not already possess witchcraft. This is a condition for all the accused elderly people who were admitted to the camp. But this very condition, rather than erase, sustains and perpetuates the belief in witchcraft, for which reason the camp exists in the first place. Thus, witch camps, in name and in practice, function as spaces where witchcraft is by intent nullified, but by effect made perpetually salient for all in the Ghanaian society. And this paradox goes on to negatively affect the care, identity, status and overall wellbeing of the elderly who have been accused and banished from their communities to the camps.

## 6.2 Identity and Status Negotiation for the Accused Elderly in Witch Camps

As we noted earlier, in the Ghanaian society, due to the reciprocal duty of care between elderly parents and their adult children, it is usually considered an act of ungratefulness to send your aged parent away to be taken care of by non-relatives. Thus, first it is inappropriate in the Ghanaian caring philosophy to send elderly relatives to witch camp communities for others to take care of them. Second, there are no professional caregivers or nurses in the various camps to attend to the needs of the elderly. Third, the elderly in the various witch camps are always forcibly evicted from their communities with little or no ties at all with their kinship members. It appears that they are basically disposed of by society, using witchcraft as an excuse, probably with the assumption that they have outlived their usefulness. Doing so therefore calls into question the general Ghanaian caring philosophy. But what is paramount here is how the identities of the displaced accused witches are constantly being negotiated within witch camp communities and the broader Ghanaian society.

Residents of the Gnani community often refer to accused witches as *tipinikpir* (elderly women) or *tiyatiib* (our grandmothers) rather than as witches. This is because after the purification ritual, they are no longer seen as witches. But this label is specifically only used for the accused elderly women and is loaded with stigma. For example, during a mass service at the Roman Catholic Church where the majority of the accused witches worshipped, the *ugbagmari* (secretary) of the church made an announcement that clarified how accused witches are referred to in the Gnani community. This was captured vividly by the *ugbagmari* as '*tiya do church kan, tipinikpir ti bi tiche na kpa nkuun lipaal*' ('the elderly women among us have a meeting immediately after church service outside'). Within the context of the community, it is understood that the *tipinikpir* does not necessarily refer to all elderly women in the church. The term only refers to elderly women who are accused and brought into the community as witches. The *Utindaan (Landowner)* similarly told me that he is in charge of taking care of '*tinatiib ni tiyaatiib bin bi n-che na*' ('our mothers and grandmothers residing in his community') when referring to the accused witches.

But referring to only the accused witches as *tipinikpir* (elderly women) in Gnani also comes with its own challenges. It takes on a pejorative meaning that stigmatizes the accused elderly women as second-class citizens of the community. The label serves as a point of differentiation between the accused and non-accused elderly women in the community. The term *bipinikpiib* (referring to elderly women) would have been the most appropriate as it is non-pejorative and has an associated dignity. That is, however, not the case. Conversations with several of the accused witches in Gnani revealed that none of them prefer to be called witches, though they do not resist any of the other labels discussed above. Although they are aware of their second-class citizen status in the Gnani witch camp, it appears they preferred its paradox to the painful memories of their former homes and communities. They continue to live with the scars of this pain on their happiness and wellbeing.

We found from our research that once the elderly are accused of witchcraft, regardless of where they live afterwards—whether in their original communities or at the witch camp—they are stripped of their pre-accusation dignity and considered second-class citizens. They are constantly negotiating for a status of recognition and acceptance, at least one with dignity. The difference though in the Gnani witch camp is that they are not perceived as evil and malicious, but rather as a vulnerable group of people who are in need of help. People then view them with pity and most often patronize them. Thus, the status of an accused witch is always being negotiated by other people, and themselves, which leads the accused to a constancy of becoming and unbecoming, always 'betwixt and between' (Turner, 1967) acceptance and rejection, happiness and pain, a sort of perpetual liminality.

## 7 Exorcizing the Exorcist: The Passivity of Controlling Witchcraft in Ghana

Perhaps a glaring issue that we have not yet addressed is the role of the state in all of this. For a long time, controlling or ending witchcraft has become a burning issue with polarized positions. While the nation-state authorities have the overall governance of the entire Ghanaian society, one key area it has faced challenges with is the issue of witchcraft. The fundamental issue at stake here is that witchcraft is considered part of the cultural discourse of the Ghanaian people, and yet the state's position is that there is no such thing as witchcraft. This potentially brings about a dilemma; how do you control something that does not exist? The state, caught in this quagmire, has only passively engaged with the issue of witchcraft beyond reactionary measures (Mabefam, 2019). We recall the case of the assemblyman who was charged for murder and is currently in prison as evidence of the state's passivity on witchcraft matters. While the reasons for the murder were based on his mother being accused of witchcraft and occurring in the process of him trying to defend the mother against lynching by her accusers, it appears the state is superficially dealing with only the murder part, thus overlooking the main cause of the problem.

The state is represented by institutions and individuals who have the responsibility to act on its behalf. However, the default position of most of these professional individuals who act on behalf of the state with the legal logic that there is no witchcraft themselves is first and foremost cultural actors. As cultural texts of their societies, they believe in witchcraft and yet are supposed to implement a law that says there is no witchcraft. This is contradictory and came out clearly while engaging with state officials in Ghana. They would usually ask 'are you asking for my personal position or as an officer of the state?' The response to our questions even if same brought about different responses and yet from the same person. This is another layer of passivity by the state represented by its officials. This is because of these officials although they may feel obliged to protect the accused, innately, they might hold the view that indeed, they are witches and their actions are reprehensible.

Drawing from the thesis of non-existence of witchcraft, the state, over the years, has considered that closing down witch camps which seem to be a physical manifestation of witchcraft in Ghana could be useful. And yet, if one were to look keenly at the outcomes of this policy over the years, it is quite disappointing on many fronts. We use the case of Bunyasi witch camp which was closed down in 2014 to illustrate our point. It has been noted that some accused witches reconvened in other camps where people are more willing to accept them after their families or communities rejected them (Igwe, 2016). An accused witch relayed that she would resist any attempt to get her back home: 'If they ask me to come back home, I won't go. Why will I go back home? Now my name has been destroyed. I cannot erase the label I have acquired'. This is due to the constant discrimination, risk of violence and exclusion of people who are accused of witchcraft in their communities. The state is not often available to provide protection when they return home.

What becomes of their lives in a situation that people often consciously or unconsciously discriminate against accused witches regardless of the state control mechanisms?

Various religious institutions in Ghana, especially Christian churches, often hold the view that witchcraft is evil. As a result, they pray towards controlling and destroying witchcraft. Nonetheless, witchcraft as we suggest does not seem to disappear. During the research, we interviewed a religious cleric about witchcraft and witches and he said that they as priests could exorcize witchcraft and would have liked it if the accused witches were brought to them. So although the church believes it can and seeks to control witchcraft, in part, their beliefs rather legitimize the existence and effect of witchcraft, thereby paradoxically rooting the relevance of witchcraft in place. But even the priest said that the church would send the accused witches back to their home community after exorcizing the witchcraft. The priest was either blind to or taking for granted that the accused witches are no longer safe in their home communities.

It is for these reasons that the witch camp community becomes relevant. This is because if the lives of accused witches are threatened in their home environment and yet they are unable to settle in different communities because of the label, where else will they go? In this instance, the witch camp becomes a refuge for people rejected by their communities. It is in this sense that although the paradoxical existence of witch camps is criticized, they play a functional role in the absence of government and society's ability to protect individuals who are accused of witchcraft.

In summary, the state's policy attempt to close down witch camps has not been successful. This is because there is a dissonance between state policy and local realities. The governance of witchcraft by the state seems to be an encroachment on cultural sovereignty. The legal antecedent of state policy is not rooted in the cultural realities of the communities and hence local people are more tilted to respect the cultural leaders as compared to state directives at the local level, and that is the clear case of witchcraft in Ghana.

# 8 Conclusion

Our ethnographic research in northern Ghana reveals a problematic aspect of cultural discourse and practices that leads to the ill-treatment and displacement of mostly elderly (women). On the one hand, the Ghanaian culture venerates the elderly as wise custodians of secular and spiritual knowledge, and tradition. On the other hand, their embodiment of status, power and tradition is resented by other sections of the society. We found that in spite of the numerous expertise the elderly possess, their possession of spiritual knowledge, which is believed can be used to good and malicious outcomes—where it is termed as witchcraft—is employed as weapon of discrimination against them. On this note, the elderly who are accused of witchcraft are believed to use their spiritual knowledge to bewitch and harm others in society and prevent people from succeeding in life, be it economic, education, political, social and even family.

In relation to the above, we demonstrated through this chapter that cultural belief systems have a significant impact on the wellbeing of the elderly in Ghana. Various religions in Ghana prescribe mechanism to determine who a witch is, through either public or private rituals. A confirmation of one as a witch through these ritualistic activities comes with consequences, including eviction from their own societies, discrimination, violence and abuse—both physical and psychological. In terms of economic life, they become poorer as they are limited in opportunities and access to economic resources.

The government of Ghana and other non-state actors over the years have tried to make policies and interventions to assist the accused and manage witchcraft in Ghana. While some good outcomes emerged from these interventions such as meeting the immediate needs of the elderly accused witches, in most of the instances, we argued that such interventions are misdirected and misplaced. For example, the state's policy of wanting to close down witch camp communities needs to be revisited. This is because, it has the potential of more negative implications for the wellbeing of the elderly who are forced to return to communities that do not want them, and yet the state is not present to ensure their security. While the state denies the existence of witchcraft, social response to people accused of witchcraft is real and the state must actively criminalize these acts. Admittedly, the discourse on witchcraft and its effect on the wellbeing of the elderly are indeed a wicked problem; that is, it is a problem difficult to contain and manage. But the reward for addressing it is happiness and a better quality of life, a universal human right, for the elderly—and for us all, because we will all get old. And for this, we must try, whatever it takes.

## References

Ashforth, A. (1998). *Witchcraft, violence, and democracy in the New South Africa* [Sorcellerie, violence et démocratie dans la Nouvelle Afrique du Sud]. Cahiers d'études Africaines, 505–532.

Baba, I. M. (2013). *Life in a witch camp. Experiences of residents in the Gnani Witch Camp in Ghana* (Master's thesis, The University of Bergen).

Byrne, C. (2011). Hunting the vulnerable: Witchcraft and the law in Malawi. *Consultancy Africa Intelligence, 16.*

Comaroff, J., & Comaroff, J. L. (1999). Occult economies and the violence of abstraction: Notes from the South African postcolony. *American Ethnologist, 26*(2), 279–303.

Comaroff, J., & Comaroff, J. L. (2000). Millennial capitalism: First thoughts on a second coming. *Public Culture, 12*(2), 291–343.

Crampton, A. (2013). No peace in the house: Witchcraft accusations as an "old woman's problem" in Ghana. *Anthropology & Aging Quarterly, 34*(2), 199–212.

De Certeau, M. (1984). *The practice of everyday life translated by Steven Rendall.* Berkeley and Los Angeles: University of California Press.

Eboiyehi, F. A. (2017). Convicted without evidence: Elderly women and witchcraft accusations in contemporary Nigeria. *Journal of International Women's Studies, 18*(4), 247–265.

Evans-Pritchard, E. E. (1937). *Witchcraft, oracles and magic among the Azande.* Oxford: The Clarendon Press.

Gaskill, M. (2010). *Witchcraft: A very short introduction* (vol. 228). Oxford University Press.

Geschiere, P. (1997). *The modernity of witchcraft: Politics and the occult in post-colonial Africa.* Charlottesville and London: University of Virginia Press.

Ghana, Action Aid. (2008). *The state and condition of alleged witches in Northern Region of Ghana.* Accra: ActionAid Ghana.

HelpAge International. (HAI, 2010). *Discrimination against older women in Burkina Faso.* Parallel report submitted to the 47th session of the Committee on the Elimination of All Forms of Discrimination against Women (CEDAW) in relation to Burkina Faso's Sixth periodic report of States parties, CEDAW/C/BFA/6, October 2009.

Igwe, L. (2016). *Do not close down 'witch camps' in Northern Ghana.* Accessed from http://www.modernghana.com/news/713689/do-not-close-down-witch-camps-in-northern-ghana.html on the 5th of November 2016.

Jesen, S., & Buur, L. (2004). Everyday policing and the occult: Notions of witchcraft, crime and 'the people'. *African Studies, 63*(2), 193–211.

Mabefam, G. M. (2019). *Witchcraft and the paradox of development: Contesting the category of the non-modern.* Unpublished Ph.D. thesis submitted to the University of Melbourne.

Machangu, H. M. (2015). Vulnerability of elderly women to witchcraft accusations among the Fipa of Sumbawanga, 1961–2010. *Journal of International Women's Studies, 16* (2), 274–284.

Mair, L. (1969). *Witchcraft.* New York: McGraw-Hill Book Company.

Mavhungu, K. (2012). *Witchcraft in post-colonial Africa: Beliefs, techniques and containment strategies.* African Books Collective.

Miguel, E. (2005). Poverty and witch killing. *The Review of Economic Studies, 72*(4), 1153–1172.

Monter, W. (2010). *The scourge of demons: Possession, lust and witchcraft in a seventeenth-century Italian convent.* By Jeffrey R. Watt, *Journal of Interdisciplinary History 40,* 605–606.

Onyinah, O. (2002). Deliverance as a way of confronting witchcraft in modern Africa: Ghana as a case history. *Asian Journal of Pentecostal Studies, 5*(1), 107–134.

Parish, J. (1999). The dynamics of witchcraft and indigenous shrines among the Akan. *Africa, 69*(3), 426–447.

Parrinder, G. (1958). *Witchcraft, a critical study of the belief in witchcraft from the records of witch hunting in Europe yesterday and Africa today.* Harmondsworth: Penguin Books.

Schubert, V., & Mabefam, M. (Forthcoming). *A comparison of contemporary perceptions of witchcraft in the west and Africa.*

Tayo, S. (2010). *An analytical assessment of the Konkomba Belief in witchcraft and the institutionalised witchcraft at Gnani (Yendi Municipality): A challenge to Christianity.* Unpublished long essay. Cape Coast: University of Cape Coast.

Thompson, E. P. (1971). The moral economy of the English crowd in the eighteenth century. *Past & Present, 50*, 76–136.

Turner, V. (1967). Betwixt and between: The liminal period in rites of passage. In V. Turner (Ed.), *The Forest of Symbols* (93–111). Ithaca, NY: Cornell University Press.

Van der Geest, S. (2002). From wisdom to witchcraft: Ambivalence towards old age in rural Ghana. *Africa, 72*(3), 437–463.

Wolfe, M. (1997). *Changing identities in early modern France.* Duke University Press.

# 10

# Housing and Ageing Well

Sarah Sinclair, Ashton de Silva, Foula Kopanidis and Stuart Thomas

## 1 Introduction

The process of ageing is shaped by life experiences, individual health factors as well as social and environmental factors which can be influenced by where people live. Housing is recognised as one of the key domains of

S. Sinclair (✉) · A. de Silva · F. Kopanidis · S. Thomas
School of Economics, Finance and Marketing, RMIT University, Melbourne, VIC, Australia
e-mail: sarah.sinclair@rmit.edu.au

A. de Silva
e-mail: ashton.desilva@rmit.edu.au

F. Kopanidis
e-mail: foula.kopanidis@rmit.edu.au

S. Thomas
e-mail: stuart.thomas@rmit.edu.au



S. Awaworyi Churchill et al. (eds.), *Measuring, Understanding and Improving Wellbeing Among Older People*,
https://doi.org/10.1007/978-981-15-2353-3_10

community life that can influence the health and wellbeing of older people (World Health Organisation [WHO], 2007). The wellbeing implications of residential housing extend beyond the built environment of the home to include the broader context of access to outdoor spaces and buildings, transportation, social participation and inclusion, civic participation and employment, community interaction and support, and health services to name a few. The importance of residential housing in the development of promotion of healthy ageing cities is outlined in the global age friendly cities guide—where housing is considered as a facilitator of health ageing across dimensions of affordability, accessibility to services, housing design and construction, and access to family and friends (WHO, 2007). In Australia, the Victorian state government has signed the WHO's age-friendly declaration signally a commitment to the provision of housing that meet the WHO's essential age-friendly city features such as:

- available and affordable housing in safe areas that are close to services and the rest of the community, which caters to the needs of the frail and disabled
- sufficient and affordable home maintenance and support services
- well-constructed, weather-resistant building stock that provides safe and comfortable shelter
- interior spaces and level surfaces allowing freedom of movement in all rooms and passageways
- affordable and available home modification options and supplies based on providers' understanding of older people's uses and needs
- clean, well-maintained, secure public and commercial rental housing. (*Source* WHO, 2007)

Access to quality, well-designed housing is considered critical in supporting older people's changing health and social needs over time (Nordbakke & Schwanen, 2014). There is growing concern that Australian housing options are not future proofed for an ageing population and much of the housing stock does not have the flexibility to adapt to changing needs of occupants over the life cycle (McLaughlin & Mills, 2008).

The term "successful" ageing is traditionally defined as the avoidance of disability or illness, maintenance of mental and physical function and active social engagement, yet it is likely that longer lives will go along with years of both good and bad health. Tesch-Römer and Wahl (2017) suggest that "the concept of successful aging should be expanded to capture desirable living situations for those who grow old in good health *and* for those who grow old with care needs" (Tesch-Römer & Wahl, 2017: 311).

In this chapter, reflecting on the connections between housing and successful ageing for seniors with and without care needs, we focus on which residential housing attributes are considered central components of a senior's health and wellbeing. Framing residential housing within an ecological context, more specifically environmental gerontology, we examine residential housing in the day-to-day context of ageing individuals with an understanding that the physical environment of the home has also a social and cultural interpretation. By examining the mechanisms through which housing can impact on wellbeing outcomes of seniors, we develop a simple conceptual framework to explore the value of good home design in supporting successful ageing outcomes, and in doing so generate both private and social value.

The first section of the chapter will review housing preferences of older Australians. We then review the type of housing advocated in the literature as best serving the needs and preferences of older households. For example, housing designs with accessibility measures (such as level access, flush access, WC on ground level and sufficient circulation space) and locations that can support wellbeing outcomes across physical, social and psychological domains. Considering the barriers in the market to provision of this type of housing, we briefly examine disconnections between community aspirations and current practices in housing markets. We question if accessible housing (built to liveable housing guidelines) has merit good attributes and warrants a re-think in planning regulatory approaches to support the development of more suitable housing in the general housing stock.

## 2 Successful Ageing and Housing

There is growing policy interest in how to facilitate healthier old age and promote successful ageing. Yet there is contention in the literature on what attributes should be considered in a definition of successful ageing (Peel, Bartlett, & McClure, 2004). Biomedical theories focus on the absence or minimisation of disease, active physical and social engagement with life (Rowe & Kahn, 1997) while psychosocial approaches emphasise life satisfaction, social participation and functioning and psychological resources (Bowling & Iliffe, 2011).

Research that has examined older people's views on what defines successful ageing for them includes factors in addition to physical and mental health such as life satisfaction, having a sense of purpose, financial security, contribution to life, a sense of humour and spirituality (Bowling, 2008). What is evident is that successfully ageing needs to be viewed multidimensionally and that many of the domains of successful ageing are interconnected across physical, functional, cognitive, social and spiritual domains (Peel et al., 2004).

As part of the promotion of successful ageing, there is acknowledgement of the importance of the built environment in supporting ageing well objectives from a public health perspective (Srinivasan, O'Fallon, & Dearry, 2003). Population health outcomes are shaped by complex interactions between individuals and the physical and social environments in which they live, work and engage (Frochen & Pynoos, 2017). As people age, and needs continue to evolve, they can become more sensitive to their environments. Both academic (Lawton, 1990) and policy literature (AIHW, 2017) highlight the important role of accessible, supportive, home environments particularly for those older people at greater risk of frailty. Housing is a provider of shelter services and possibly capital in the formal provision of care services for its residents, but for homeowners it is also a stock of wealth, wealth that can be drawn down on to supplement income if needed over retirement.

Yet beyond the standard market value approach there is a paucity of research conceptualising how one might value the positive externalities of and social value implicit in "good" residential home design and locational attributes, as facilitators of an environment to age successfully in.

## 3 The Australian Demographic Trajectory and Implications for the Housing System

The number of people in Australia aged 65 years and over has increased from one in every seven people in 2011 (14%) to nearly one in every six people (16%) in 2016 (Australian Bureau of Statistics [ABS], 2018). Older Australians as a collective are a financially significant cohort, with 54% of the household wealth in Australia held by those aged over (Lourey, McLoughlin, & Taylor, 2016). A growing number of seniors with significant housing assets represent an influential consumption group. Yet an expanding senior population will also place pressure on publicly funded, age-related expenditures such as health and pensions (Kudrna, 2016). This budgetary pressure will increase the institutional expectation that older Australians should be responsible for planning, managing and paying for services where possible as they age, with means tested support from the public sector (Department of Health, 2017).

The extent of both public and private age-related expenditures will be dependent on how "well" people age, both physically and financially. Hence, there is growing policy and societal emphasis on "positive" and "active" ageing, with a focus on health and improved quality of life (Humpel, O'Loughlin, Wells, & Kendig, 2010) and concurrently, an interest in optimising private financial wellbeing, through financial literacy programmes (Worthington, 2013) and superannuation (Wang, Koo, & O'Hare, 2016). The family home is for many older Australians their major asset—a source of financial security, investment, retirement savings/superannuation. For some baby boomers, the notion of bequeathing the family home to children is still an important one—although there is evidence that bequest motives for retaining the family home are changing (Olsberg, 2012). Accumulated housing equity can be used to support retirement consumption and income needs and ease financial stress in later retirement (Jefferson, Austen, Ong, Haffner, & Wood, 2017; Lusardi & Mitchell, 2007; Ong, 2008; de Silva, Sinclair, Fard, & Thomas, 2015) [although current trend suggests there will be growing numbers of seniors that won't own their own home by retirement].

More generally, Judd, Liu, Easthope, Davy, and Bridge (2014) highlight the necessity to understand housing utilisation as people age and the social and cultural complexities of human attitudes and behaviour regarding housing liveability in Australia. They find the home represents more than a "machine for living"—but is tied up in symbolism of autonomy and independence particularly when occupants are faced with increasing frailty or decreasing capacity as a result of ageing (Judd et al., 2014). The home in the context of the "Australian Dream" is symbolically laden with memories and meaning and strong emotional affiliations.

Housing can have direct and indirect implications on government health expenditures. A UK government report highlights the economic importance of housing in the context of ageing demographics adding that "suitable housing can significantly improve life in older age while unsuitable housing can be the source of multiple problems and costs. Poor housings is estimated to create hazards that cost the National health system 2.5 billion per annum" (Government Office for Science, 2016: 9). While the UK context may not be directly comparable to the Australian context in men and women over 65, falls remain the leading reason for older people being admitted to hospital (38%) with most hospitalised fall cases (72%) occurring in either the home or aged care setting (AIHW, Kreisfeld, Pointer, & Bradley, 2017).

## 4 The New Middle Age and Changing Attitudes to Ageing "Well"

Growth in the number of older people is a global phenomenon. There are over seven million Australians aged 50–75 years in the "new middle age", and increased longevity is driving extended middle age rather than extended old age (Edgar et al., 2017). According to the 2014–2015 National Health Survey (NHS), nearly three-quarters (73%) of older Australians (aged 65 and over) reported they had good, very good or excellent health. Two in five (39%) older people self-assessed their health as being very good or excellent (ABS, 2015). Older Australians feel "middle aged", not old and have cognitive identities younger than their chronological age with 75% of Australians reporting feeling at least 5–10 years younger (Kohlbacher & Chéron, 2012).

The advent of this longer middle age has necessitated a rethink of the social, cultural and marketing attitudes to ageing. The transition of baby boomers to older ages signals both a quantitative change in numbers aged over 65 but also, as Hugo, (2014) states, a shift in attitudes, resources and expectations relating to post retirement years. The Australian context is particularly interesting as older Australians are culturally and linguistically diverse with one in three older people born overseas many from non-English speaking countries.

Economic activity that serves the needs of this new middle age demographic is likely to be transformative over the coming decades, and social and financial systems and institutions will need to adapt to changing economic trends. Edgar et al. (2017) advocate for a reorganisation of how work, education, health, and housing systems interact to facilitate healthy active ageing and to recognise older households as a valuable economic and social resource (Edgar et al., 2017). This coming generation of older Australians have a diversity of tastes, demands, aspirations and expectations on how they want to live their lives and as a result, to succeed in this setting both industry and public service providers will need develop innovations to meet these needs and do so efficiently.

Population ageing is thus likely to have implications for the functioning of the housing market in Australia with housing demand reflecting the preferences of baby boomers incorporating retirement plans, family considerations, available amenities, lifestyle preferences and of course financial constraints (Clark & Onaka, 1983; Painter, Gabriel, & Myers, 2001; Painter & Lee, 2009).

An interesting typology of baby boomers that captures preferences for housing paths by Pinnegar, van Den Nouwelant, Judd, and Randolph (2012) suggests a high degree of diversity within the baby boomer group. Housing paths of seniors are varied and the authors highlight that a perceived lack of supply of housing for seniors is often responded to with a focus on specialised housing such as retirement villages and aged care facilities rather than the broader housing market system. While downsizing and "right sizing" are often seen as a desirable option for seniors the importance of housing as a stock of wealth in the household asset portfolio may deter downsizing transitions and encourage ageing in place in the family home (Pinnegar et al., 2012). Inevitably, the choice made by this growing cohort of seniors will shape the wider housing system in the years to come.

## 4.1 Property Wealth

The rate of home ownership for older Australians remains high but is declining overtime, and this decline in home ownership is coupled with higher rates of mortgage debt at retirement than observed in previous generations. In 2003–2004, 79% of older people (65+) owned their homes without a mortgage; this had declined to 71.7% in 2015–2016 (ABS, 2017b). This reduction in homeownership rates is likely to have measurable effects on wellbeing (Coulson & Li, 2013; Wood, Smith, Ong, & Cigdem, 2013). This debt burden may be a catalyst to more households downsizing or moving to alternate housing as they get closer to retirement. Older Australians may also be using retirement savings to reduce mortgage debt on retirement (Yates & Bradbury, 2010). In 2010, those Australians who had not retired had a household debt of $119,000 as compared to $55,000 for those who had retired, with superannuation being considerably lower for retired households (about $60,000 lower for retired) (Kelly Research, 2012).

Australians are also increasingly working to older ages. In January 2018, Australians aged 65 and over had a workforce participation rate of 13% (17% for men and 10% for women), compared with 8% in 2006 (12% for men and 4% for women). Most people retiring in the next few years will rely partially or substantially on the age pension for some or all their retirement as they have inadequate super savings. There is still a significant proportion of the population who do not have any superannuation, with around one in four men and one in three women reporting they have no superannuation savings coupled with rising inequality in property wealth distributions (Clare, 2017).

## 5 Preferences for Ageing in Place—What Is Needed to Support This

Historically, Australia has a strong culture of homeownership, coupled with a high value on personal autonomy, both of which are reflected in the stated preferences of older homeowners to age "successfully" while remaining in place in their own homes and communities.

The term ageing-in-place is variously defined but is generally interpreted as meaning remaining living in their own homes and communities, with some level of independence of other family members (Davey, de Joux, Nana, & Arcus, 2004). The term *place* has several dimensions that are interrelated: a physical dimension that can be seen and touched like home or neighbourhood, a social dimension involving relationships with people and the ways in which individuals remain connected to others, an emotional and psychological dimension, which has to do with a sense of belonging, attachment, and a cultural dimension, which has to do with older people's values, beliefs, ethnicity, and symbolic meanings (Iecovich, 2014). The home is not just the building that is lived in, it enables a person to preserve a social identity. From this perspective, the home reflects an extension of the self, individualisation, enabling preservation of integrity of the self and promoting a sense of personhood (Fang et al., 2016; Sixsmith & Sixsmith, 2008; Yang, 2009). Many people are fearful of the alternative of moving to shared living environment or institutional settings, such as nursing homes and high-care facilities. Relocation often entails losing social relationships, changes in daily routines and lifestyles, leaving behind personal possessions, which they cannot take with them due to small spaces in the residential units, and loss of independence (Iecovich, 2014).

# 6 Consistent Desire to Age in Their Own Homes and Communities

A key component of ageing in place is adaptable, flexible housing that accommodates the resident's needs as they change. Maintaining autonomy and independence in old age is an objective for both individuals and policy makers however current housing stock may not be supporting this objective. Retrofitting older housing stock to provide older households with supports to facilitate independence can be effective however often expensive and invasive. Byles et al. (2014) as part of the Housing and Independence Living Study (HAIL) find that of the 400 interviewees in their sample, most homes were built prior to current legislative or building standards, and despite recent modifications, do not meet Australian adaptable housing (AS 4299) guidelines (Byles et al., 2014). The authors identified that many of the homes would not accommodate increased frailty or disability of occupants into the future. Occupational therapy related literature highlights how traditional residential designs disable people as they age and create challenges to older homeowners' safety and independence. The physical design of a home can have negative implications across a range of domains both physical and social (de Jonge, Jones, Phillips, & Chung, 2011; Kendig, Clemson, & Mackenzie, 2012).

Beyond the physical safety needs, the work of de Jonge et al. (2011) highlights the value assigned to the house location as a facilitator of social connectedness in addition to the capacity of the house to facilitate provision of care to loved ones and to pets as important themes assigned by Australians to their living environments.

> Older people have an overwhelming desire to continue to live independently in the community – control, personal autonomy, flexibility and lifestyle choices are paramount. (Olsberg, 2012: 144)

For older people, where they "age in place depends more upon attachment to location, rather than the family home" per se (Olsberg & Winters, 2005: 4). This would suggest that there is interaction between Pinnegars "local adaptors" and "ageing in place" groups when broadening the definition of ageing in place to mean ageing in ones own home rather than the family home per say. This importance to remain socially connected to place and community may dominate over the physical restrictions presented by the design of the home in the event of a decline in physical competence. Location of housing with proximity to family, friends and health services was particularly important to both lone and couple households over 65 (Emlet & Moceri, 2012; Weidmann & Kelly, 2011).

Downsizing is one means of releasing home equity (Judd et al., 2014). Olsberg and Winters' (2005) findings indicate that only around one in 10 homeowners aged 50+ years will extract housing equity by downsizing. Downsizing remains an uncommon path for older Australians and primary reasons for not downsizing are a desire to age in place and a perceived lack of alternatives in the market (Productivity Commission, 2015). In addition, "there is a general lack of affordable downsizing options for older Australians, due in large part to the red tape and inconsistencies within state and territory land planning regimes" (Productivity Commission, 2015: 2).

If the motivation for downsizing is financially motivated then it may be that smaller properties are a step up in quality and the move is a trade off in housing attributes rather than a release of equity. When coupled with the stress and transactions costs of moving (Easthope, 2004) older people may choose to remain in a home that is not suitable to support them if they experience increased frailty (lower competence). Selling the family home could impact on age pension entitlements, (de Silva et al., 2015) creating another incentive to remain in the family home.

For those that do downsize, survey analysis suggests that the most common factor influencing their decision was a desire for a change in lifestyle, followed by an inability to maintain the home and/or garden. Financial circumstances were important to a comparatively small number of downsizers (Judd et al., 2014).

## 7 Livable Housing Guidelines—Universal Design and Lifetime Homes

As identified by the WHO the design of the house, housing stock more generally, and its cost, form, density and location can create or erode community capacity to age well (de Silva, Sinclair, & Angelopoulos, 2016). Homes built for young families now add to the current stock of housing and may eventually become homes for older households with increasing frailty, hence the importance of designing "lifetime homes".

Universal design principles focus on safety, ease of movement and attractive design for all ages and abilities. The introduction of Australia's *Livable Housing Design Guidelines* in 2012 is a move towards improving the adaptable and flexible nature of housing stock to align with the needs of all generations. The objective was to create a national standard of design elements that can be applied in new housing to improve function for all and avoid costly retrofitting should household circumstances change. The livable housing guidelines (LHG) are a non-statutory standard incorporating 15 design criteria intended to support the development of mainstream housing to meet the changing needs of residents over their lifetimes (Livable Housing Australia, 2012).

The guidelines provide technical advice and guidance on the features of a house that ensure it will be:

- Easier to enter
- Safer to move in and around
- More capable of easy and cost-effective adaptation
- Designed to better anticipate and adapt to the needs and abilities of those living in the home.

The guidelines have three performance levels: Silver, Gold and Platinum. A minimum of 7 criteria must be satisfied to meet the minimum standard—silver accreditation.

**The seven core design features elements in the silver level they are:**

1. A safe continuous and step free path of travel from the street entrance and/or parking area to a dwelling entrance that is level.

2. At least one, level (step-free) entrance into the dwelling.
3. Internal doors and corridors that facilitate comfortable and unimpeded movement between spaces.
4. A toilet on the ground (or entry) level that provides easy access.
5. A bathroom that contains a hobless shower recess.
6. Reinforced walls around the toilet, shower and bath to support the safe installation of grabrails later.
7. Stairways are designed to reduce the likelihood of injury and also enable future adaptation.

The gold level provides more generous dimensions for most of the core livable housing design elements and introduces additional elements in areas such as the kitchen and bedroom. All 15 elements are featured in the platinum level. This level describes design elements that would better accommodate ageing in place and people with higher mobility needs. (*Source* Livable Housing Guidelines [2012])

Healthy active baby boomers may not immediately appreciate the need to outlay additional costs upfront for what may be deemed "specialist" housing. However, as laid out in the National Dialogue on Universal Design and the *Livable Housing Design Guidelines*, a wide range of Australians benefit from universally designed homes, including:

- families with young children who need safer homes with easy access for strollers
- people with injuries that limit their mobility would require less hospitalisation if they could safely move around their home while recovering
- ageing baby boomers planning for their future needs
- people vulnerable to slip, trip and fall injuries in their homes
- people with disabilities, and their families, friends and relatives
- home care workers and family and friends who provide in-home care and support. (*Source* Livable Housing Australia, 2012)

Using various methodologies, there is scope to explore the impact and value of *Livable Housing Design* Guidelines as the needs of the population shift and policy emphasis and user wishes increasingly favour ageing in place. Illawarra Retirement Trust customers, for example, showed that on average, seniors living in a purpose-built residential community require less access to both Residential Aged Care (RAC) and Community Services (CS), later in life compared with their community peers living in un-modified accommodation (O'Brien & Grey, 2012).

# 8 Housing as a Facilitator of Ageing Well

## 8.1 Environmental Gerontology

Environmental gerontology is a field of research that seeks to understand the relationship between older persons and their physical and social environments. It places emphasis on the day-to-day activities and given that older people spend around ¾ of their daytime in the home and immediate home environment, housing as an ecological environment is a focus of research in this space.

> The house is both a physical structure constructed through established cultural practices as well as a place infused with pronounced intimacy with one's partner, social interactions, and the symbolization of attachment, normalcy, and loss. (Wahl & Oswald, 2010: 112)

Older people have a desire to age while continuing to live independently in their own homes and communities and that is connected with maintaining control, personal autonomy and flexibility around lifestyle choices Yet, research suggests that while ageing in place may bring social and psychological benefit, UK studies have also shown that ageing in place can be a negative experience of isolation and loneliness often due to weaknesses in levels of informal support, poor physical environment of the home and limited neighbourhood and social network, which undermine the person's ability to live independently (Sixsmith & Sixsmith, 2008).

Seminal works by Lawton (1977) assert that the person–environment system is fundamental to defining the quality of later life (Lawton, 1977, 1990). The proposed environmental docility hypothesis stated that the more competent the person, the less dependent they are on environmental circumstances. More recently, ageing well has been conceptualised as a person environment dynamic, where the physical environment can impose significant constraints in late life, or it may also enhance opportunities for ageing well, as new housing solutions and new technologies support declining competencies (Lawton & Nahemow, 1973; Oswald et al., 2007; Peace, Holland, & Kellaher, 2011).

The competence environmental press model put forward by Powell in the late 1970s is relevant today in helping us understand the interaction of the individual and their core competencies and their interactions with the physical residence and community environment (Lawton, 1977). Adaption levels incorporate the feelings of people to changes in their environmental demands which either cause them to increase theory competence or reduce the environmental press (Perry, Andersen, & Kaplan, 2014). This may include adaption of the physical building or relocating to a more suitable home. A very useful systematic review of the literature relating to relocation or housing transitions of older frail adults by Roy, Dubé, Després, Freitas, and Légaré (2018) identifies a total of 71 factors that influence the housing decision making of older adults (Crisp, Windsor, Butterworth, & Anstey, 2013; Roy et al., 2018). While the work of Granbom, Löfqvist, Horstmann, Haak, and Iwarsson (2014) suggests that key predictors of transitions in higher needs care in old age are deficiencies in cooking, cognitive deficits and accessibility problems (Granbom et al., 2014).

## 8.2 Well-Designed Homes, Smart Technologies and Wellbeing

Universal design coupled where relevant with technological solutions such as smart home appliances reshape the "environmental press" of the traditional household and compensate for possible person–environment mismatches. This also applies for many increasingly smart assistive devices, which now offer a full new potential of maintaining autonomy and participation.

There is also strong evidence that improvements in residential physical environment can facilitate the activities of daily living for older households, raise the effectiveness and efficiency of care, reduce the incidence of frailty and disability through reduced accidents and falls and enable older people to live independently despite limitations in their functional abilities (Gitlin, 2003; Slaug, Chiatti, Oswald, Kaspar, & Schmidt, 2017; Wahl, Fänge, Oswald, Gitlin, & Iwarsson, 2009; Wahl & Oswald, 2010). A study by Iwarsson (2005) examining elderly people (aged 75–84) living in their homes measuring their ability to carry out activities of daily living ADL (Eating, Bathing, Dressing, Toileting, Transferring, Maintaining Continence) finds that the level of person-environment fit and ADL dependence correlate significantly. Reiterating that a well-designed house for the elderly significantly improves the elderly's wellbeing (Iwarsson, 2005).

## 8.3 Lifetime Homes—UK Assessment of Health Benefits

A report commissioned in the UK to assess the equivalent of the LHG referred to as the lifetime homes standard employed a hazard reduction model to try to estimate the potential cost reduction to society of building to the lifetime homes building standard. Focusing on housing and health, their model estimated the health cost benefits of a reduction in injury caused by hazards in a dwelling. Indirect health benefits were considered to be those that promote psychological wellbeing and activity for dwelling residents (Roys, 2012). The lifetime homes standards differ somewhat to the LHG but there are similarities. Direct health benefits were assumed via the reduction in accidents such as falls on the stairs, falls on the level, accessibility issues, fear of crime and personal hygiene/sanitation and ergonomics.

The indirect health benefits for occupants focus on the promotion of psychological wellbeing and activity. Ensuring that occupants can maintain a good quality of life means that the dwelling itself must be functional for all occupants and that no additional stress and anxiety should be caused to any household member who is elderly, or who has become temporarily incapacitated or disabled. Promotion of wellbeing and activity was facilitated via the lifetime home standards by increased independence, a reduction in the need for external assistance, reduced stress-related illnesses, a reduction in the fear of crime, increased psychological wellbeing and supporting the development of stable communities.

A Communities and Local Government report (2008) in addition to the work of Roys (2012) suggests that implementing the lifetime homes standard would have the following impacts on health and costs attributed to health.

- reduce or delay the need for people to move to residential care
- reduce the demand for temporary residential care
- ensure that people are discharged from hospital into suitable accommodation instead of remaining in hospital in much needed acute hospital beds because their accommodation is unsuitable
- reduce the need for home care for disabled people. (Department for Communities and Local Government, 2008; Roys, 2012)

## 8.4 The Need for Services at Home—Australia

Despite over 70% of +65 identifying as having good health, forty per cent of older people reported needing assistance as they aged (ABS, 2018). Much of the care and support for older people is provided by family members, friends or neighbours (ABS, 2015) with 80% of older people accessing some form of government-funded aged care service before death. Government recurrent expenditure on aged care services was $18.4 billion in 2017–2018 or $4572 per older person (AIHW, 2015).

The proportion of all older Australians who needed assistance with at least one activity decreased to 38.6% in 2015, down from 41.9% in 2012. Assistance was most commonly needed for tasks (22.9%), such as taking medications and property maintenance (20.2%) (ABS, 2017a). Older Australians are less reliant on family to assist in their day-to-day care and given that they very much want to remain living independently in their own homes, indicating that their use of services (including those rendered by their living accommodation) in older ages will differ to those of previous generations.

## 9 Conceptualising Housing Built to Livable Housing Guidelines (LHG) as a Merit Good

Given the growing need for some level of care services delivered within the context of the home environment over the lifecycle we posit that the quality of the home environment can have merit good attributes, creating benefits which are both private and social. The residential home design attributes (as measured by the LHG) can create an environment that supports ageing well outcomes and maintains agility to adapt to the needs of its residents' overtime. The person–environment (P/E) relationship is dynamic.

Examining the concept of value in residential home, both in its design and location attributes, as a facilitating factor to successful ageing, we suggest that the quantity of LHG housing may be under supplied in the market because the implicit value has both a private and public component. Current supply in the market is driven by private demand for housing with these specific attributes. The value of livable housing can be split into three components: market value, social value and future value for the individual. Market value is directly observed via market price, and specific attributes can be measured using a hedonic type analysis (Cheshire & Sheppard, 2017). Social value can capture the value of the LHG beyond those directly experienced by the home owner and can be captured by evaluation methods similar to other types of externalities such as vaccination and preventative medicine and capture benefits such as reduced public expenditure on care services. The future benefits of livable housing for the individual include improved accessibility, cost effectiveness and better wellbeing due to more comfortable ageing. However, these benefits are not fully realised by consumers due to information asymmetry, uncertainty and the general preferences for the current consumption over the future consumption (Hsiao, 1995).

Following on from the UK assessment of lifetime homes we posit that there are four main testable forms of value implicit in housing built with universal design principles[1] and incorporating some locational service and amenity attributes.

1. Well-designed housing may reduce the need for care as it reduces the likelihood of accidents and falls in the home (*Physical/Functional/Cognitive wellbeing*)
2. Good design may reduce the level of care required if capabilities decrease through supporting autonomy in the home (*Physical/Functional/Cognitive wellbeing*)
3. The home may be perceived as capital in the care giving process and as such can support the ease and efficiency of care provision when required within the home (*all domains*)
4. Housing location may support the development and maintenance of cultural and social capital (*social wellbeing*).

There are both social and private values in the increased wellbeing outcomes if LHG housing can be shown to reduce the need for care (generating efficiency gains in ageing well outcomes).

Should there be specific social value in universal designed housing over and above the market value it may justify calibrations in policy settings to provide incentives to new housing providers to incorporate more of these features into home designs. These incentives may be via streamlined planning process amendments like those recently implemented for residential aged care facilities, where they are no longer assessed as standard residential buildings, but rather as unique built form designed to support appropriate outcomes. The streamlined planning process would reduce costs for producers and increase the supply of LHG housing in the market.

The discussion presented in this chapter highlights the importance of housing to the physical, social and emotional wellbeing of older people as they age. Australians have demonstrated a strong preference to age in

[1] Livable Housing Guidelines are applied in the Australian context to capture the various aspects of "Good" design.

their own homes, neighbourhoods and communities, and often due to barriers to housing transitions in later life such as the stress of moving, transaction costs, lack of appropriate housing to downsize, they choose to remain in their own homes. The findings of Byles et al. (2014) are just one example which illustrates that often these homes are not supportive and adaptable to the changing needs of occupants as they age and may present challenges to maintaining independence over time (Byles et al., 2014). Employing the concept of accessible housing design embodied in the Australia context as "livable homes" can provide the housing conditions necessary to improve the physical, social and cognitive wellbeing of occupants. The design features can facilitate increased mobility, accessibility and independence and in doing so reduce the need for and dependence on public services. Further research is needed to measure the social benefit implicit in good sustainable future proofed housing design in the context of an ageing society.

## References

Australian Bureau of Statisitics (ABS). (2015). Disability, ageing and carers, Australia. *4430.0—Disability, ageing and carers, Australia: Summary of findings, 2015*.

Australian Bureau of Statisitics (ABS). (2017a). *A profile of older people in Australia*. Cat. No. 4430. Canberra: Australian Bureau of Statisitics.

Australian Bureau of Statisitics (ABS). (2017b). Changes in wealth over time. Cat. No. 6253. Canberra: Australian Bureau of Statisitics.

Australian Bureau of Statisitics (ABS). (2018). *Census of population and housing: Reflecting Australia—Stories from the census 2016*. Canberra: Australian Bureau of Statisitics.

Australian Institute of Health and Welfare (AIHW). (2015). *Use of aged care services before death*. Australian Institute of Health and Welfare: 42.

Australian Institute of Health and Welfare (AIHW). (2017, October 12). *Pathways to permanent residential aged care in Australia: A pathways in aged care (PiAC) analysis of people's aged care program use before first entry to permanent residential aged care in 2013–2014*. https://www.aihw.gov.au/reports/aged-care/permanent-residential-aged-care-2013-14/contents/table-of-contents.

AIHW, Kreisfeld, R., Pointer, S., & Bradley, C. (2017). Injury research and statistics. *Trends in hospitalisations due to falls by older people, Australia 2002–2003 to 2012–2013.*

Bowling, A. (2008). Enhancing later life: How older people perceive active ageing? *Aging and Mental Health, 12*(3), 293–301.

Bowling, A., & Iliffe, S. (2011). Psychological approach to successful ageing predicts future quality of life in older adults. *Health and Quality of Life Outcomes, 9*(1), 13. http://hqlo.biomedcentral.com/articles/10.1186/1477-7525-9-13.

Byles, J. E., Mackenzie, L., Redman, S., Parkinson, L., Leigh, L., & Curryer, C. (2014). Supporting housing and neighbourhoods for healthy ageing: Findings from the housing and independent living study (HAIL). *Australasian Journal on Ageing, 33*(1), 29–35. https://doi.org/10.1111/j.1741-6612.2012.00646.x.

Cheshire, P., & Sheppard, S. (2017). On the price of land and the value of amenities. In *The economics of land use* (pp. 315–335). Taylor and Francis.https://doi.org/10.4324/9781315240114-21.

Clare, R. (2017). *Superannuation account balances by age and gender.* www.superannuation.asn.au (February 18, 2019).

Clark, W. A. V., & Onaka, J. (1983). Life cycle and housing adjustment as explanations of residential mobility. *Urban Studies, 20*(1), 47–57.

Coulson, N. E., & Li, H. (2013). Measuring the external benefits of homeownership. *Journal of Urban Economics, 77*(C), 57–67.

Crisp, D. A., Windsor, T. D., Butterworth, P., & Anstey, K. J. (2013). What are older adults seeking? Factors encouraging or discouraging retirement village living. *Australasian Journal on Ageing, 32*(3), 163–170.

Davey, J., de Joux, V., Nana, G., & Arcus, M. (2004). *Accommodation options for older people in Aotearoa/New Zealand.* http://citeseerx.ist.psu.edu/viewdoc/download?doi=10.1.1.460.8794&rep=rep1&type=pdf (July 23, 2019).

de Jonge, D. M., Jones, A., Phillips, R., & Chung, M. (2011). Understanding the essence of home: Older people's experience of home in Australia. *Occupational Therapy International, 18,* 39–47.

Department for Communities and Local Government. (2008). Communities and Local Government—*Lifetime homes, lifetime neighbourhoods: A national strategy for housing in an ageing society.* http://eprints.whiterose.ac.uk/74127/.

Department of Health. (2017, October 17). *Legislated review of aged care 2017.* ISBN: 978-1-76007-325-1. Online ISBN: 978-1-76007-326-8. Publications No. 11825. https://agedcare.health.gov.au/sites/g/files/net1426/f/documents/08_2017/legislated_review_of_aged_care_2017.pdf.

de Silva, A., Sinclair, S., & Angelopoulos, S. (2016). Retirees, creatives and housing market complexity: Challenges for policy-makers. *Australian Economic Review, 49*(3), 340–351.

de Silva, A., Sinclair, S, Fard, A., & Thomas, S. (2015). *Exploring home equity release options for retirees: Opportunities for optimising retirement income.* Report for Australian Centre of Financial studies. https://australiancentre.com.au/publication.

Easthope, H. (2004). A place called home. *Housing, Theory and Society, 21*(3), 128–138.

Edgar, D., Patricia, E., Bob, B., Katherine, B., Briony, D., & Chris, L. (2017). *The new middle age: Ways to thrive in the longevity economy | APO.* https://apo.org.au/node/112756 (February 18, 2019).

Emlet, C. A., & Moceri, J. T. (2012). The Importance of Social Connectedness in Building Age-Friendly Communities. *Journal of Aging Research, 2012,* 1–9. https://doi.org/10.1155/2012/173247.

Fang, M. L., Woolrych, R., Sixsmith, J., Canham, S., Battersby, L., & Sixsmith, A. (2016). Place-making with older persons: Establishing sense-of-place through participatory community mapping workshops. *Social Science and Medicine, 168,* 223–229. https://doi.org/10.1016/j.socscimed.2016.07.007.

Frochen, S., & Pynoos, J. (2017). Housing for the elderly: Addressing gaps in knowledge through the lens of age-friendly communities. *Journal of Housing for the Elderly, 31*(2), 160–177.

Gitlin, L. N. (2003). Conducting research on home environments: Lessons learned and new directions. *Gerontologist, 43*(5), 628–637.

Government Office for Science. (2016). *Future of an Ageing Population.* https://assets.publishing.service.gov.uk/government/uploads/system/uploads/attachment_data/file/535187/gs-16-10-future-of-an-ageing-population.pdf (June 25, 2019).

Granbom, M., Löfqvist, C., Horstmann, V., Haak, M., & Iwarsson, S. (2014). Relocation to ordinary or special housing in very old age: Aspects of housing and health. *European Journal of Ageing, 11*(1), 55–65. http://link.springer.com/10.1007/s10433-013-0287-3 (July 3, 2019).

Hsiao, W. C. (1995). Abnormal Economics in the health sector. *Health Policy, 32,* 125–129.

Hugo, G. (2014). *The demographic facts of ageing in Australia.* Appendix Q for Aged Care Financing Authority Second Annual Report.

Humpel, N., O'Loughlin, K., Wells, Y., & Kendig, H. (2010). The health of Australian baby boomers. *Australasian Journal on Ageing, 29*(1), 8–13. http://www.ncbi.nlm.nih.gov/pubmed/20398080 (September 12, 2017).

Iecovich, E. (2014). Aging in place: From theory to practice. *Anthropological Notebooks, 20*(1), 21–33.

Iwarsson, S. (2005). A long-term perspective on person-environment fit and ADL dependence among older Swedish adults. *Gerontologist, 45*(3), 327–336.

Jefferson, T., Austen, S., Ong, R., Haffner, M., & Wood, G. (2017). Housing equity withdrawal: Perceptions of obstacles among older Australian home owners and associated service providers. *Journal of Social Policy, 46*(3), 623–642.

Judd, B., Liu, E., Easthope, H., Davy, L. & Bridge, C. (2014). *Downsizing amongst older Australians.* AHURI Final Report No. 214, Australian Housing and Urban Research Institute Limited, Melbourne. https://www.ahuri.edu.au/research/final-reports/214.

Kelly Research. (2012). *Household savings and retirement where has all my super gone? A report on superannuation and retirement for CPA Australia.* https://melbourneinstitute.unimelb.edu.au/assets/documents/hilda-bibliography/other-publications/2012/Kelly_household-savings-retirement.pdf (June 26, 2019).

Kendig, H., Clemson, L., & Mackenzie, L. (2012). Older people: Well-being, housing and neighbourhoods. In *International encyclopedia of housing and home* (pp. 150–155). http://www.sciencedirect.com/science/article/pii/B9780080471631000187 (September 10, 2017).

Kohlbacher, F., & Chéron, E. (2012). Understanding 'silver' consumers through cognitive age, health condition, financial status, and personal values: Empirical evidence from the world's most mature market Japan. *Journal of Consumer Behaviour, 11*(3), 179–188. http://doi.wiley.com/10.1002/cb.382 (July 3, 2019).

Kudrna, G. (2016). Economy-wide effects of means-tested pensions: The case of Australia. *The Journal of the Economics of Ageing, 7,* 17–29.

Lawton, M. P. (1990). Residential environment and self-directedness among older people. *American Psychologist, 45*(5), 638–640.

Lawton, M. P. (1977). An ecological theory of aging applied to elderly housing. *Journal of Architectural Education, 31*(1), 8–10.

Lawton, M. P., & Nahemow L. (1973). Ecology and the aging process: Psychology of adult development and aging. In *Psychology of adult development and aging* (pp. 619–674).

Livable Housing Australia. (2012). Livable housing design guidelines. *Reproduction* (May), 1–34. https://livablehousingaustralia.org.au (October 17, 2017).

Lourey, E., McLoughlin, C., & Taylor, P. E. (2016). *The mundanities of life: Older consumers' views from the national seniors social survey.* Melbourne. https://nationalseniors.com.au/system/files/06161862PAC_TheMundanitiesOfLife_PACReport_REV2.pdf (September 2, 2017).

Lusardi, A., & Mitchell, O. S. (2007). Baby boomer retirement security: The roles of planning, financial literacy, and Housing wealth. *Journal of Monetary Economics, 54*(1), 205–224.

McLaughlin, T., & Mills, A. (2008). Where will we live when we get older? *Quality in Ageing, 9*(3), 15–21.

Nordbakke, S., & Schwanen, T. (2014). Well-being and mobility: A theoretical framework and literature review focusing on older people. *Mobilities, 9*(1), 104–129. http://www.tandfonline.com/doi/abs/10.1080/17450101.2013.784542 (August 25, 2017).

O'Brien, D., & Grey, F. (2012). *Aged care in Australia: A report for Carabott Holt architects.*

Olsberg, D. (2012). Older people: Well-being. In *International encyclopedia of housing and home* (pp. 143–149).

Olsberg, D., & Winters, M. (2005) *Ageing in place: Intergenerational and intrafamilial housing transfers and shifts in later life.* AHURI Final Report No. 88, Australian Housing and Urban Research Institute Limited, Melbourne. https://www.ahuri.edu.au/research/final-reports/88.

Ong, R. (2008). Unlocking housing equity through reverse mortgages: The case of elderly homeowners in Australia. *European Journal of Housing Policy, 8*(1), 61–79.

Oswald, F., Wahl, H. W., Schilling, O., Nygren, C., Fänge, A., Sixsmith, A., … Iwarsson, S. (2007). Relationships between housing and healthy aging in very old age. *Gerontologist, 47*(1), 96–107.

Painter, G., Gabriel, S., & Myers, D. (2001). Race, immigrant status, and housing tenure choice. *Journal of Urban Economics, 49*(1), 150–67. http://www.sciencedirect.com/science/article/pii/S0094119000921880 (July 14, 2015).

Painter, G., & Lee, K.-O. (2009). Housing tenure transitions of older households: Life cycle, demographic, and familial factors. *Regional Science and Urban Economics, 39*(6), 749–760.

Peace, S., Holland, C., & Kellaher, L. (2011). 'Option recognition' in later life: Variations in ageing in place. *Ageing and Society, 31*(5), 734–757.

Peel, N., Bartlett, H., & McClure, R. (2004). Healthy ageing: How is it defined and measured? *Australasian Journal on Ageing, 23*(3), 115–119.

Perry, T. E., Andersen, T. C., & Kaplan, D. B. (2014). Relocation remembered: Perspectives on senior transitions in the living environment. *Gerontologist, 54*(1), 75–81.

Pinnegar, S., van Den Nouwelant, R., Judd, B., & Randolph, B. (2012). *Understanding housing and location choices of retiring australians in the "baby Boom" generation: Scoping report prepared for the national housing supply council.* Commonwealth of Australia. http://192.195.49.161/PublicationsAndMedia/Publications/2012/housing-in-the-baby-boom-generation (October 10, 2017).

Productivity Commission. (2015). *Housing decisions of older Australians.* Commission Research Paper, Canberra.

Rowe, J. W., & Kahn, R. L. (1997). Successful aging. *The Gerontologist, 37*(4), 433–440.

Roy, N., Dubé, R., Després, C., Freitas, A., & Légaré, F. (2018). Choosing between staying at home or moving: A systematic review of factors influencing housing decisions among frail older adults. *PLoS ONE, 13*(1), e0189266. https://doi.org/10.1371/journal.pone.0189266.

Roys, M. (2012). *Assessing the health benefits of lifetime homes.* www.communities.gov.uk (February 19, 2019).

Sixsmith, A., & Sixsmith, J. (2008). Ageing in place in the United Kingdom. *Journal of International Ageing, 32,* 219. https://doi.org/10.1007/s12126-008-9019-y.

Slaug, B., Chiatti, C., Oswald, F., Kaspar, R., & Schmidt, S. M. (2017). Improved housing accessibility for older people in Sweden and Germany: Short term costs and long-term gains. *International Journal of Environmental Research and Public Health, 14*(9), 964.

Srinivasan, S., O'Fallon, L. R., & Dearry, A. (2003). Creating healthy communities, healthy homes, healthy people: Initiating a research agenda on the built environment and public health. *American Journal of Public Health, 93*(9), 1446–1450.

Tesch-Römer, C., & Wahl, H.-W. (2017). Toward a more comprehensive concept of successful aging: Disability and care needs. *The Journals of Gerontology Series B, 72*(2), 310–318. https://doi.org/10.1093/geronb/gbw162.

Wahl, H., Fänge, A., Oswald, F, Gitlin, L., & Iwarsson, S. (2009, June). The home environment and disability-related outcomes in aging individuals: What is the empirical evidence? *The Gerontologist, 49*(3), 355–367. https://doi.org/10.1093/geront/gnp056.

Wahl, H., & Oswald, F. (2010). Environmental perspectives on ageing. In D. Dannefer & C. Phillipson (Eds.), *The SAGE handbook of social gerontology* (pp. 111–124). London: Sage. https://doi.org/10.4135/9781446200933.n8.

Wang, H., Koo, B., & O'Hare, C. (2016). Retirement planning in the light of changing demographics. *Economic Modelling, 52*(PB), 749–763.

Weidmann, B., & Kelly, J. F. (2011). *What matters most? Housing preferences across the Australian population.* Melbourne: Grattan Institute.

World Health Organisation (WHO). (2007). *Checklist of essential features of age-friendly cities outdoor spaces and buildings.* http://www.who.int/ageing/publications/Age_friendly_cities_checklist.pdf (October 10, 2017).

Wood, G., Smith, S. J., Ong, R., & Cigdem, M. (2013). *The edges of home ownership.* AHURI Final Report No. 216. Australian Housing and Urban Research Institute Limited, Melbourne. https://www.ahuri.edu.au/research/final-reports/216.

Worthington, A. C. (2013). Financial literacy and financial literacy programmes in Australia. *Journal of Financial Services Marketing., 18,* 227. https://doi.org/10.1057/fsm.2013.18.

Yang, F. (2009). Consumption over the life cycle: How different is housing? *Review of Economic Dynamics, 12*(3), 423–443.

Yates, J., & Bradbury, B. (2010). Home ownership as a (Crumbling) fourth pillar of social insurance in Australia. *Journal of Housing and the Built Environment, 25*(2), 193–211.

# 11

# Life, Liberty and the Pursuit of Happiness: Examining the Role of Personal and Country-Level Freedom in Well-Being

Sook Ning Chua, Sefa Awaworyi Churchill and Richard Koestner

## 1 Introduction

"They may take away our lives, but they'll never take our freedom!" cried William Wallace in the Academy Award winning film, *Braveheart*. His cry reflects the great value people place on their freedom, willing to sacrifice even their own lives to gain freedom. Freedom is about having

S. N. Chua (✉)
Department of Psychological Science, National Institute of Education, Nanyang Technological University, Singapore, Singapore
e-mail: sookning.chua@nie.edu.sg

S. Awaworyi Churchill
School of Economics, Finance & Marketing, RMIT University, Melbourne, VIC, Australia
e-mail: sefa.awaworyichurchill@rmit.edu.au

R. Koestner
Department of Psychology, McGill University, Montréal, QC, Canada
e-mail: richard.koestner@mcgill.ca



S. Awaworyi Churchill et al. (eds.), *Measuring, Understanding and Improving Wellbeing Among Older People*,
https://doi.org/10.1007/978-981-15-2353-3_11

choices—the opportunity to choose and capacity to choose between two viable alternatives (Lau, Hiemisch, & Baumeister, 2015; Westcott, 1992; Veenhoven, 2000). It has been argued that people have an intrinsic need to be free and to experience agency in their lives (deCharms, 1968; Ryan & Deci, 2017). Such is the importance of freedom to man, that Sartre believed freedom to be the essence of being human. Indeed, people who experience personal freedom of choice in their lives report higher levels of happiness than those who do not (Diener, Diener, & Diener, 2009; Inglehart, Foa, Peterson, & Welzel, 2008; Welzel & Inglehart, 2010; Verme, 2009). More than just personal freedom, however, the larger cultural and sociopolitical context also has a significant impact on individual's life (Bronfenbrenner, 1977; Bronfenbrenner & Morris, 1998). Past studies have shown that people in democratic nations tend to report higher subjective well-being as people have the freedom to express and participate in the evolution of their society (Downie, Chua, & Koestner, 2007; Inglehart et al., 2008). Little research has looked at their separate and unique contributions to well-being. This paper looks at the importance of personal and country freedom and the interactive effects of both levels of freedom on well-being from a lifespan perspective.

Freedom at the national level can be understood in terms of democracy—or civil liberties and political rights (Bollen, 1990; Tilly, 2007). While there are some subtle differences, civil liberties and political rights have often been viewed together as characteristics of a democratic nation and collectively represent the level of freedom experienced by a country. Briefly, political rights refer to the electoral process, political pluralism, political participation and the functioning of the government; civil liberties refer to freedom of expression and beliefs, personal autonomy, organizational and individual rights and independence and fairness of the law. Civil liberties and political rights rarely deviate more than 2 points apart and are highly correlated about 0.80–0.90 (Armstrong, 2011).

Although a free society may facilitate a personal sense of control, this may not always be the case. For instance, Ted lives in a free country but has little say in where he works (at a factory) or what he does (at the production line). There is little room for creativity, self-expression or choice. Such a person is limited in his options in where he can live based on the prices of real estate in his area. Yet he lives in a country where elections are free, the judiciary is autonomous and fair, and the government functions efficiently. Examples of low personal freedom in a free country include Japan and Italy. On the other hand, John experiences a high level of personal freedom and control at home but lives under a dictatorship which suppresses the freedom of the press, curtails the independence of the judiciary system and limits freedom of expression. It may be that John's overall well-being is only marginally impacted by systemic freedom. People adjust to the limits of the system, carve pockets of control in their lives and function so as to experience freedom in an unfree nation. Examples of high personal freedom and partial country freedom include Singapore and Qatar. Conversely, people may report low levels of personal freedom in a country that is free. Thus, we sought to answer two questions: 1. What are the unique contributions of personal and national freedom on well-being and 2. What is the interactive effect of personal and national freedom on well-being?

## 2 Freedom: Universal or Relative Importance?

The issue of personal freedom and agency is particularly salient during the later stages of life (Rodin, 1986). Although there are positive changes with age such as gaining wisdom and life experience, normal aging is also accompanied with increased limitations in functioning and activities (Moore, Rosenberg, & Fitzgibbon, 1999; Wilkie, Peat, Thomas, & Croft, 2007). There are physical changes which negatively impacts daily functioning such as decreases in executive control functioning (Royall, Palmer, Chiodo, & Polk, 2004) and increases in chronic health conditions (Moore et al., 1999). Personal freedom means that people have to invest time, effort and resources to make decisions and to risk failure and as people get older, they may not want the responsibility that comes with freedom or have the resources to commit to such freedom. From a developmental perspective, aging-related losses and role changes are accompanied with an increase in secondary control strategies and a decrease in primary control strategies to maintain life satisfaction and self-esteem (Heckhausen, 1997). Primary control refers to exerting control over the environment to fit one's own needs; secondary control refers to fitting one's needs to the environment (Rothbaum, Weisz, & Snyder, 1982). For instance, across education and health status, older people expressed a lower desire for control over their health and a greater belief in ability of powerful others to control their health (Smith et al., 1988). People adaptively focus and reserve energy for areas that they have the most control (Lachman & Leff, 1989; Rothbaum et al., 1982). They may thus give up the importance of freedom in certain areas of their lives and take control through secondary sources.

Advocates of the universal importance of agency and freedom, however, would argue that the freedom and choice contribute to well-being regardless of life stage (Collopy, Dubler, Zuckerman, Crigger, & Campbell, 1990; Ryan & Deci, 2017; Kasser & Ryan, 1999). For instance, even within highly structured and regulated environments like nursing homes, people had higher well-being and lived longer when they volitionally chose to stay in a nursing home and when they had a sense of choice and volition in their daily activities (Kasser & Ryan, 1999). Nursing home environments that offer opportunities for freedom and choice promoted psychological adjustment, particularly for individuals who are high functioning and have the capacity and competency to be self-determined (Collopy, 1988; O'Connor & Vallerand, 1994; Thomasma, 1984).

Interestingly, there is some evidence that certain individuals appear to do better in environments that are more controlling than in environments that offer opportunities for freedom and choice (O'Connor & Vallerand, 1994). Nursing home residents who reported low levels of self-determination in important life domains had higher levels of psychological adjustment in nursing homes that did not provide opportunities for freedom and choices compared to nursing homes that did provide opportunities for freedom. Individuals with high levels of self-determination appeared to be unaffected by the nursing home environment. The authors argue that self-determination is not universally beneficial and that the person-environment fit is an important consideration when examining the effects of freedom on well-being. The person-environment fit hypothesis is also consistent with recent research showing that personality factors are better suited to certain cultures (Geeraert,

Li, Ward, Gelfand, & Demes, 2019). In general, people who were high in self-monitoring, prevention focus and need for structure adapted better to restrictive characterized by strong and rigidly imposed norms and low tolerance for deviant behaviors (Geeraert et al., 2019; Gelfand et al., 2011).

In this study, we expected that personal and country-level freedom are independently positively associated with well-being among the elderly. However, we also expected a significant interaction between personal and country-level freedom, such that the people with a low sense of personal control would report higher well-being in countries with low political and civic freedom, compared to free countries. In contrast, people with a high sense of personal control would report higher well-being in free countries compared to restricted countries that were not free.

# 3 Method

## 3.1 Data

Our study draws on data from various sources. Individual-level data is sourced from the World Values Survey (WVS). The WVS presents surveys for nationally representative samples in approximately 100 countries. Surveys capture changes in social values and how such changes impact political and socioeconomic outcomes. The WVS currently has data on six waves of surveys and we draw on data from all six waves. Table 1 presents an overview of the survey waves with regard to the

**Table 1** Overview of survey waves

| Wave | Year survey was conducted |
|---|---|
| Wave 1 | 1981–1984 |
| Wave 2 | 1990–1994 |
| Wave 3 | 1995–1998 |
| Wave 4 | 1999–2004 |
| Wave 5 | 2005–2009 |
| Wave 6 | 2010–2014 |

time period each survey wave was conducted. Data on our macroeconomic variable, GDP per capita, is sourced from the World Bank's World Development Indicators (WDI) database while country-level freedom and rights are drawn from the Freedom House database.

In order to merge our survey data with country-level data, we take the average of observations for country-level data for periods corresponding with the six waves of the WVS. Thus, for data on GDP per capita and Freedom House data, we form a panel which is based on the average of the years corresponding with each survey wave. Given that our study examines the well-being of older people, we focus on respondents that are at least 50 years old. Overall, we have approximately 83, 300 observations across 93 countries as our working sample. List of countries included in our analysis are reported in Appendix Table 5.

### 3.1.1 Dependent Variable: Subjective Well-Being

Our dependent variable is consistent with the existing literature and measures self-reported subjective well-being (see, e.g., Angner, 2010; Awaworyi Churchill & Mishra, 2016; Diener & Oishi, 2000). The literature presents several ways to measure subjective well-being including happiness and life satisfaction (Pinquart & Sörensen, 2000). Given the data at hand, we focus on subjective happiness and life satisfaction as measures of well-being. The WVS provides information on individual life satisfaction and happiness through the answers to two questions: (1) "All things considered, how satisfied are you with your life as a whole these days? 1 means you are 'completely dissatisfied' and 10 means you are 'completely satisfied'; where would you put your satisfaction with your life as a whole?"; and (2) taking all things together, would you say you are "very happy," "quite happy," "not very happy" and "not at all happy"? 4 means "very happy," 3 means "quite happy," 2 means "not very happy," 1 means "not at all happy."[1]

Following Inglehart et al. (2008), we generate a composite index of subjective well-being using happiness and life satisfaction. We take the

[1]The coding we use transposed the original coding in the WVS dataset where 1 means "very happy," 2 means "quite happy," 3 means "not very happy," 4 means "not at all happy."

mean of individual responses to the happiness and life satisfaction questions to produces an index of subjective well-being. Given that happiness is measured on a 4-point scale while life satisfaction is on a 10-point scale, we multiply happiness by 2.5 before taking the mean of both indicators. We use the index of subjective well-being in our main regressions. For robustness, we also run regressions with the individual well-being indicators, i.e., happiness and life satisfaction.

### 3.1.2 Main Explanatory Variables

The WVS provides information on individual freedom through the answers to the question: "*how much freedom of choice and control do you have over your life? On a scale where 1 means 'no choice at all' and 10 means 'a great deal of choice' where would you put your freedom*?" Country-level freedom indicators include indices capturing: (1) How much civil liberties citizens of a country is perceived to have and (2) the level of political rights in the country.[2] Given the high correlation between civil liberties and political rights, we take the average of both variables as our measure of country-level freedom. We include interaction terms which capture the interaction between individual freedom and country-level freedom. We also include GDP per capita as a proxy for country-level economic development and wealth (national income). Interactions between GDP per capita and country-level freedom are also included as additional covariates.

### 3.1.3 Covariates

We control for other relevant factors, discussed in the literature, that are likely to affect an individual's happiness or life satisfaction: national GDP, gender, marital status, employment status, income, education, age,

[2]The Freedom House rating scores for civil liberties and political rights are original coded from 1 to 7, where 1 equals most free and 7 equals least free. In our regressions, to allow for ease of interpretation, we transpose this such that 1 equals least free and 7 most free.

health status and other community and family factors (see, e.g., Awaworyi Churchill & Mishra, 2016; Dolan, Peasgood, & White, 2008; Helliwell & Wang, 2011).

Our measures of gender, marital status, health status and employment status are dummy variables for respondents who are male, married, in good health and unemployed, respectively. Age is a continuous variable capturing the age of respondents while age squared is the quadratic term of age. Our measure of income is an income scale which, compared to continuous income values, addresses the problems associated with variations in relative income and currency value across different countries. Thus, we adopt an income scale which reflects 10 income categories with the lowest category being 1 and the highest being 10. Education captures respondents that have completed tertiary education either for a degree or non-degree program.

We also control for the importance of religion to the respondent, financial freedom and fear associated with various issues. For religion, the WVS asks if religion is important, and respondents are coded as one if they agree that religion is important. Our measure of financial freedom (*money*) is a dummy variable which equals one if a respondent has in the past gone without money to afford basic needs. Dummy variables are also included to capture respondents' fear of or worry about terrorist attack and civil war. Lastly, we include dummy variables that reflect whether respondents have felt unsafe from crime in the past (*unsafe*) and whether or not it is important for a respondent to help people nearby (*help*). To control for country and time fixed effects associated with the various waves of the survey, dummies for these are included.

Table 2 presents a description of variables together with summary statistics. Appendix Table 6 presents an overview of mean individual freedom scores in each country against Freedom House country-level civil liberties and political rights as well as GDP per capita and visually represented in Appendix Table 7. Appendix Table 8 presents a correlation matrix for variables the main variables included in our regressions.[3]

[3]Given space constraints and the large number of variables, we limit this table to main variables of interest.

**Table 2** Description of variables and summary statistics

| Variable | Descriptions | Mean | SD |
|---|---|---|---|
| Subjective well-being | Composite index of subjective well-being | 7.12 | 1.87 |
| Life satisfaction | All things considered, how satisfied are you with your life as a whole these days? 1 means you are "completely dissatisfied" and 10 means you are "completely satisfied" where would you put your satisfaction with your life as a whole? | 6.59 | 2.43 |
| Happiness | Taking all things together, would you say you are "very happy," "quite happy," "not very happy" and "not at all happy"? 1 means "very happy," 2 means "quite happy," 3 means "not very happy," 4 means "not at all happy" | 3.06 | 0.75 |
| Individual freedom | How much freedom of choice and control do you have over your life? On a scale where 1 means "no choice at all" and 10 means "a great deal of choice" | 6.85 | 2.41 |
| Civil liberty | Freedom House country civil liberties index | 3.21 | 1.71 |
| Political rights | Freedom House country political rights index | 3.31 | 1.99 |
| CLPR | Mean of civil liberty and political right | 3.27 | 1.82 |
| Freedom*CLPR | Interaction term between individual freedom and CLPR | 22.07 | 15.06 |
| GDP per capita | Log of real GDP per capita in constant 2010 dollars | 8.81 | 1.38 |
| GDP/capita*CLPR | Interaction term between GDP per capita and political rights | 27.15 | 14.22 |
| Male | Dummy variable equals to 1 if respondent is male | 0.48 | 0.50 |
| Married | Dummy variable equals to 1 if respondent is married | 0.64 | 0.48 |
| Unemployed | Dummy variable equals to 1 if respondent is unemployed | 0.09 | 0.28 |
| Education | Dummy variable equals to 1 if respondent has a tertiary education (either degree and non-degree) | 0.22 | 0.41 |
| Income | Scale of income | 4.67 | 2.33 |
| Age | Age of respondent | 40.48 | 16.21 |
| Age squared | Square of age/100 | 19.01 | 14.71 |
| Money | Dummy variable equals to 1 if respondent has in the past gone without money | 0.87 | 0.34 |

(continued)

**Table 2** (continued)

| Variable | Descriptions | Mean | SD |
|---|---|---|---|
| Unsafe | Dummy variable equals to 1 if respondent has in the past felt unsafe from crime | 0.83 | 0.38 |
| Helper | Dummy variable equals to 1 if It is important for respondent to help people nearby | 0.98 | 0.13 |
| Religion | Dummy variable equals to 1 if religion is important to respondent | 0.68 | 0.47 |
| Terrorism | Dummy variable equals to 1 if respondent worries about a terrorist attack | 0.17 | 0.38 |
| Civil war | Dummy variable equals to 1 if respondent worries about a civil war | 0.15 | 0.35 |
| Good health | Dummy variable equals to 1 if respondent self-assesses their general health as good/very good | 0.65 | 0.47 |

# 4 Empirical Model and Strategy

In order to examine the impact of individual freedom and country-level characteristics on subjective well-being, we estimate a model consistent with the existing literature (see, e.g., Di Tella, MacCulloch, & Oswald, 2003):

$$WB_{ji} = \alpha + \sum_{l} \gamma_l \boldsymbol{F}_{l,ji} + \sum_{m} \varphi_m \boldsymbol{C}_{m,j} + \sum_{n} \beta_n \boldsymbol{X}_{n,ji} + \varepsilon_{ji}$$

where $i$ indexes the individuals and $j$ indexes countries, $WB$ is the measure of subjective well-being, $F_l$ is a vector of our main explanatory variables (i.e., individual-level freedom and associated interaction terms), $C_m$ is a set of country-level variables including GDP per capita and indices of freedom. $X_n$ is a set of control variables or personal characteristics of respondents described earlier, $\gamma_l$, $\varphi_m$ and $\beta_n$ are parameters to be estimated, and $\varepsilon$ is the random error term. This model estimates the effects of our explanatory variable on individual-level well-being. We run ordinary least square (OLS) regressions but given the ordinal nature of our dependent variables, we also estimate the model using ordered logit regressions (Awaworyi Churchill & Mishra, 2016; Portela, Neira, & del Mar Salinas-Jiménez, 2013).

# 5 Empirical Results

Table 3 presents OLS and ordered logit regression results for effects on well-being. Columns 1 and 2 present results for OLS regressions while Columns 3 and 4 present results for ordered logit regressions. Results in Columns 1 and 3 are based on a model that only examines the effects of individual-level characteristics while those in Columns 2 and 4 include country-level variables and interaction terms.[4]

[4]The results discussed in this section focus mostly on regression with the most complete specification, which include both individual-level and country-level factors (Column 2). Both OLS and ordered logit results are consistent. Thus, we focus on ordered logit regressions for interpretation.

**Table 3** Freedom and subjective well-being

| Variables | (1) SWB | (2) SWB | (3) SWB | (4) SWB |
|---|---|---|---|---|
| Individual freedom | 0.219*** | 0.274*** | 0.276*** | 0.326*** |
| | (0.003) | (0.004) | (0.003) | (0.005) |
| CLPR | | 0.461*** | | 0.576*** |
| | | (0.029) | | (0.032) |
| Freedom*CLPR | | 0.005*** | | 0.005*** |
| | | (0.001) | | (0.001) |
| GDP per capita | | 0.288*** | | 0.301*** |
| | | (0.012) | | (0.013) |
| GDP/capita* CLPR | | 0.030*** | | 0.032*** |
| | | (0.003) | | (0.003) |
| Male | −0.136*** | −0.114*** | −0.157*** | −0.126*** |
| | (0.011) | (0.012) | (0.013) | (0.013) |
| Married | 0.407*** | 0.407*** | 0.458*** | 0.430*** |
| | (0.013) | (0.014) | (0.015) | (0.015) |
| Unemployed | −0.273*** | −0.207*** | −0.288*** | −0.190*** |
| | (0.027) | (0.030) | (0.030) | (0.032) |
| Age | 0.021*** | 0.011 | 0.028*** | 0.012 |
| | (0.008) | (0.009) | (0.009) | (0.009) |
| Age squared | −0.005 | 0.000 | −0.008 | 0.001 |
| | (0.006) | (0.007) | (0.007) | (0.007) |
| Income | 0.104*** | 0.093*** | 0.115*** | 0.098*** |
| | (0.003) | (0.003) | (0.003) | (0.003) |

| Variables | (1) SWB | (2) SWB | (3) SWB | (4) SWB |
|---|---|---|---|---|
| Money | −0.131*** | −0.233*** | −0.148*** | −0.244*** |
| | (0.022) | (0.023) | (0.025) | (0.025) |
| Unsafe | −0.296*** | −0.159*** | −0.332*** | −0.159*** |
| | (0.022) | (0.024) | (0.026) | (0.025) |
| Helper | 0.209*** | 0.165*** | 0.241*** | 0.202*** |
| | (0.043) | (0.046) | (0.047) | (0.048) |
| Religion | 0.231*** | 0.233*** | 0.268*** | 0.264*** |
| | (0.013) | (0.013) | (0.015) | (0.014) |
| Terrorism | 0.041 | −0.131*** | −0.056* | −0.143*** |
| | (0.026) | (0.027) | (0.030) | (0.029) |
| War | −0.095*** | −0.013 | −0.112*** | −0.004 |
| | (0.027) | (0.027) | (0.031) | (0.030) |
| Good health | 0.796*** | 0.902*** | 0.893*** | 0.956*** |
| | (0.012) | (0.013) | (0.014) | (0.014) |
| Country dummies | Yes | Yes | Yes | Yes |
| Wave dummies | Yes | Yes | Yes | Yes |
| Observations | 83,299 | 73,730 | 83,299 | 73,730 |
| $R^2$ | 0.389 | 0.318 | – | – |

Columns 1 and 2 report OLS regression results
Columns 3 and 4 report ordered logit regression results
Robust standard errors in parentheses
***$p < 0.01$, **$p < 0.05$, *$p < 0.1$

Overall, we find that higher levels of individual freedom are associated with increases in subjective well-being among older people. Specifically, from column (4), we find that the coefficient on our measure of individual freedom is 0.326, implying a 0.326 higher subjective well-being, on a scale of 1–10, if respondents thought they had complete freedom of choice and control over their life.

Turning to country-level freedom, we find a positive association between freedom and well-being. Thus, an increase in country-level freedom (i.e., civil liberties and political rights) is associated with an increase in subjective well-being. This effect is stronger in magnitude compared to the effect of personal freedom on well-being. Specifically, we find that the coefficient explaining the effects of country-level freedom on well-being is about double the effects of personal freedom.

GDP per capita (our proxy for national income) enters the model significant with a positive coefficient. This finding is consistent with past findings (Di Tella et al., 2003) and suggests that an increase in national income is associated with an increase in subjective well-being.

The interaction term between individual freedom and country-level freedom is positive and statistically significant. A simple slopes analysis showed that people with low personal freedom had higher well-being in countries with low freedom compared to countries with high freedom. In contrast, people with high personal freedom tended to do better in countries with high freedom compared to countries with low freedom. This supports the person-environment fit hypothesis, such that individuals benefit most from civil and political liberties when the environment fits their personal situation.

To examine the robustness of our results, we examine the impact of our explanatory variables on the individual indicators of well-being used in our composite index. These results are presented in Table 4. Columns 1 and 2 report results for effects on life satisfaction and Columns 3 and 4 for effects on happiness. Regressions in odd columns (1 and 3) present results for a model that only examines the effects of individual-level characteristics while even columns (2 and 4) include country-level variables and interaction terms.

Overall, we find that results here are consistent with those from our main regression, where higher levels of individual freedom are associated

**Table 4** Further analysis

| Variables | (1) Satisfaction | (2) Satisfaction | (3) Happiness | (4) Happiness |
|---|---|---|---|---|
| Individual freedom | 0.311*** | 0.351*** | 0.156*** | 0.201*** |
| | (0.004) | (0.005) | (0.003) | (0.005) |
| CLPR | | 0.145*** | | 0.309*** |
| | | (0.032) | | (0.037) |
| Freedom*CLPR | | 0.002 | | 0.006*** |
| | | (0.001) | | (0.001) |
| GDP per capita | | 0.265*** | | 0.237*** |
| | | (0.012) | | (0.014) |
| GDP/capita* CLPR | | 0.018*** | | 0.036*** |
| | | (0.003) | | (0.004) |
| Male | −0.140*** | −0.114*** | −0.141*** | −0.105*** |
| | (0.012) | (0.013) | (0.014) | (0.015) |
| Married | 0.294*** | 0.269*** | 0.563*** | 0.545*** |
| | (0.015) | (0.015) | (0.017) | (0.017) |
| Unemployed | −0.259*** | −0.207*** | −0.256*** | −0.123*** |
| | (0.030) | (0.032) | (0.035) | (0.037) |
| Age | 0.032*** | 0.020** | 0.014 | 0.004 |
| | (0.009) | (0.009) | (0.010) | (0.011) |
| Age squared | −0.012* | −0.005 | −0.000 | 0.005 |
| | (0.007) | (0.007) | (0.008) | (0.008) |
| Income | 0.108*** | 0.090*** | 0.085*** | 0.073*** |
| | (0.003) | (0.003) | (0.003) | (0.003) |
| Money | −0.154*** | −0.255*** | −0.081*** | −0.133*** |
| | (0.024) | (0.024) | (0.029) | (0.029) |
| Unsafe | −0.248*** | −0.069*** | −0.352*** | −0.237*** |
| | (0.025) | (0.024) | (0.030) | (0.030) |
| Helper | 0.178*** | 0.172*** | 0.247*** | 0.153*** |
| | (0.047) | (0.048) | (0.055) | (0.056) |
| Religion | 0.206*** | 0.152*** | 0.280*** | 0.350*** |
| | (0.014) | (0.014) | (0.017) | (0.016) |
| Terrorism | 0.042 | −0.130*** | 0.057 | −0.138*** |
| | (0.029) | (0.028) | (0.035) | (0.034) |
| War | −0.123*** | −0.020 | −0.093*** | −0.031 |
| | (0.030) | (0.029) | (0.036) | (0.035) |
| Good health | 0.672*** | 0.724*** | 0.960*** | 1.022*** |
| | (0.014) | (0.014) | (0.016) | (0.016) |
| Country dummies | Yes | Yes | Yes | Yes |
| Wave dummies | Yes | Yes | Yes | Yes |
| Observations | 83,299 | 73,730 | 83,299 | 73,730 |

Robust standard errors in parentheses
***$p < 0.01$, **$p < 0.05$, *$p < 0.1$

with increases in subjective well-being. Specifically, from column (2), we find that the coefficient on our measure of individual freedom is 0.351, implying a 0.351 higher individual life satisfaction, on a scale of 1–10, if respondents thought they had complete freedom of choice and control over their life. Similarly, from column (4), we find that the coefficient on our measure of individual freedom is 0.201, which implies a 0.201 increase in perceived individual happiness, on a four-point scale, if respondents thought they had complete freedom of choice and control over their life. Results for country-level freedom and interaction terms are also consistent.

# 6 Discussion

The United Nations has identified population aging as one of the most important social issues in this century. The population size of individuals aged 60 and over is increasing faster than all other age groups and is expected to triple by 2010 to 3.1 billion (United Nations, 2017). The Second World Assembly on Aging has called for policymakers to create environments that support and facilitate healthy aging (United Nations, 2008). In this study, we examine the relationship between personal and country-level freedom on well-being. It is important to note that the correlation between personal freedom and country freedom is small ($r = .007$), indicating that there is little overlap between the two variables. We found that both levels of freedom positively contribute to well-being, with country-level freedom having nearly two times the effect on well-being compared to that of personal freedom.

We also found a significant interaction between personal and country-level freedom. People who had low personal control had greater life satisfaction when living in countries with limited political and civic liberties, compared to living in free countries. It may be that individuals with low levels of personal freedom have adapted to the restrictions of the system by giving up primary control strategies and adopting secondary control strategies (Heckhausen, 1997). This allows them to gain a sense of life satisfaction and happiness while living in a restrictive and controlling system. For people with low personal freedom, they may benefit more from systems with limited freedom as they can focus on their own quality of life rather than participating in the larger society. They need not take personal responsibility for the well-being of the system, or feel guilty for not being involved, given that the system does not afford them the opportunities to do so. Thus, rather than contributing to their sense of well-being, political and civil liberties are perceived as an added burden.

There was a non-significant trend where people with high personal control had higher well-being in free countries. This is consistent with the findings of O'Conner and Vallerand (1994) showing that self-determined individuals were less affected by nursing home environments. Future research could look at whether what agentic and self-determined individuals do in controlling situations. Importantly, our results hold even after controlling for income, which supports past research showing that income and agency have independent effects of well-being on a personal (Creed & Klisch, 2005) and national level (Acemoglu, Johnson, Robinson, & Yared, 2008).

One of the limitations is that we could not identify what factors contribute to a low sense of personal control (e.g., health, finances), nonetheless this study has important implications for the literature on healthy aging and well-being. An environment that promotes both personal and system freedom appears to be optimal for well-being. People have a sense of personal control in an environment that encourages and values their participation. The impact of personal and system freedom cannot be overstated, given the main effect sizes are much greater than the interaction effect size. This shifts the focus to a much more practical one—not whether freedom is beneficial but how to enhance the benefits of freedom on well-being. Freedom is not valued when it is experienced as chaotic and unstructured. For instance, opportunities for participation and choices in schools need to be offered in a manner that meets the students' needs (Katz & Assor, 2007). They have to be relevant to the students' interests and goals, optimally challenging and congruent with personal values. For individuals with a low sense of personal control, system liberties can feel anxiety-provoking rather than freeing. Freedom may mean that the responsibility lies solely on an individual's knowledge of and agency to make full use of opportunities provided. People with low personal freedom may experience the many choices and information as irrelevant and overwhelming (Moller, Deci, & Ryan, 2006). Thus, system freedom needs to be accompanied with increased accessibility to help them navigate and fully participate in the system to the extent that the elderly are able to and that they want to. For individuals who are aging and need to prioritize limited resources, the choice not to choose and control must be respected as well, while working with them to build and maintain a sense of self-determination in life domains that are personally meaningful.

## Appendix

See Tables 5, 6, 7, and 8.

**Table 5** List of countries

| Albania | Ghana | Philippines |
|---|---|---|
| Algeria | Great Britain | Poland |
| Andorra | Guatemala | Qatar |
| Argentina | Hungary | Romania |
| Armenia | India | Russia |
| Australia | Indonesia | Rwanda |
| Azerbaijan | Iran | Saudi Arabia |
| Bahrain | Iraq | Serbia |
| Bangladesh | Italy | Singapore |
| Belarus | Japan | Slovakia |
| Bosnia | Jordan | Slovenia |
| Brazil | Kazakhstan | South Africa |
| Bulgaria | Kuwait | South Korea |
| Burkina Faso | Kyrgyzstan | Spain |
| Canada | Latvia | Sweden |
| Chile | Lebanon | Switzerland |
| China | Libya | Tanzania |
| Colombia | Lithuania | Thailand |
| Croatia | Macedonia | Trinidad and Tobago |
| Cyprus | Malaysia | Tunisia |
| Czech Republic | Mali | Turkey |
| Dominican Republic | Mexico | Uganda |
| Ecuador | Moldova | Ukraine |
| Egypt | Montenegro | United States |
| El Salvador | Morocco | Uruguay |
| Estonia | Netherlands | Uzbekistan |
| Ethiopia | New Zealand | Venezuela |
| Finland | Nigeria | Viet Nam |
| France | Norway | Yemen |
| Georgia | Pakistan | Zambia |
| Germany | Peru | Zimbabwe |

**Table 6** Mean values of relevant explanatory variables against individual freedom mean scores

| Countries | Individual freedom | GDP per capita | Civil liberty | Political rights |
|---|---|---|---|---|
| Albania | 5 | 4261 | 4 | 4 |
| Algeria | 7 | 4343 | 5 | 6 |
| Andorra | 8 | 45,393 | 1 | 1 |
| Argentina | 7 | 6722 | 1 | 2 |
| Armenia | 6 | 1787 | 4 | 5 |
| Australia | 8 | 45,668 | 1 | 1 |
| Azerbaijan | 6 | 4523 | 5 | 6 |
| Bahrain | 7 | 22,259 | 5 | 6 |
| Bangladesh | 6 | 417 | 4 | 4 |
| Belarus | 6 | 13,447 | 1 | 1 |
| Bosnia | 6 | 2960 | 4 | 5 |
| Brazil | 8 | 10,048 | 3 | 2 |
| Bulgaria | 6 | 4131 | 4 | 2 |
| Burkina Faso | 6 | 525 | 4 | 6 |
| Canada | 8 | 47,753 | 1 | 1 |
| Chile | 7 | 13,791 | 2 | 2 |
| China | 7 | 2081 | 6 | 7 |
| Colombia | 8 | 5789 | 4 | 3 |
| Croatia | 6 | 12,162 | 4 | 4 |
| Cyprus | 8 | 21,989 | 1 | 1 |
| Czech Republic | 6 | 15,728 | 2 | 1 |
| Dominican Republic | 7 | 3981 | 2 | 2 |
| Ecuador | 8 | 3783 | 3 | 2 |
| Egypt | 6 | 2658 | 4 | 6 |
| El Salvador | 8 | 2857 | 4 | 3 |
| Estonia | 6 | 15,885 | 2 | 2 |
| Ethiopia | 6 | 396 | 5 | 6 |
| Finland | 8 | 35,069 | 1 | 1 |
| France | 7 | 40,906 | 2 | 1 |
| Georgia | 6 | 3426 | 5 | 4 |
| Germany | 7 | 35,708 | 1 | 1 |
| Ghana | 7 | 1535 | 3 | 3 |
| Great Britain | 7 | 36,251 | 1 | 1 |
| Guatemala | 7 | 2748 | 4 | 3 |
| Hungary | 6 | 9342 | 5 | 2 |

(continued)

**Table 6** (continued)

| Countries | Individual freedom | GDP per capita | Civil liberty | Political rights |
|---|---|---|---|---|
| India | 6 | 29,741 | 1 | 1 |
| Indonesia | 7 | 578 | 4 | 2 |
| Iran | 7 | 4074 | 6 | 6 |
| Iraq | 6 | 2404 | 6 | 7 |
| Italy | 6 | 36,699 | 2 | 1 |
| Japan | 6 | 42,715 | 2 | 1 |
| Jordan | 7 | 2859 | 4 | 5 |
| Kazakhstan | 7 | 9874 | 5 | 6 |
| Kuwait | 8 | 40,163 | 5 | 5 |
| Kyrgyzstan | 7 | 821 | 5 | 5 |
| Latvia | 6 | 9763 | 2 | 2 |
| Lebanon | 7 | 6729 | 5 | 6 |
| Libya | 7 | 11,310 | 7 | 7 |
| Lithuania | 6 | 11,978 | 2 | 1 |
| Macedonia | 6 | 3201 | 3 | 3 |
| Malaysia | 7 | 8441 | 4 | 4 |
| Mali | 6 | 352 | 3 | 3 |
| Mexico | 8 | 7534 | 3 | 4 |
| Moldova | 6 | 1016 | 4 | 4 |
| Montenegro | 6 | 1528 | 4 | 2 |
| Morocco | 6 | 1875 | 4 | 5 |
| Netherlands | 7 | 46,598 | 1 | 1 |
| New Zealand | 8 | 31,302 | 1 | 1 |
| Nigeria | 7 | 361 | 3 | 5 |
| Norway | 7 | 58,674 | 1 | 1 |
| Pakistan | 6 | 873 | 5 | 4 |
| Peru | 7 | 4357 | 4 | 3 |
| Philippines | 7 | 1475 | 3 | 3 |
| Poland | 7 | 13,376 | 2 | 2 |
| Qatar | 8 | 73,546 | 5 | 6 |
| Romania | 7 | 6352 | 5 | 4 |
| Russia | 6 | 7904 | 6 | 7 |
| Rwanda | 7 | 609 | 5 | 7 |
| Saudi Arabia | 7 | 14,887 | 7 | 7 |
| Serbia | 6 | 3849 | 2 | 2 |
| Singapore | 7 | 49,155 | 4 | 5 |
| Slovakia | 6 | 12,231 | 1 | 2 |

(continued)

**Table 6** (continued)

| Countries | Individual freedom | GDP per capita | Civil liberty | Political rights |
|---|---|---|---|---|
| Slovenia | 8 | 20,764 | 2 | 1 |
| South Africa | 7 | 7537 | 2 | 2 |
| South Korea | 7 | 6939 | 3 | 2 |
| Spain | 7 | 29,851 | 2 | 1 |
| Sweden | 7 | 35,910 | 1 | 1 |
| Switzerland | 7 | 73,065 | 1 | 1 |
| Tanzania | 6 | 474 | 6 | 5 |
| Thailand | 7 | 3774 | 4 | 3 |
| Trinidad and Tobago | 8 | 15,932 | 3 | 2 |
| Tunisia | 7 | 2714 | 4 | 5 |
| Turkey | 6 | 7538 | 3 | 4 |
| Uganda | 7 | 318 | 4 | 5 |
| Ukraine | 6 | 1757 | 2 | 3 |
| United States | 8 | 34,113 | 1 | 1 |
| Uruguay | 8 | 8843 | 1 | 1 |
| Uzbekistan | 8 | 1552 | 6 | 7 |
| Venezuela | 8 | 14,054 | 2 | 5 |
| Viet Nam | 7 | 409 | 7 | 7 |
| Yemen | 6 | 1041 | 6 | 6 |
| Zambia | 7 | 917 | 5 | 5 |
| Zimbabwe | 6 | 773 | 6 | 6 |

*Notes* Mean scores by countries. Original coding for Freedom House rating maintained. For civil liberties and political rights, 1 = most free and 7 = least free. For individual freedom, 1 = least freedom of control and choice and 9 = most freedom of control and choice

**Table 7** Standardized scores of personal and country freedom. Countries are arranged according to standardized scores of country, with countries on the right being more free than countries on the left on the Y-axis

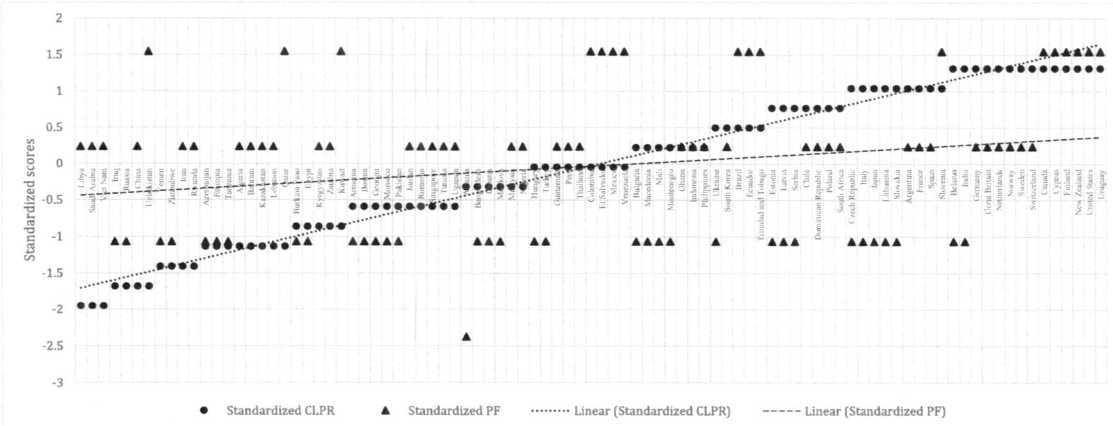

**Table 8** Correlation matrix

| | A | B | C | D | E | F | G |
|---|---|---|---|---|---|---|---|
| A | – | | | | | | |
| B | 0.3829 | – | | | | | |
| C | 0.2317 | 0.1509 | – | | | | |
| D | 0.1463 | −0.0710 | −0.0412 | – | | | |
| E | 0.1515 | −0.0739 | −0.0371 | 0.9265 | – | | |
| F | 0.1520 | 0.0739 | 0.0397 | −0.9784 | −0.9843 | – | |
| G | 0.1667 | 0.0802 | 0.0637 | −0.6136 | −0.6224 | −0.6299 | – |

*Notes* A—Subjective well-being; B—Individual freedom; C—Income; D—Civil liberty; E—Political rights; F—CLPR; G—GDP per capita. All correlations are significant at a $p < 0.01$

# References

Acemoglu, D., Johnson, S., Robinson, J. A., & Yared, P. (2008). Income and democracy. *American Economic Review, 98,* 808–842.

Angner, E. (2010). Subjective well-being. *The Journal of Socio-Economics, 39,* 361–368.

Armstrong, D. A. (2011). Stability and change in the Freedom House political rights and civil liberties measures. *Journal of Peace Research, 48,* 653–662.

Awaworyi Churchill, S., & Mishra, V. (2016). Trust, social networks and subjective wellbeing in China. *Social Indicators Research, 132,* 313–339.

Bollen, K. A. (1990). Political democracy: Conceptual and measurement traps. *Studies in Comparative International Development, 25,* 7–24.

Bronfenbrenner, U. (1977). Toward an experimental ecology of human development. *American Psychologist, 32*(7), 513–531.

Bronfenbrenner, U., & Morris, P. A. (1998). The ecology of developmental processes. In W. Damon & R. M. Lerner (Eds.), *Handbook of child psychology: Theoretical models of human development* (pp. 993–1028). Hoboken, NJ, USA: Wiley.

Collopy, B. J. (1988). Autonomy in long term care: Some crucial distinctions. *The Gerontologist, 28*(Suppl), 10–17.

Collopy, B., Dubler, N., Zuckerman, C., Crigger, B. J., & Campbell, C. S. (1990). Special supplement: The ethics of home care—Autonomy and accommodation. *The Hastings Center Report, 20,* 1–16.

Creed, P. A., & Klisch, J. (2005). Future outlook and financial strain: Testing the personal agency and latent deprivation models of unemployment and well-being. *Journal of Occupational Health Psychology, 10,* 251–260.

DeCharms, R. C. (1968). *Personal causation: The internal affective determinants of behavior.* New York: Academic Press.

Di Tella, R., MacCulloch, R. J., & Oswald, A. J. (2003). The macroeconomics of happiness. *Review of Economics and Statistics, 85,* 809–827.

Diener, E., Diener, M., & Diener, C. (2009). Factors predicting the subjective well-being of nations. In *Culture and well-being* (pp. 43–70). Dordrecht: Springer.

Diener, E., & Oishi, S. (2000). Money and happiness: Income and subjective well-being across nations. In E. Diener & E. M. Suh (Eds.), *Culture and subjective well-being* (pp. 185–218). Cambridge, MA, USA: The MIT Press.

Dolan, P., Peasgood, T., & White, M. (2008). Do we really know what makes us happy? A review of the economic literature on the factors associated with subjective well-being. *Journal of Economic Psychology, 29,* 94–122.

Downie, M., Koestner, R., & Chua, S. N. (2007). Political support for self-determination, wealth, and national subjective well-being. *Motivation and Emotion, 31,* 174–181.

Geeraert, N., Li, R., Ward, C., Gelfand, M., & Demes, K. A. (2019). A tight spot: How personality moderates the impact of social norms on sojourner adaptation. *Psychological Science, 30,* 333–342.

Gelfand, M. J., Raver, J. L., Nishii, L., Leslie, L. M., Lun, J., Lim, B. C., … & Aycan, Z. (2011). Differences between tight and loose cultures: A 33-nation study. *Science, 332,* 1100–1104.

Heckhausen, J. (1997). Developmental regulation across adulthood: Primary and secondary control of age-related challenges. *Developmental Psychology, 33,* 176–187.

Helliwell, J. F., & Wang, S. (2011). Trust and well-being. *Journal of Wellbeing, 1,* 42–78.

Inglehart, R., Foa, R., Peterson, C., & Welzel, C. (2008). Development, freedom, and rising happiness: A global perspective (1981–2007). *Perspectives on Psychological Science, 3,* 264–285.

Kasser, V. G., & Ryan, R. M. (1999). The relation of psychological needs for autonomy and relatedness to vitality, well-being, and mortality in a nursing home. *Journal of Applied Social Psychology, 29,* 935–954.

Katz, I., & Assor, A. (2007). When choice motivates and when it does not. *Educational Psychology Review, 19,* 429–442.

Lachman, M. E., & Leff, R. (1989). Perceived control and intellectual functioning in the elderly: A 5-year longitudinal study. *Developmental Psychology, 25,* 722–728.

Lau, S., Hiemisch, A., & Baumeister, R. F. (2015). The experience of freedom in decisions–Questioning philosophical beliefs in favor of psychological determinants. *Consciousness and Cognition, 33,* 30–46.

Moller, A. C., Deci, E. L., & Ryan, R. M. (2006). Choice and ego-depletion: The moderating role of autonomy. *Personality and Social Psychology Bulletin, 32,* 1024–1036.

Moore, E., Rosenberg, M. W., & Fitzgibbon, S. H. (1999). Activity limitation and chronic conditions in Canada's elderly, 1986–2011. *Disability and Rehabilitation, 21,* 196–210.

O'Connor, B. P., & Vallerand, R. J. (1994). Motivation, self-determination, and person environment fit as predictors of psychological adjustment among nursing home residents. *Psychology and Aging, 9,* 189–194.

Pinquart, M., & Sörensen, S. (2000). Influences of socioeconomic status, social network, and competence on subjective well-being in later life: A meta-analysis. *Psychology and Aging, 15,* 187–224.

Portela, M., Neira, I., & del Mar Salinas-Jiménez, M. (2013). Social capital and subjective wellbeing in Europe: A new approach on social capital. *Social Indicators Research, 114,* 493–511.

Rodin, J. (1986). Aging and health: Effects of the sense of control. *Science, 233,* 1271–1276.

Rothbaum, F., Weisz, J. R., & Snyder, S. S. (1982). Changing the world and changing the self: A two-process model of perceived control. *Journal of Personality and Social Psychology, 42,* 5–37.

Royall, D. R., Palmer, R., Chiodo, L. K., & Polk, M. J. (2004). Declining executive control in normal aging predicts change in functional status: The Freedom House Study. *Journal of the American Geriatrics Society, 52,* 346–352.

Ryan, R. M., & Deci, E. L. (2017). *Self-determination theory: Basic psychological needs in motivation, development, and wellness.* New York: Guilford Publications.

Smith, R. A. P., Woodward, N. J., Wallston, B. S., Wallston, K. A., Rye, P., & Zylstra, M. (1988). Health care implications of desire and expectancy for control in elderly adults. *Journal of Gerontology: Psychological Sciences, 43,* P1–P7.

Thomasma, D. C. (1984). Freedom, dependency, and the care of the very old. *Journal of the American Geriatrics Society, 32,* 906–914.

Tilly, C. (2007). *Democracy.* Retrieved from https://www.cambridge.org/core/books/democracy/26A098816E37F7FB60873348D1BBEBD3.

United Nations. (2008). *The Madrid International Plan of Action on Ageing: Guiding framework and toolkit for practitioners and policy makers.* New York: Department of Economic and Social Affairs.

United Nations. (2017). *World population ageing 2017—Highlights* (ST/ESA/SER.A/397). New York: Department of Economic and Social Affairs, Population Division.

Veenhoven, R. (2000). Freedom and happiness: A comparative study in forty-four nations in the early 1990s. In E. Diener & E. M. Suh (Eds.), *Culture and subjective well-being* (pp. 257–288). Cambridge, MA, USA: The MIT Press.

Verme, P. (2009). Happiness, freedom and control. *Journal of Economic Behavior & Organization, 71,* 146–161.

Welzel, C., & Inglehart, R. (2010). Agency, values, and well-being: A human development model. *Social Indicators Research, 97,* 43–63.

Westcott, M. R. (1992). The discursive expression of human freedom. *American Behavioral Scientist, 36,* 73–87.

Wilkie, R., Peat, G., Thomas, E., & Croft, P. (2007). Factors associated with participation restriction in community-dwelling adults aged 50 years and over. *Quality of Life Research, 16,* 1147–1156.

# 12

# Innovation and Subjective Wellbeing Among Older People

Sefa Awaworyi Churchill and Anne-Laure Mention

## 1 Background

The effects of innovation are widely known, and across various levels of society, many have come to embrace the importance of innovation. The early concept of innovation in economics suggests that innovation comprises elements of technological advancement, research and development (R&D), creativity, new products, services and processes that can have economy-wide effects (see, e.g., Grossman & Helpman, 1991; Schumpeter, 1942; Solow, 1956). The rapid pace of innovation and

S. Awaworyi Churchill (✉)
School of Economics, Finance and Marketing, RMIT University, Melbourne, VIC, Australia
e-mail: sefa.awaworyichurchill@rmit.edu.au

A.-L. Mention
Research and Innovation, College of Business, RMIT University, Melbourne, Australia
e-mail: anne-laure.mention@rmit.edu.au



S. Awaworyi Churchill et al. (eds.), *Measuring, Understanding and Improving Wellbeing Among Older People*,
https://doi.org/10.1007/978-981-15-2353-3_12

technological change is, thus, argued to have direct relevance for both public policy and welfare.

We examine the effects of innovation on subjective wellbeing. Despite the large body of literature that examines the impact of innovation, very little is known about the effects of innovation on wellbeing. Traditionally, macroeconomic indicators such as economic growth have been used to access the wellbeing of a country and by extension its citizens. Thus, a large body of literature has examined the link between innovation and economic growth (see, e.g., Bilbao-Osorio & Rodríguez-Pose, 2004; Scherer, 1986; Solow, 1956; Verspagen, 2006). However, given that subjective wellbeing measures are now increasingly being used to monitor progress and evaluate policy (Fujiwara & Campbell, 2011; Sachs, Becchetti, & Annett, 2016), it is important to understand the effects of innovation on subjective wellbeing. Further, innovation has become part of public policy agendas in many countries, and a part of government efforts to improve welfare and reduce inequality around the world. Indeed, the OECD's Observatory of Public Sector Innovation (OPSI) initiative, aimed at reviewing ways governments are improving lives through innovation, attests to the widespread adoption of innovation.

Conceptually, innovation may either promote or hinder subjective wellbeing depending on the channels of influence. For instance, the positive effects of innovation on economic growth, discussed in the literature, suggest that innovation is likely to have a positive effect on subjective wellbeing via the economic growth channel given the established positive link between economic growth and individual wellbeing (Helliwell, 2003). However, despite its popularity and acceptance as an important engine for economic growth, innovation has also been criticized since the Luddite riots of the nineteenth century. The objection of Luddites was not to a lack of economic efficiency through technological innovation but to efficiency derived from innovation that may have harmful social consequences. Thus, while innovation may be considered as essential for productivity and economic progress, it has also been associated with job loss and unemployment (Ugur, Awaworyi Churchill, & Solomon, 2018), which are known to negatively influence subjective wellbeing (Awaworyi Churchill & Mishra, 2017). Put differently, innovation has been associated with job loss and unemployment, and may thus negatively influence wellbeing through this channel.

We study whether an individual's wellbeing is enhanced by the level of innovation in the country in which they live. Specifically, we examine the impact of country-level innovation on the subjective wellbeing of older people with the aim of identifying if innovation is an important factor to focus on when shaping policy to influence the wellbeing of older people. Using cross-country data from two waves of the World Values Survey (WVS) and the Global Innovation Index (GII) to measure country-level innovation, we find that innovation is positively associated with subjective wellbeing. This result is robust to the use of the recorded number of patents per country as an alternative measure of innovation.

Our study contributes to a very small body of literature that examines the link between subjective wellbeing and innovation (Dolan & Metcalfe, 2012; Engelbrecht, 2014, 2018). Using data on Britain, Dolan and Metcalfe (2012) present empirical evidence to show that creativity, measured by self-reported creativity and working in creative environments, is correlated with wellbeing. Engelbrecht (2014, 2018) proposes conceptual models that explain the link between innovation and subjective wellbeing, and demonstrates the many ways in which this link can be established. We contribute to this literature by providing the first cross-country empirical study that examines the impact of country-level innovation on the individual subjective wellbeing of older people.

## 2 Data and Variables

Our data comes from three sources. Individual level data are sourced from the WVS, which presents nationally representative samples that capture socioeconomic and political values of respondents in approximately 100 countries. The WVS data are based on survey questionnaires that are designed to capture the beliefs and values of respondents across different countries, how they change over time and how they may impact social, economic, and political factors. Specifically, the WVS monitors and reports information on issues related to religion, democracy, tolerance, gender equality, work, family, national identity, culture, diversity, politics and subjective wellbeing, among others. The first wave of the WVS was launched in 1981 followed by five subsequent waves. However, our study is restricted only to the last two waves—the fifth (2005–2009) and sixth (2010–2014) waves—given that data on our main measures of innovation are only available from 2007. Data on innovation are drawn from the GII database, and the World Bank's World Development Indicators database.

Given that our study focuses on older people, we restrict our sample to respondents that are at least 50 years old.[1] Regressions with the largest number of observation include a sample size of 27,182 across 58 countries. A list of countries included in the analysis is reported in Table 4.

## 2.1 Dependent Variables

Consistent with the existing literature, our dependent variable is a measure of self-reported subjective wellbeing (see, e.g., Angner, 2010; Awaworyi Churchill & Mishra, 2016; Diener & Oishi, 2000). The literature presents several ways to measure subjective wellbeing including happiness, life satisfaction and perceptions of self-esteem (Pinquart & Sörensen, 2000). Given the data at hand, we focus on life satisfaction as our main measure of wellbeing. The WVS provides information on individual life satisfaction through the answers to the question: (1) "All things considered, how satisfied are you with your life as a whole these days? 1 means you are 'completely dissatisfied' and 10 means you are 'completely satisfied'; where would you put your satisfaction with your life as a whole?"

In robustness checks, we also use a measure of subjective happiness, which is based on the WVS question: Taking all things together, would you say you are "very happy," "quite happy," "not very happy" and "not at

[1] Given that there are different cutoffs, in terms of age, for those considered as part of the elderly population, we use 50 years which is consistent with recent World Health Organization discussions which consider life expectancy in the developing world.

all happy"? (1) means "very happy," (2) means "quite happy," (3) means "not very happy," (4) means "not at all happy."

## 2.2 Main Explanatory Variable

An important challenge for academics and policymakers is how best to measure innovation. In economics, the traditional measures of innovation inputs have been expenditure-based variables such as investment in R&D or R&D expenditures as a share of GDP. However, recent efforts have led to the development of composite indices such as the GII, which is an annual ranking of countries reflecting their capacity for, and success in, innovation. This index published by Cornell University, INSEAD, and the World Intellectual Property Organization in partnership with other institutions is argued to capture the multi-dimensional nature of innovation. The index comprises of two sub-indices focused on the innovation input and output.[2] We use the GII as our measure of innovation given its multi-dimensional nature. The GII is on a 0–100 scale but prior to 2011 was on a 1–7 scale.[3]

In robustness checks, we use country-level patent information, drawn from the World Bank's World Development Indicators database, to examine the robustness of our results. Specifically, patent is measured as the number of patent applications per year made by residents with a national patent office. A patent provides protection for an invention, defined as a product or process that offers a new technical solution to a problem or provides a new way of doing something. This is an important measure of innovation output.

[2] Details on index construction can be found at https://www.globalinnovationindex.org/about-gii#framework.

[3] We convert the scores on previous versions of the index to correspond with a 0–100 scale.

## 2.3 Control Variables

Endogenous growth theories suggest that the interaction between innovation and relevant economic factors induces economic growth (Grossman & Helpman, 1991), and thus, innovation has direct effects on economic growth, which in turn affects subjective wellbeing (Becker, Rayo, & Krueger, 2008; Frijters, Haisken-DeNew, & Shields, 2004). Thus, to isolate the effects of innovation on subjective wellbeing, we include GDP per capita as a proxy to control for economic performance.

At the individual level, we control for factors that the existing literature has associated with self-reported subjective wellbeing including income, marital status, gender, age, employment status, religion, and general health, among others (Awaworyi Churchill & Mishra, 2017; Biswas-Diener & Diener, 2006; Helliwell & Putnam, 2004; Helliwell & Wang, 2011).

Our measure of income is an income scale, which reflects 10 income categories with 1 representing the lowest income group and 10 the highest income group. The use of an income scale instead on income values addresses problems associated with different currencies used in different countries as well as with potential variations in relative wealth across countries (Awaworyi Churchill, Appau, & Farrell, 2019). For marital status, gender and employment status, we include dummy variables for respondents who are married, male, and unemployed, respectively. We include age and the quadratic term of age as additional covariates.

Additionally, we control for religion through the WVS questions which ask if religion is important to respondents. We include a dummy variable which equals one when respondents agree that religion is important. We also control for financial freedom by introducing a dummy which equals one if a respondent has in the past gone without money to afford basic needs. Other controls include dummy variables that capture respondents' worry or fear of terrorism and crime. Lastly, we include a dummy variable to capture self-reported health and another to capture whether respondents consider help they extend to others to be important.

In order to control for country-level fixed effects, we also include country dummies. We also control for year fixed effects which correspond with the waves of the surveys, and particularly, the years during which respondents are interviewed. Table 5 presents a list and description of variables used in the analysis.

## 3 Empirical Strategy

We estimate a subjective wellbeing equation consistent with the literature that has examined the impact of macro-level variables on individual level subjective wellbeing (Tella, MacCulloch, & Oswald, 2003). Specifically, we estimate the following wellbeing equation:

$$WB_{ij} = f\left(I_j, G_j, X_{ij}, \varepsilon_{ij}\right)$$

where $i$ indexes the individuals and $j$ indexes countries. $WB$ is the measure of subjective wellbeing, $I$ is the measure of innovation while $G$ is GDP per capita. $X$ is a set of individual level control variables, and $\varepsilon$ is the random error term. The existing literature on the determinants of subjective wellbeing uses either ordinary least squares (OLS) or ordered logit regressions. To ensure robustness, we estimate the above model using both OLS and ordered logits, and find that, consistent with the literature (Ferrer-i-Carbonell & Frijters, 2004), findings are not sensitive to treating subjective wellbeing as ordinal or cardinal. As a further robustness check on our results, we also adopt the Lewbel (2012) 2SLS approach. Lewbel (2012) proposes a heteroskedasticity-based approach to address endogeneity using internally generated instruments. This method is used in the subjective wellbeing literature to address endogeneity given the difficulty in finding valid external instruments (Awaworyi Churchill & Mishra, 2017).[4]

[4]See Lewbel (2012) for more details.

# 4 Results

Table 1 presents results for the association between innovation and sub-

**Table 1** Innovation and wellbeing (baseline results)

| Variables | (1)<br>OLS | (2)<br>Ordered logit |
|---|---|---|
| Global Innovation Index | 0.250*** | 0.289*** |
| | (0.076) | (0.083) |
| GDP per capita | 0.365 | 0.657* |
| | (0.359) | (0.389) |
| Income | 0.137*** | 0.157*** |
| | (0.005) | (0.006) |
| Male | −0.115*** | −0.140*** |
| | (0.019) | (0.022) |
| Married | 0.428*** | 0.478*** |
| | (0.022) | (0.026) |
| Unemployed | −0.176*** | −0.166*** |
| | (0.044) | (0.049) |
| Age | 0.042*** | 0.043*** |
| | (0.014) | (0.016) |
| Age squared | −0.022** | −0.019 |
| | (0.011) | (0.012) |
| Money | −0.342*** | −0.387*** |
| | (0.026) | (0.031) |
| Unsafe | −0.265*** | −0.327*** |
| | (0.026) | (0.030) |
| Help | 0.235*** | 0.272*** |
| | (0.058) | (0.064) |
| Religion | 0.231*** | 0.279*** |
| | (0.024) | (0.027) |
| Terrorism | −0.045* | −0.057** |
| | (0.023) | (0.027) |
| General health | 0.956*** | 1.082*** |
| | (0.021) | (0.025) |
| Year/wave dummies | Yes | Yes |
| Country dummies | Yes | Yes |
| Observations | 27,182 | 27,182 |
| $R^2$ | 0.315 | |

Robust standard errors in parentheses
***$p < 0.01$, **$p < 0.05$, *$p < 0.1$

jective wellbeing. Columns 1 and 2 present results for OLS and ordered logit regressions, respectively. Across both columns, we find evidence of a positive association between innovation and subjective wellbeing with similar effect sizes. In Column 1, we find that the coefficient on innovation is 0.250 while in Column 2, the coefficient is 0.289 both statistically significant at the 1% significance level. These results suggest that innovation is associated with a 0.250–0.289 higher life satisfaction.

The coefficients on our control variables show directions of effect sizes consistent with the existing literature. From Column 2, at the 10% significance level, we find a positive effect of GDP per capita on subjective wellbeing. This result suggests that living in a country with higher national income or higher economic development, as proxied by GDP per capita, is associated with higher levels of life satisfaction. This finding is consistent with previous studies that examined the impact of GDP per capita on subjective wellbeing (Tella et al., 2003).

Results also suggest that individual level income is positively associated with subjective wellbeing. Respondents with higher level of individual income, therefore, tend to report higher subjective wellbeing. Male respondents tend to have lower subjective wellbeing compared to female respondents while married respondents, compared to those that are single and divorced, tend to have higher subjective wellbeing. Unemployed respondents tend to report lower levels of subjective wellbeing compared to those employed. We find evidence of an inverted U-shaped relationship for age, a finding which is not consistent with one strand of the existing literature (Awaworyi Churchill & Mishra, 2017; Helliwell & Wang, 2011), but may be explained by our sample focused only on older people. Results further show that feeling unsafe because of crime or terrorism and lack of financial freedom is negatively associated with subjective wellbeing. On average, respondents draw utility from religion and helping others, and thus findings suggest that respondents that find religion and helping people nearby important tend to report higher levels of subjective wellbeing. Good general health is also associated with higher subjective wellbeing.

Table 2 presents results for a series of checks to examine the robustness of our results. Panel A reports results using an alternative measure

**Table 2** Robustness checks

| Variables | (1)<br>OLS | (2)<br>Ordered logit |
|---|---|---|
| *Panel A—Alternative measure of innovation* | | |
| Patents | 0.027*** | 0.031*** |
| | (0.004) | (0.004) |
| Observations | 25,363 | 25,363 |
| *Panel B—Alternative measure of wellbeing* | | |
| Global Innovation Index | 0.043*** | 0.119*** |
| | (0.010) | (0.029) |
| Observations | 26,963 | 26,963 |
| *Panel C—Ages up to 65 years* | | |
| Global Innovation Index | 0.398*** | 0.449*** |
| | (0.087) | (0.095) |
| Observations | 18,742 | 18,742 |
| *Panel D—Ages above 65 years* | | |
| Global Innovation Index | −0.188 | −0.162 |
| | (0.163) | (0.193) |
| Observations | 8440 | 8440 |

Robust standard errors in parentheses
***$p < 0.01$, **$p < 0.05$, *$p < 0.1$

of innovation. Here, we use number of patent applications per country, drawn from the World Bank database, as an alternative measure of innovation. Panel B reports results using an alternative measure of subjective wellbeing. Here, we use a measure of self-reported happiness instead of happiness to examine if our results are robust to the measure of subjective wellbeing. In both cases, we find that results are consistent.

In Panels C and D, we extend our results to examine if the effects of innovation differ across age groups. To do this, we consider the average retirement age across countries (65 years) as the cut-off point and examine if our results differ between the sub-sample of those below this age, and those above this age. Previous research has shown that openness to new ideas and being open minded changes with age with much older people being less open to new innovative ideas (Gopnik, Griffiths, & Lucas, 2015; Roberts, Walton, & Viechtbauer, 2006). If this is true, we might expect that innovation could negatively influence the wellbeing of much older people. Panel C of Table 2 reports results for the effects of innovation on respondents that are up to 65 years, while Panel D reports results for respondents that are above 65 years. Our results suggest that the effects of innovation on subjective wellbeing remain positive in the younger age group but wanes out, with a statistically insignificant effect observed for the older age group.

Table 3 presents Lewbel 2SLS results. Panel A reports results for the effects of the GII, while Panel B presents results for the effects of patent. Column 1 across both panels reports results for the full sample. Columns 2 and 3 report results for the relatively younger and older sub-samples, respectively. Overall, we find that the effects of the GII from the Lewbel 2SLS regressions are consistent with those from our main results, although there is evidence to suggest that endogeneity generates considerable upward bias in our baseline results. Thus, Lewbel 2SLS estimates appear to be relatively smaller in magnitude compared to both OLS and ordered logit regression results. Similar patterns are observed in Panel B for the effects of patents. However, we now observe a positive and statistically significant effect of patents in the older sub-sample, albeit smaller than the estimate observed for the younger sub-sample.

**Table 3** Lewbel 2SLS results

| Variables | (1)<br>Full sample | (2)<br>Up to 65 | (3)<br>Above 65 |
|---|---|---|---|
| *Panel A—Effects of Global Innovation Index* | | | |
| Global Innovation Index | 0.020*** | 0.041*** | 0.002 |
| | (0.006) | (0.009) | (0.006) |
| Observations | 27,182 | 18,742 | 8440 |
| $R^2$ | 0.218 | 0.209 | 0.237 |
| *First stage statistics* | | | |
| *F*-statistics | 49.46 | 47.41 | 18.87 |
| $R^2$ | 0.0537 | 0.0714 | 0.0763 |
| *Panel B—Effects of Patents* | | | |
| Patents | 0.062*** | 0.102*** | 0.038** |
| | (0.013) | (0.019) | (0.016) |
| Observations | 25,363 | 17,410 | 7953 |
| $R^2$ | 0.215 | 0.202 | 0.245 |
| *First stage statistics* | | | |
| *F*-statistics | 78.20 | 53.38 | 49.27 |
| $R^2$ | 0.0808 | 0.0782 | 0.1272 |

Robust standard errors in parentheses
***$p < 0.01$, **$p < 0.05$, *$p < 0.1$

# 5 Discussion and Conclusion

Research on the interplay between subjective wellbeing and innovation is still at its infancy. This research contributes to the empirical evidence on the relationship between subjective wellbeing and innovation, focusing on older populations and adopting a multiple country perspective. In doing so, it builds on prior literature that has investigated this relationship in a single country setting (see, e.g., Dolan and Metcalfe [2012] and their survey of the British population), and extends it through the analysis of a specific age group. Understanding how to improve the older generations' wellbeing is a timely issue for policymakers across developed and emerging economies. This is particularly the case given higher life expectancy across several countries. The World Health Organization forecasts that the proportion of the world's population over 60 will almost double, from 12 to 22% between the 2015–2050 window, and that seniors (aged 60+) will outnumber children under 5 in 2020.

Our research underpins the strong association between the overall innovativeness level of an economy, as captured by both the multidimensional GII and the patenting activity, and measures of subjective wellbeing, happiness and self-reported happiness. A sub-sample analysis suggests that this finding is particularly true for those aged up to 65. However, the association in the case of those aged above 65 is statistically insignificant. While exploring the reasons behind this finding is beyond the scope of the current study, we call for further research to understand the factors influencing this relationship. Correlations have been established, but the exact nature of the effects of a properly functioning innovation ecosystem on individual wellbeing remains to be investigated. Single country setting analysis could shed some light on those effects, by controlling other typical factors (such as culture, social identity). Finland, repeatedly named as the "most happy country" (*The Economist*), could be an interesting case.

Further research could also explore the effects of the different innovation types (technological versus non technological, social, etc.) on the subjective wellbeing of older generations, identifying the moderators and mediators affecting those relationships.

# Appendix

See Tables 4 and 5.

**Table 4** List of countries included in analysis

| | |
|---|---|
| Algeria | Mali |
| Argentina | Mexico |
| Armenia | Morocco |
| Australia | Netherlands |
| Azerbaijan | New Zealand |
| Bahrain | Niger |
| Brazil | Norway |
| Burkina Faso | Pakistan |
| Chile | Peru |
| China | Philippines |
| Colombia | Poland |
| Cyprus | Qatar |
| Ecuador | Russian Federation |
| Egypt | Rwanda |
| Estonia | Singapore |
| Georgia | South Africa |
| Germany | Spain |
| Ghana | Sweden |
| Hong Kong | Switzerland |
| Hungary | Thailand |
| Iceland | Trinidad and Tobago |
| Iran | Tunisia |
| Japan | Turkey |
| Jordan | Ukraine |
| Kazakhstan | United States |
| Kuwait | Uruguay |
| Kyrgyzstan Republic | Yemen |
| Lebanon | Zambia |
| Malaysia | Zimbabwe |

**Table 5** Description and summary statistics

| Variable | Description | Mean | SD |
|---|---|---|---|
| Life satisfaction | All things considered, how satisfied are you with your life as a whole these days? 1 means you are "completely dissatisfied" and 10 means you are "completely satisfied" where would you put your satisfaction with your life as a whole? | 7.211 | 1.837 |
| Happiness | Taking all things together, would you say you are "very happy," "quite happy," "not very happy" and "not at all happy"? 1 means "very happy," 2 means "quite happy," 3 means "not very happy," 4 means "not at all happy" | 6.477 | 2.374 |
| Global Innovation Index | Global Innovation Index scores | 43.44 | 12.08 |
| Patent | Log of number of patent applications | 7.364 | 2.753 |
| GDP per capita | Log of real GDP per capita | 9.092 | 1.346 |
| Age | Age of respondent | 61.82 | 8.918 |
| Age squared | Square of age/100 | 39.01 | 11.61 |
| Income | Scale of income | 4.526 | 2.146 |
| Male | Dummy variable equals to 1 if respondent is male | 0.482 | 0.500 |
| Married | Dummy variable equals to 1 if respondent is married | 0.701 | 0.458 |
| Money | Dummy variable equals to 1 if respondent has in the past gone without money | 0.557 | 0.497 |
| Unsafe | Dummy variable equals to 1 if respondent has in the past felt unsafe from crime | 0.456 | 0.498 |
| Help | Dummy variable equals to 1 if it is important for respondent to help people nearby | 0.973 | 0.161 |
| Religion | Dummy variable equals to 1 if religion is important to respondent | 0.665 | 0.472 |
| Terrorism | Dummy variable equals to 1 if respondent worries about a terrorist attack | 0.471 | 0.499 |
| Unemployed | Dummy variable equals to 1 if respondent is unemployed | 0.0596 | 0.237 |
| Good health | Dummy variable equals to 1 if respondent self-assesses their general health as good/very good | 0.538 | 0.499 |

## References


Angner, E. (2010). Subjective well-being. *The Journal of Socio-Economics, 39*(3), 361–368.

Awaworyi Churchill, S., Appau, S., & Farrell, L. (2019). Religiosity, income and wellbeing in developing countries. *Empirical Economics, 56*(3), 959–985. https://doi.org/10.1007/s00181-017-1380-9.

Awaworyi Churchill, S., & Mishra, V. (2016). Trust, social networks and subjective wellbeing in China. *Social Indicators Research, 132,* 1–27.

Awaworyi Churchill, S., & Mishra, V. (2017). Trust, social networks and subjective wellbeing in China. *Social Indicators Research, 132*(1), 313–339. https://doi.org/10.1007/s11205-015-1220-2.

Becker, G. S., Rayo, L., & Krueger, A. B. (2008). Economic growth and subjective well-being: Reassessing the Easterlin paradox—Comments and discussion. *Brookings Papers on Economic Activity, 2008,* 88–102.

Bilbao-Osorio, B., & Rodríguez-Pose, A. (2004). From R&D to innovation and economic growth in the EU. *Growth and Change, 35*(4), 434–455.

Biswas-Diener, R., & Diener, E. (2006). The subjective well-being of the homeless, and lessons for happiness. *Social Indicators Research, 76*(2), 185–205. https://doi.org/10.1007/s11205-005-8671-9.

Diener, E., & Oishi, S. (2000). Money and happiness: Income and subjective well-being across nations. In *Culture and subjective well-being* (pp. 185–218).

Dolan, P., & Metcalfe, R. (2012). The relationship between innovation and subjective wellbeing. *Research Policy, 41*(8), 1489–1498.

Engelbrecht, H.-J. (2014). A general model of the innovation—Subjective well-being nexus. *Journal of Evolutionary Economics, 24*(2), 377–397. https://doi.org/10.1007/s00191-014-0343-y.

Engelbrecht, H.-J. (2018). The (social) innovation–subjective well-being nexus: Subjective well-being impacts as an additional assessment metric of technological and social innovations. *Innovation: The European Journal of Social Science Research, 31*(3), 317–332.

Ferrer-i-Carbonell, A., & Frijters, P. (2004). How important is methodology for the estimates of the determinants of Happiness?*. *The Economic Journal, 114*(497), 641–659. https://doi.org/10.1111/j.1468-0297.2004.00235.x.

Frijters, P., Haisken-DeNew, J. P., & Shields, M. A. (2004). Money does matter! Evidence from increasing real income and life satisfaction in East Germany following reunification. *American Economic Review, 94*(3), 730–740.

Fujiwara, D., & Campbell, R. (2011). *Valuation techniques for social cost-benefit analysis: Stated preference, revealed preference and subjective well-being approaches—A discussion of the current issues.* London: HM Treasury.

Gopnik, A., Griffiths, T. L., & Lucas, C. G. (2015). When younger learners can be better (or at least more open-minded) than older ones. *Current Directions in Psychological Science, 24*(2), 87–92. https://doi.org/10.1177/0963721414556653.

Grossman, G. M., & Helpman, E. (1991). *Innovation and growth in the global economy.* Cambridge: MIT Press.

Helliwell, J. F. (2003). How's life? Combining individual and national variables to explain subjective well-being. *Economic Modelling, 20*(2), 331–360. https://doi.org/10.1016/S0264-9993(02)00057-3.

Helliwell, J. F., & Putnam, R. D. (2004). The social context of well-being. *Philosophical Transactions of the Royal Society B: Biological Sciences, 359*(1449), 1435.

Helliwell, J. F., & Wang, S. (2011). Trust and well-being. *Journal of Wellbeing, 1*(1), 42–78.

Lewbel, A. (2012). Using heteroscedasticity to identify and estimate mismeasured and endogenous regressor models. *Journal of Business & Economic Statistics, 30*(1), 67–80. https://doi.org/10.1080/07350015.2012.643126.

Pinquart, M., & Sörensen, S. (2000). Influences of socioeconomic status, social network, and competence on subjective well-being in later life: A meta-analysis. *Psychology and Aging, 15*(2), 187–224. https://doi.org/10.1037/0882-7974.15.2.187.

Roberts, B. W., Walton, K. E., & Viechtbauer, W. (2006). Patterns of mean-level change in personality traits across the life course: A meta-analysis of longitudinal studies. *Psychological Bulletin, 132*(1), 1–25. https://doi.org/10.1037/0033-2909.132.1.1.

Sachs, J., Becchetti, L., & Annett, A. (2016). *World happiness report 2016* (Vol. 2). New York: UN Sustainable Development Solutions Network.

Scherer, F. M. (1986). *Innovation and growth: Schumpeterian perspectives.* Cambridge: MIT Press.

Schumpeter, J. A. (1942). *Capitalism, Socialism and Democracy.* New York and London: Harper & Brothers.

Solow, R. (1956). A contribution to the theory of economic growth. *Quarterly Journal of Economics, 70*(1), 65–94.

Tella, R. D., MacCulloch, R. J., & Oswald, A. J. (2003). The macroeconomics of happiness. *The Review of Economics and Statistics, 85*(4), 809–827. https://doi.org/10.1162/003465303772815745.

Ugur, M., Awaworyi Churchill, S., & Solomon, E. (2018). Technological innovation and employment in derived labour demand models: A hierarchical meta-regression analysis. *Journal of Economic Surveys, 32*(1), 50–82. https://doi.org/10.1111/joes.12187.

Verspagen, B. (2006). Innovation and economic growth. In J. Fagerberg & D. C. Mowery (Eds.), *The oxford handbook of innovation.* New York: Oxford University Press.

# 13

# Improving the Wellbeing of Old People: Thoughts and Reflections

Samuelson Appau and Sefa Awaworyi Churchill

In this book, we have an ensemble of incredible scholarship that have addressed how we can better understand, measure and improve the wellbeing of older people using empirical and conceptual research. The studies included in the volume have spanned different fields including anthropology, economics, consumer research and sociology, with global data from the World Values Survey and country-specific data from both developed and developing countries including Australia, China, Ghana and the UK. The chapters in this book have also considered varied micro and macro level factors that affect the wellbeing of older people

S. Appau · S. Awaworyi Churchill (✉)
School of Economics, Finance & Marketing, RMIT University, Melbourne, VIC, Australia
e-mail: sefa.awaworyichurchill@rmit.edu.au

S. Appau
e-mail: samuelson.appau@rmit.edu.au



S. Awaworyi Churchill et al. (eds.), *Measuring, Understanding and Improving Wellbeing Among Older People*,
https://doi.org/10.1007/978-981-15-2353-3_13

including occupation and retirement, housing and homelessness, gambling, height, religion and cultural discourses, ethnic diversity and discrimination, social support, personal freedom and independence, and country-level freedom and innovation. More than simply specifying how these factors affect the wellbeing of the aged, the authors have variously reflected on ways individuals, societies, practitioners and policymakers can apply this knowledge to better understand and improve the wellbeing of the aged. The chapters in this book therefore offer a wonderful collage of knowledge and direction for scholars and practitioners alike who work or seek to work in this space.

In this concluding chapter, we discuss two overarching themes that build on the multiple contributions offered by the chapters in this book. First, we examine the role of discourses of ageism in scientific and popular discourse and how these discourses can negatively influence and affect even well-intended policies and interventions. We then advocate for policies and interventions aimed at improving the wellbeing of old people to adopt an intersectionality lens to better capture disadvantages older people may have due to other vulnerable social identities—like gender and ethnicity—which may be invisible to policy aimed solely at old age.

## 1 Interrogating Discourses of Ageism

Discourse is a powerful tool that frames the beliefs, actions and representation of people in any given society (Foucault, 1979). Negative discourses about any group in society can lead to prejudices, stigmatization and marginalization of that group (Goffman, 1963; Gullette, 2004). In many places, there is a discourse of ageism that frame older people as unproductive, dependent, having slow physical mental capabilities, and demonstrating regressive tastes and habits (Day & Hitchings, 2011; Goffman, 1963; Gullette, 2004). Three chapters in this book have also offered evidence about how prejudice and discrimination against older Chinese people (Agyekumhene et al.), stigmatization of old women as witches in Northern Ghana (Mabefam and Appau), and perceptions of dependency about older Australians (Franco) affect the wellbeing of the old people concerned. It is therefore important to reflect on how old age is framed in scientific and popular discourse so that well-meaning efforts to support older people do not reinforce these ageist perceptions, and/or result in unintended consequences.

Since the early twentieth century, the medical field has framed old age as a pathological decline from the capabilities of younger people (Fennell, Phillipson, & Evers, 1988). This has led to the stigmatization and marginalization of older people in society that has become entrenched and perpetuated in media, fashion, advertising, cinema and popular culture (Binstock, 2005; Gullette, 1997). The stigmatization of old age in such popular media is conversely sharpened by the veneration of youth. Whereas old age is depicted as the moniker of decay, ugliness and decline, youth is depicted as embodying beauty, strength and life. Put differently, youth is desirable; old age is not (Barnhart & Peñaloza, 2012; Rozario & Derienzis, 2009). This can even result in discrimination in the labour markets as research shows that older people struggle to change jobs because employers maintain a bias in hiring younger people (Manger, 2014).

It is therefore no surprise that ageing people do not want to identify as old. Research shows that many people of old age do not identify with their chronological age, and do not self-identify as old even if others identify them as such (Barnhart & Peñaloza, 2012). Some research suggests that old people do not want to be considered and served separately as a demographic or market/social segment in the marketplace (Barnhart & Peñaloza, 2012; Marrs 1984; Tepper 1994). Being categorized as old comes with a lot of stigma and older people avoid the categorization or deliberately engage in habits and practices to combat the associated stigma. For example, in this book, Franco's chapter unveils how older Australians desire independence and attempt to achieve such independence through the use of technology. We surmise that their desire for independence is necessary to combat the stigma of dependence associated with old age. In addition, we can see how learning to use technology also helps mitigate the "teaching old new tricks" stigma associated with old people and technology adoption. Thus, as stakeholders including policymakers seek to understand and improve the wellbeing of the aged, it is important that the prejudices and stigmatization with which old age is represented in various scientific and policy discourses are interrogated.

Policymakers and practitioners need to be reflexive about their own possible ageist assumptions and biases that underlie policies aiming to help old people. Policies and interventions seeking to improve the wellbeing older people must also be well-devised to ensure they do not reinforce such stigma about older people. Ignoring such important factors is likely increase the risk of such policies failing. Particularly, where those identified as old do not self-identify as such and therefore subvert or refuse any policy interventions, social privileges and support offered towards improving their wellbeing, no matter how well-intentioned, may fail.

For instance, in their study of the UK winter welfare policy to assist old people keep warm in winter, Day and Hitchings (2011) argued that welfare policies tend to reinforce pathological assumptions about the ageing body and also promote the stigma of the old as dependent people who need help. They also found that some old people adopted countervailing practices like opening their windows during winter nights to keep their rooms from being "stuffy"—even if this made their rooms colder—because it helped them counter stigma of their failing bodies unable to keep their houses fresh (Day & Hitchings, 2011). Tepper (1994) also found that Americans who qualified for senior citizen discounts offered by retailers refused to claim the discounts to avoid the stigma and self-devaluation attached to old age. Older people in Uganda also refused to access needed health care services early due to experiences of ageism they face with health care workers (Schatz, Seeley, Negin, & Mugisha, 2018).

Thus, policy makers must seek to use policies to disarm ageist stigma that may be inherent in the policy design, and offer solutions that do support rather than patronize older people. As Mabefam and Appau's chapter on witchcraft accusation against old people in Ghana suggest, in cases where stigma is entrenched in cultural discourse, more political will may be needed to have a lasting impact. Sinclair et al.'s chapter in this book also advocates for empathetic housing design that suits the corporal limitations of older people. We suggest that such housing design adjustments must be done collaboratively with old people themselves, rather than offering them adjustments that would only reinforce stigma about their bodies and capabilities to manage their homes.

More importantly, it is imperative to reflect on and confront the perpetuation of ageism in our societies. Stigma associated with old age is internalized at an early age and then manifested throughout life even into old age (Gullette, 2004). Older people too have self-stigma, and this may affect their self-esteem and wellbeing (Day & Hitchings, 2011). All things being equal, we will all grow old, and it is important to reconsider the scientific and popular discourse on old age, especially in regard to the meanings we assign to "old bodies" in the media, advertising, marketplace products and offerings like Botox and aged care facilities, and in business and public policies. In this regard, Mabefam and Appau's chapter highlights how some solutions that seek to address the symptoms of ageism are ineffective if the underlying discourse of ageism itself is not addressed with a concerted effort to eradicate it.

## 2 Towards an Intersectionality Lens

People have multiple social identities and belong in multiple social categories such as being adults, Christians, homeless, immigrants and middle-class. Similarly, old age is experienced in tandem with other social identities including gender, socio-economic status and ethnicity. Some old people have other vulnerable social identities, like gender, that intersect to create heightened disadvantages, and yet may be invisible to policy or interventions that address only old age. For example, witchcraft accusation in Africa has been labelled "a problem for older women" (see, Mabefam and Appau's chapter). The stigmatization of old bodies affects women more often than men, and older women's bodies receive more negative depictions and judgements in popular discourse than older men (Black & Brown, 2016). Older women who get abused by their partners remain invisible to researchers, law enforcement and policymakers because it is assumed that partner violence mostly affects young women and abuse of the elderly is committed by younger people (Bhatia & Soletti, 2019). Thus, it is important that research, policy and other interventions aimed at understanding and improving the wellbeing of old people take an intersectionality lens that recognizes other vulnerable social identities of older people that may amplify disadvantages that they may face.

Developed in feminist research, intersectionality examines how a person's overlapping social identities interact to create multiple disadvantages for the person, and which may not be apparent when examined only through a singular categorical lens such as income or disability (Cole, 2009; Corus et al., 2016; Crenshaw, 1991; McCall, 2001). Intersectionality also considers how multiple social processes and experiences such as racism, ageism and gender discrimination play an important role in structuring social identities and the ensuing stigmatization, vulnerabilities and prejudices that people categorized into these structures experience (Choo & Ferree, 2010; Crenshaw, 1991; Davis, 2008). Thus, intersectionality scholars contend that policy conversations on, for example, racism often misunderstand the actual nature of vulnerabilities experienced by the racial subject, due to the failure of the anti-racism policy to acknowledge other intersectional vulnerabilities resulting from say gender and low-income (Corus et al., 2016; Crenshaw, 1991; Davis, 2008).

For our purposes, an intersectional lens challenges any assumption that older people are a homogenous group and that all of them may have the same vulnerabilities or challenges that can be well addressed with similar interventions. The chapters in this book unveil multiple dimensions of vulnerabilities that may intersect to mutually affect an older person's wellbeing. We also see how multiple social processes including housing insecurity, social support, witchcraft beliefs and accusations, and technology usage capabilities affect the wellbeing of old people. Awaworyi Churchill and Farrell's chapter in this book on gambling is particularly revealing as the authors suggest that multiple vulnerabilities—age, retirement and mental health problems—underlie older people's addiction to gambling. But research on gambling addiction may not consider the mutually reinforcing impact of these intersecting vulnerabilities.

We recommend then that future research that seeks to measure and understand the wellbeing of old people needs to consider it from an intersectionality lens in order to better unveil other mutually reinforcing disadvantages due to other vulnerable social identities of older people. For example, the experiences of older gays and lesbians within contexts where same-sex relations are legal, contested or illegal offer an interesting space for future research into the intersectionality of age, gender, sexuality and processes of homophobia (see also Cronin & King, 2010). Other social identities and categories of potential vulnerabilities experienced by old people that future research could explore include immigration (and residence status), weight and body size, mental health, and physical and learning disabilities. As a methodological and analytical approach, intersectionality is a useful toolkit for researchers in problematizing, measuring and analysing research on the wellbeing of older people.

Policies and interventions aimed at improving the wellbeing of older people also need to carefully understand how different segments of social identities may affect the effectiveness of policies in achieving the desired results. For example, the UK winter fuel payment policy provides all old people with financial aid to spend on heating during winter (Day & Hitchings, 2011). However, this policy does not consider vulnerabilities that low-income households may face, and which might result in the use of such financial aid or funds on other basic household needs like food rather than on heating. It also overlooks homeless old people or those living with housing insecurity, who are most vulnerable during winter but remain invisible to this policy (see discussions in Elkins, Farrell and Fry's chapter). An intersectional lens to policy on improving the wellbeing of older persons thus requires a more comprehensive problematization of whatever issue the policy seeks to address, and will involve multiple stakeholders. Demanding as it may be, a policy considered through an intersectional lens is more likely to be effective, and mitigate unintended consequences than one that is not (Corus et al., 2016)

## References


Barnhart, M., & Peñaloza, L. (2012). Who are you calling old? Negotiating old age identity in the elderly consumption ensemble. *Journal of Consumer Research, 39*(6), 1133–1153.

Bhatia, P., & Soletti, A. (2019). Hushed voices: Views and experiences of older women on partner abuse in later life. *Ageing International, 44*(1), 41–56.

Black, P., & Brown, A. (2016). Is fifty really the new thirty? The stigma of age as a form of strain and its role in drug and alcohol abuse and dependence by women. *Deviant Behavior, 37*(9), 1052–1063.

Binstock, R. H. (2005). Old age policies, politics, and ageism. *Generations, 29*(3), 73–78.
Choo, H. Y., & Ferree, M. M. (2010). Practicing intersectionality in sociological research: A critical analysis of inclusions, interactions, and institutions in the study of inequalities. *Sociological Theory, 28*(2), 129–149.
Cole, E. R. (2009). Intersectionality and research in psychology. *American Psychologist, 64*(3), 170.
Corus, C., Saatcioglu, B., Kaufman-Scarborough, C., Blocker, C., Upadhyaya, S., & Appau, S. (2016). Transforming poverty-related policy with intersectionality. *Journal of Public Policy & Marketing, 35*(2), 211–222.
Crenshaw, K. (1991). Mapping the margins: Intersectionality, identity politics, and violence against women of color. *Stanford Law Review, 43*(6), 1241–1299.
Cronin, A., & King, A. (2010). Power, inequality and identification: Exploring diversity and intersectionality amongst older LGB adults. *Sociology, 44*(5), 876–892.
Davis, K. (2008). Intersectionality as buzzword: A sociology of science perspective on what makes a feminist theory successful. *Feminist Theory, 9*(1), 67–85.
Day, R., & Hitchings, R. (2011). 'Only old ladies would do that': Age stigma and older people's strategies for dealing with winter cold. *Health and Place, 17*(4), 885–894.
Fennell, G., Phillipson, C., & Evers, H. (1988). *The sociology of old age.* Philadelphia: Open University Press.
Foucault, M. (1979). *Discipline and punish: The birth of the prison.* London: Penguin.
Goffman, E. (1963). *Stigma: Notes on the management of spoiled identity.* Englewood Cliffs, NJ: Prentice Hall.
Gullette, M. M. (1997). *Declining to decline: Cultural combat and the politics of the midlife.* Charlottesville: University of Virginia Press.
Gullette, M. M. (2004). *Aged by culture.* Chicago: University of Chicago Press.
Manger, C. (2014). Endogenous age discrimination. *Journal of Population Economics, 27*(4), 1087–1106.
Marrs, C. H. (1984). Developing a profitable program for the senior market. *Journal of Retail Banking, 6*(1 & 2), 25–35.
McCall, L. (2001). *Complex inequality: Gender, class, and race in the new economy.* New York: Routledge.

Rozario, P. A., & Derienzis, D. (2009). 'So forget how old I am!' Examining age identities in the face of chronic conditions. *Sociology of Health & Illness, 31*(4), 540–553.

Schatz, E., Seeley, J., Negin, J., & Mugisha, J. (2018). They 'don't cure old age': Older Ugandans' delays to health-care access. *Ageing & Society, 38*(11), 2197–2217.

Tepper, K. (1994). The role of labeling processes in elderly consumers' responses to age segmentation cues. *Journal of Consumer Research, 20*(4), 503–519.

# Index




S. Awaworyi Churchill et al. (eds.), *Measuring, Understanding and Improving Wellbeing Among Older People*,
https://doi.org/10.1007/978-981-15-2353-3

The manufacturer's authorised representative in the EU is Springer Nature Customer Service Centre GmbH, Europaplatz 3, 69115 Heidelberg, Germany. If you have any concerns regarding our products, please contact ProductSafety@springernature.com

Printed and bound by CPI Group (UK) Ltd, Croydon, CR0 4YY
25/09/2026
02222902-0009